Pro Encryption in SQL Server 2022

Provide the Highest Level
of Protection for Your Data

Matthew McGiffen

Apress®

Pro Encryption in SQL Server 2022: Provide the Highest Level of Protection for Your Data

Matthew McGiffen
Bristol, UK

ISBN-13 (pbk): 978-1-4842-8663-0   ISBN-13 (electronic): 978-1-4842-8664-7
https://doi.org/10.1007/978-1-4842-8664-7

Managing Director, Apress Media LLC: Welmoed Spahr
Acquisitions Editor: Jonathan Gennick
Development Editor: Laura Berendson
Coordinating Editor: Gryffin Winkler

Cover image designed by Freepik (www.freepik.com)

Distributed to the book trade worldwide by Springer Science+Business Media LLC, 1 New York Plaza, Suite 4600, New York, NY 10004. Phone 1-800-SPRINGER, fax (201) 348-4505, e-mail orders-ny@springer-sbm.com, or visit www.springeronline.com. Apress Media, LLC is a California LLC and the sole member (owner) is Springer Science + Business Media Finance Inc (SSBM Finance Inc). SSBM Finance Inc is a **Delaware** corporation.

For information on translations, please e-mail booktranslations@springernature.com; for reprint, paperback, or audio rights, please e-mail bookpermissions@springernature.com.

Apress titles may be purchased in bulk for academic, corporate, or promotional use. eBook versions and licenses are also available for most titles. For more information, reference our Print and eBook Bulk Sales web page at http://www.apress.com/bulk-sales.

Any source code or other supplementary material referenced by the author in this book is available to readers on GitHub.

Printed on acid-free paper

For Lisa and Alby.

Table of Contents

About the Author xiii

About the Technical Reviewer xv

Acknowledgments xvii

Introduction xix

Part I: Understanding the Landscape 1

Chapter 1: Purpose of Encryption and Available Tools 3

What Is the Purpose of Encryption? 4

Encryption and Data Protection Regulation 5

Overview of the Tools Available in SQL Server 7

TDE 8

Backup Encryption 9

Always Encrypted 9

TLS 9

Hashing and Salting 10

Encryption Functions 10

EKM 10

Recommended Approach to Encryption 11

Encryption in the Cloud 12

Summary 13

Part II: At-Rest Encryption 15

Chapter 2: Introducing Transparent Data Encryption 17

What Is TDE? 17

Understanding Keys and Certificates 22

Database Encryption Key (DEK)... 24

Certificate and Associated Asymmetric Key Pair........................... 24

Database Master Key (DMK) 24

Service Master Key (SMK) 25

Understanding the Need for the Hierarchy... 25

How Secure Is TDE?... 27

What Are We Protected From?... 28

How Easy Is It to Break Down the Encryption?............................. 28

Summary.. 29

Chapter 3: Setting Up TDE.. 31

Creating the Keys and Certificate 31

Creating the Database Master Key (DMK) 32

Creating the Certificate.. 33

Creating the Database Encryption Key (DEK) 34

Encrypting the Database.. 35

Securing the Root Keys.. 37

Encrypting Existing Data with TDE.. 39

Benchmarking TDE Performance on Your Server 39

Monitoring for Problems... 42

What If You Run into Any Performance Problems During the Scan? 43

What If the Encryption Scan Fails?... 44

Taking Backups While Encryption Is in Progress........................... 45

Summary.. 45

Chapter 4: Managing TDE 47

Migrating or Recovering a TDE-Protected Database......................... 47

Create a Database Master Key (DMK) If One Doesn't Exist 48

Restore the Certificate and Private Key.. 48

Restore the Database 49

Recovering a TDE Database Without the Certificate 50

Setting Up a New SQL Instance Using the Same Service Account as the Old Instance 51

Restore Your Backup of Master from the Old Instance onto the New Instance.................... 51

Reboot Your New Server: The Whole Server, Not Just SQL 52

Backup Your Certificate and Private Key – and Don't Lose Them This Time 52

Key Rotation 53

Creating a New Certificate 54

Rotating the Certificate 55

Impact of TDE on Performance 55

Where Do We See an Overhead? 56

How to Estimate the Performance Impact for Your Server? 56

TDE and Backups 60

Backup Performance 60

Backup Compression 61

Backup Compression Issues 62

TDE and High Availability 62

Summary 63

Chapter 5: Backup Encryption 65

Setting Up Backup Encryption 66

Creating a Test Database 66

Create the Database Master Key (DMK) 66

Creating the Certificate 67

Permissions 67

Working with Encrypted Backups 68

Taking an Encrypted Backup 68

Restoring an Encrypted Backup 69

Backup Encryption Performance 70

Backup Encryption and Compression 72

Summary 73

Part III: Column Encryption using Always Encrypted 75

Chapter 6: Introducing Always Encrypted 77

SQL Server 2016 vs. SQL Server 2019 and Beyond 78

How Does Always Encrypted Work? 78

Encryption Hierarchy 79

Encryption in Practice 79

Summary 82

Chapter 7: Setting Up Always Encrypted 85

Create Keys and Certificates 85

Creating the Certificate and Column Master Key 85

Creating the Column Encryption Key (CEK) 89

Create an Encrypted Column 92

Summary 94

Chapter 8: Executing Queries Using Always Encrypted 97

Performing a Basic Insert and Select 97

Connecting to the Database 97

Inserting Data 99

Reading Data 102

Looking at What Happens in the Background 103

What Happens with an Insert Query 103

What Happens with a Select Query 108

Issuing a Query with a Predicate Against an Encrypted Column 108

Indexes and Statistics on Encrypted Columns 112

Working with Stored Procedures 113

Querying Always Encrypted Data from Your Application 116

Working with Direct Queries 117

Working with Stored Procedures 119

Summary 121

Chapter 9: Encrypting Existing Data with Always Encrypted 123

Encrypting Data Using the Always Encrypted Wizard 124

Encrypting Data Using PowerShell 129

Encrypting Data Using the Import and Export Wizard 133

Summary 142

Chapter 10: Limitations with Always Encrypted..**145**

SQL Server Only Ever Sees Encrypted Data.. 145

Strong Encryption Isn't Predictable 147

Deterministic vs. Randomized 147

Data Types... 148

Miscellaneous 149

Summary.. 149

Chapter 11: Key Rotation with Always Encrypted **151**

CMK Rotation 151

Rotating the CMK Using the SSMS GUI.. 153

Rotating the CMK Using T-SQL 158

Rotating the CMK Using PowerShell... 160

Rotating the CMK Using PowerShell with Role Separation 162

Rotating the CEK 164

Summary.. 167

Chapter 12: Considerations When Implementing Always Encrypted..................**169**

Choosing What Data to Encrypt... 169

Source Control and Release Management.. 170

ETL 175

Performance 176

Client Drivers 177

Summary.. 178

Part IV: Column Encryption using Always Encrypted with Enclaves **181**

Chapter 13: Introducing Always Encrypted with Enclaves...................................**183**

Attestation... 184

Executing Queries That Use the Enclave... 185

The Attestation Process.. 185

The Query Execution Process.. 188

Summary.. 190

Chapter 14: Setting Up Always Encrypted with Enclaves 191

Setting Up Your VMs 192

Setting Up Networking 200

Install and Configure Host Guardian Service (HGS) 203

Install SQL Server and Configure as a Guarded Host 203

Summary 205

Chapter 15: In-Place Encryption with Always Encrypted Enclaves 207

Setting Up Our Test Database and Keys 208

In-Place Encryption and Decryption of Data 211

Performance of In-Place Encryption 214

CEK Rotation 215

Summary 217

Chapter 16: Rich Querying with Always Encrypted Enclaves 219

Setting Up Your Database and Data 221

Rich Querying 222

Indexes on Columns with Randomized Encryption 227

Reading from an Index 228

Updating an Index When Data Is Modified 231

Index Rebuilds 232

Database Recovery After Failure or Shutdown 233

Joins 235

Summary 242

Chapter 17: Setting Up TPM Attestation 245

Prerequisites for Your SQL Server to Support TPM Attestation 246

Artifacts That Are Required by Attestation 246

TPM Endorsement Key Certificate 247

TPM Baseline 247

Code Integrity Policy 247

Installing and Configuring HGS 247

Configuring the SQL Server 248

Install the Attestation Client Components 249

Making Sure VBS Is Configured Correctly... 249

Configure the Attestation URL 250

Configuring a Code Integrity Policy 251

Collect and Register Attestation Artifacts.. 252

Check SQL Server Can Attest Successfully 253

Configure the Enclave Type in SQL Server... 255

Summary... 256

Part V: Completing the Picture **257**

Chapter 18: Encryption In Transit Using Transport Layer Security **259**

How TLS Works 260

Obtaining a Certificate to Use for TLS 260

Setting Up TLS on Your SQL Server.. 263

Performance 268

Summary... 268

Chapter 19: Hashing and Salting of Passwords.. **269**

Hashing... 269

Salting... 270

Using the HASHBYTES Function... 271

Storing Passwords Using HASHBYTES and a Salt Value 272

Summary... 275

Chapter 20: Extensible Key Management (EKM) **277**

Creating the Required Objects in Azure 278

Creating the Resource Group... 278

Creating the Azure Active Directory App Registration.................................... 280

Creating the Key Vault 283

Setting Up TDE to Use Azure Key Vault.. 286

Creating the Key for TDE... 286

Setting Up the SQL Server 287

Working with Always Encrypted and EKM 290

    Creating a CMK in Azure Key Vault 290

    Encrypting Columns and Working with Data 293

    Working with Azure Key Vault from Your Application................................ 295

Summary.. 295

Chapter 21: Other Methods of Column Encryption 297

Encryption Using a Symmetric Key... 298

    Your Key Hierarchy 298

Working with Automated Key Management... 300

    Creating the Keys 300

    Encrypting and Decrypting Data.. 301

    Using an Authenticator 303

Where the DMK Is Not Protected by the SMK 306

Where the Symmetric Key Is Just Protected by a Password 307

Working with and Indexing Encrypted Columns 308

Migrating or Restoring a Database with Column Encryption 310

Temporary Keys 312

Encryption by Passphrase... 313

Protection of Key Passwords Being Sent to SQL Server 314

Summary.. 315

Appendix A: Glossary of Terms 317

Appendix B: Encryption in the Cloud 331

Appendix C: Encryption Algorithms 335

Index.. 343

About the Author

Matthew McGiffen is a Data Architect with over 20 years' experience working on SQL Server and associated technologies. Matthew has also had the opportunity to collaborate with Microsoft during the development of some of the latest enhancements in encryption. He is the author of a popular blog on SQL Server and has written articles for SQL Server Central. In his spare time, Matthew is an amateur chess player and pianist.

About the Technical Reviewer

 In 1998, **Tom Norman** changed his career focus to begin working with SQL Server after working in the airline industry for 14 years. He has worked in all aspects of SQL Server including administration, database development, BI, and reporting services. Working in the finance and compliance industry, he has specialized in data protection and encryption for PII, PCI, and HIPAA data while adhering to GDPR, CCPA, and other government laws and regulations. His working career has included working for an international corporation serving multiple international clients while working in the United States and Europe.

Tom has spoken at many community events including SQL Saturday, Denver Code Camp, PASS Data Summit, and PASS Virtual events. You can find his presentations on YouTube with this one on encryption at `https://www.youtube.com/watch?v=GCXiLgbAzIA`. Tom was the Leader of the PASS Virtualization chapter, President of the Denver SQL Server User Group, and Vice President of the Raleigh SQL Server group.

Data protection, especially encryption, is the hallmark of his career while working in SQL Server since SQL Server 2000. However, new governing laws have expanded the requirement to protect the data more. He has now expanded into the classification of the data in the database, which is now required by new laws. In addition to protecting the data, he has built a strong consistent database code deployment process.

Acknowledgments

This has been my first time writing something of this scale, so the support from the team at Apress has been invaluable. They include Jonathan Gennick, Gryffin Winkler, Jill Balzano, and Laura Berendsen among others. Huge thanks to the technical reviewer Tom Norman for valuable insights and for saving me from the embarrassment of errors that might otherwise have made it into publication.

Thanks also to Steve Mitchell, who was my boss at the time Apress first contacted me with the idea of writing a book, for the encouragement and the push to go ahead. Also to my colleague Jon Bird, a DBA with decades of experience, for allowing me to bounce questions and thoughts off him. And a general thank you to my current employer Iress, who have been supportive of me writing this book – though I'm sure our legal team would like me to stress that all opinions and advice expressed in this book are solely my own and should not be considered to be the opinions or advice of Iress.

Thanks most of all to my wife Lisa, who has been hugely supportive of me undertaking this project throughout, despite us having a young baby to look after as I started writing. Thanks, too, to our parents whose support has been invaluable at this time. That's Lisa's parents Angela and Stephen Tozer and my mum and dad Gill and Mike.

Finally, thanks to my son Alby for being more fun to be with every day – and for finally sleeping through the night. That certainly helped get this book over the finish line!

Introduction

When it comes to data, the level of protection we have over it is more important now than it has ever been. The rate of cyberattacks is greater every year along with the level of sophistication of those attacks, and the cost to companies globally is in the trillions and growing every year. Add to that the increasing amount of data protection regulation, and it becomes a topic we really can't ignore.

Encryption is a critical component in protecting your data from falling into the wrong hands. A good encryption strategy means that our data is safe even if our access controls are breached. Since 2016 Microsoft has been doing excellent work in adding to the encryption feature set within SQL Server, making encryption more secure, easier to use, and accessible to everyone who uses the product.

It used to be that implementing a bulletproof encryption strategy for your data was hard and expensive in terms of both licensing and the development resource required to implement. With the addition of Always Encrypted and with Transparent Data Encryption being made available in the standard edition of the product, everyone can – and should – be thinking about encryption of their data.

I've been interested in encryption since I was a kid playing around with substitution and other ciphers and have always taken an interest in the advances in encryption within technology. I started to take a deep dive into encryption within SQL Server in 2016 when Always Encrypted came out and wrote about it in some detail on my blog. Then in 2019 I was able to be involved in a private preview of Always Encrypted with Enclaves. That gave me access to the team within Microsoft working on the product from which I was able to gain real insight about how it worked and the thinking that had gone into it. Thanks to Jakub Szymaszek, Ryan Puffer, and the rest of the team for answering all my questions and helping to troubleshoot when I was having difficulty setting things up.

My mindset is that when I work with something new, I prefer to understand it from the bottom up. I was the same way when I studied math. I really wanted to have the base principles solid so that everything above it made sense. In this book I hope to impart to you the same level of knowledge of the encryption features within SQL Server. I'm a strong believer that if you understand how something works, then the rest comes naturally. I'm not a great fan of memorizing lots of facts. Always Encrypted, for instance, has a bunch of natural restrictions; if you have a solid foundation of how it works, then you don't need to remember most of them – they become intuitive, alongside any other restrictions that haven't made it into the documentation.

Who This Book Is For

I adhere to the idea that if you can't explain something in simple terms, then you don't truly understand it. Variations of that statement are often attributed to Einstein or the famed American physicist Richard Feynman. In my writing, here and in my blog, I've tried to explain things in a manner that keeps it simple while still getting to the most complex of ideas. At the end of the day, any complex concept can always be broken down into a number of simple ones. I personally don't enjoy technology writing that makes my head hurt, and I hope I've managed to – on the whole – avoid that here.

As such, this book should be accessible to readers who don't know the first thing about encryption and contains detail that is new even to those with a good level of experience working with encryption in SQL Server. There is some prerequisite knowledge though. The reader will need a decent level of knowledge around working with SQL Server.

The book also focuses heavily on the Always Encrypted feature that was introduced in SQL 2016 and added to in 2019 and 2022. As such you'll get more out of the book if you are working with 2016 or higher.

The book will be useful to you if you work with SQL Server as a developer, architect, or DBA and contains information you need to know whatever direction you are coming at it from.

How the Book Is Structured

If you read the book from start to finish, you will know, and hopefully understand, everything there is to know about encrypting your data within SQL Server. At the same time, I've tried to make the discussion of each encryption feature as standalone as possible. So if you want to leap into looking at Always Encrypted, for instance, that will work fine. Or if you have an urgent need to understand Extensible Key Management (EKM), then that chapter should give you everything you need to know.

The book is broken into five parts, so working through the parts of most interest to you will also work well. Here is a brief summary of what is covered.

Part I: Understanding the Landscape

Chapter 1, "Purpose of Encryption and Available Tools," discusses what we are hoping to achieve through encryption and why. We then look in brief at the tools available and how they should fit into your overall strategy.

Part II: At-Rest Encryption

Here we look at the tools you can use to encrypt your data where it is stored on the disk. We take a deep dive into Transparent Data Encryption (TDE) as well as covering the separate Backup Encryption feature.

Chapter 2, "Introducing Transparent Data Encryption," gives a background about TDE; we cover what it is, how it works, and what it protects you from.

Chapter 3, "Setting Up TDE," goes over the steps of setting up TDE and how to avoid any pitfalls. We also look at TDE performance and how you can assess the impact on your servers.

Chapter 4, "Managing TDE," looks at topics you need to be aware of to manage TDE over time. This includes key rotation as well as how to recover the database in case of failure.

Chapter 5, "Backup Encryption," shows how you set up Backup Encryption and how to work with encrypted backups. You only need to use Backup Encryption though if you can't use TDE for some reason.

Part III: Column Encryption Using Always Encrypted

This part is a comprehensive look at the Always Encrypted feature, introduced in SQL Server 2016, that allows you to encrypt your columns of data with the maximum level of security and the minimum amount of application rework.

Chapter 6, "Introducing Always Encrypted," discusses what Always Encrypted is and how it protects you. We also go into detail about how it works in practice.

Chapter 7, "Setting Up Always Encrypted," goes through the steps of setting up Always Encrypted and creating encrypted columns. Each step is discussed at length, so you fully understand what is going on.

Chapter 8, "Executing Queries Using Always Encrypted," looks at how you work with data in encrypted columns. We look at basic querying patterns as well as what happens behind the scenes. Then we cover how you work with Always Encrypted through stored procedures and application code.

Chapter 9, "Encrypting Existing Data with Always Encrypted," covers the different methods you can use to encrypt existing data with Always Encrypted. We look at how they work as well as discussing the issues you may face.

Chapter 10, "Limitations with Always Encrypted," discusses what you can't do with encrypted data and explains why.

Chapter 11, "Key Rotation with Always Encrypted," talks about how to manage the periodic refreshing of your encryption keys.

Chapter 12, "Considerations When Implementing Always Encrypted," covers other things you want to think about before you implement encryption. That includes source code and release management, ETL, and performance.

Part IV: Column Encryption Using Always Encrypted with Enclaves

Having looked at the "basic" version of Always Encrypted, we now take an in-depth look at how the version with enclaves differs and how you work with it.

Chapter 13, "Introducing Always Encrypted with Enclaves," explains what using enclaves with Always Encrypted means to us, what it enables you to do, and how it works.

Chapter 14, "Setting Up Always Encrypted with Enclaves," focuses on how you can set up Always Encrypted with Enclaves in a lab environment.

Chapter 15, "In-Place Encryption with Always Encrypted Enclaves," looks at the new functionality that enclaves offer us in terms of in-place encryption and decryption. We also discuss performance and look at how the same functionality can be used to rotate your column encryption keys.

Chapter 16, "Rich Querying with Always Encrypted Enclaves," covers the new querying functionality offered with enclaves. We look at what happens in the background when you issue queries that are executed in the enclave as well as talking extensively about indexes and how they work.

Chapter 17, "Setting Up TPM Attestation," goes through the steps of setting up TPM attestation for the highest level of security, where you are protected against even the most sophisticated hardware and software attacks. We go through the steps in detail as well as looking at how you can troubleshoot if you run into issues.

Part V: Completing the Picture

In addition to the big features like TDE and Always Encrypted, there are other items that should be included in a comprehensive encryption strategy. We cover those in this part as well as looking at other methods that are available for encrypting data.

Chapter 18, "Encryption In Transit Using Transport Layer Security," looks at how you encrypt network traffic so that data is protected even when it leaves the database.

Chapter 19, "Hashing and Salting of Passwords," discusses the best practice for storing passwords.

Chapter 20, "Extensible Key Management (EKM)," shows how you can centrally manage your encryption keys in an external store. We look at how you can set up both TDE and Always Encrypted to work with keys stored in Azure Key Vault.

Chapter 21, "Other Methods of Column Encryption," looks at methods of column encryption within SQL Server that predate Always Encrypted. It's recommended that you should use Always Encrypted for encrypting your columns of data, but there may be edge cases where you need to use one of these methods instead.

Appendixes

We round off the book with a few reference sections that may be of use, or of interest, to the reader.

Appendix A, "Glossary of Terms," is the collection of all the terms related to encryption we've used in the book, so you've got them in one place if you need to look them up quickly.

Appendix B, "Encryption in the Cloud," looks at how the features discussed in the book differ if you're working in a cloud-based scenario. The features are by and large the same, but there are differences in some cases. We discuss what those differences are if you're working in Azure or AWS.

Appendix C, "Encryption Algorithms," goes into brief detail about the history of the encryption algorithms we use within SQL Server and looks at how they work.

Downloading the Code

There are numerous code samples throughout this book to demonstrate the concepts and syntax, as well as to provide demos that you can – and I hope will – repeat for yourself. All the code can be downloaded from `www.github.com/apress/ pro-encryption-sql-server-2022`.

Contacting the Author

I'm more than happy to take questions and keen to hear if you think I've got anything wrong. The best ways to contact me are through my Twitter handle (@MattMcGiffen) or via my blog (`https://matthewmcgiffen.com/`). If you follow me on either of those platforms, you'll also be kept up to date with anything else I write on the topic of encryption or SQL Server in a wider sense.

PART I

Understanding the Landscape

CHAPTER 1

Purpose of Encryption and Available Tools

SQL Server has had the native ability to encrypt data since SQL Server 2005. This included functionality that could be used to encrypt individual items and columns of data as well as the Transparent Data Encryption (TDE) feature which was available with the enterprise edition of SQL Server and could be used to encrypt all data where it is stored on disk. We then didn't see significant additions to the features available for encryption until 2016 when Microsoft added Always Encrypted for column encryption. In SQL Server 2019 Microsoft made TDE available in standard edition, and also in SQL Server 2019 the ability to use enclaves was added to Always Encrypted to improve the available functionality for interacting with encrypted data. Finally in SQL Server 2022 further enhancements were made to the set of functionality available when working with Always Encrypted with enclaves.

We can see Always Encrypted (which was introduced in 2016) as the successor to previous methods of column encryption, and we will spend a good portion of this book going into a high level of detail on Always Encrypted. As such you will get the best value out of this book if you are on SQL 2016 or higher – though we do cover the older methods in brief.

In this chapter we're going to look at the purpose of encryption, why you might want to encrypt data, and what you should hope to achieve by doing so. We'll also discuss briefly how data protection regulation might factor into your plans. Then we'll look at an overview of the tools available and discuss how you should use them in concert to provide as secure an implementation as possible.

© Matthew McGiffen 2022
M. McGiffen, *Pro Encryption in SQL Server 2022*, https://doi.org/10.1007/978-1-4842-8664-7_1

What Is the Purpose of Encryption?

On the face of it, this is a very obvious question with a very obvious answer. We want to prevent data from falling into the wrong hands. In practice, it gets a little more complicated. Exactly what types of attacks do you wish to be protected against? It's good if we make sure our data is encrypted where it is stored on the disk, but that doesn't help us if an attacker gains direct access to write queries against the database. We might encrypt data held in columns, but does that still protect us if the unencrypted data is being passed back across the network to our application and an attacker is intercepting our network traffic?

Another question is why are you considering encryption in the first place? Often projects consider encryption because relevant regulation, or client requirements, demand it. All too often in these cases, encryption is considered as a binary option, is data encrypted or not. Often what happens is that the bare minimum is done to tick the checkbox and move on. Data might be encrypted, but the protection offered is of value in only limited scenarios.

When we think about what scenarios we wish to be protected against it makes sense to consider where data exists and might therefore be vulnerable. By that I'm not talking about where specific data is held, but rather the types of locations:

- On disk, mainly in data files and backup files

- In memory on the database server

- In transit across the network

- In your application

- Files stored outside of the database, perhaps on a file share

In this book we'll look at how the tools available in SQL Server can protect the first three. We won't however look at it once it reaches your application; that's for your application developers to consider. We also don't talk about files stored outside of the database – but you should think about how you want to protect such items if you have them.

Encryption is only one line of defense and should go hand in hand with a well-defined and implemented approach to security. Your first line of defense is always going to be access controls, making sure that only the right users and applications can access your data and servers in the first place. Some might say that if you have access controls in place, then why do you need encryption at all. The answer is that there is always the potential for access controls to be breached. The best approaches to security are always multilayered, and on top of access control and encryption, it is good to have auditing in place so you can see who is accessing your systems and what they are doing, as well as having alerting in place for suspicious activity.

Even though we have a good toolset for encryption available to us in SQL Server, it doesn't come totally for free. Encrypting and decrypting data requires CPU, and so it does have some performance overhead; we'll discuss that when talking about each tool, and in many cases, we'll try to look at how you can quantify what level of overhead you might be looking at.

We also will generally have an increase in management overhead, for instance, where we need to manage encryption keys. When implementing encryption it is important to consider how you will manage it on an ongoing basis. One of the worst scenarios you can encounter with encryption is where an individual sets up encryption without telling anyone else where the keys are backed up and then that individual leaves the organization, and if we have a server failure, we may never be able to recover our encrypted data.

The last impact is on functionality; we'll talk about this a lot when we look at column encryption: where we only store encrypted values in the database that limits how you can interact with them, for instance, searching against such columns or performing calculations. Due to this, an important part of your encryption strategy will be deciding what data to encrypt and how you're going to work with it once it is encrypted.

When choosing what to encrypt we are usually most focused on personally identifiable information (PII) as well as items deemed particularly sensitive. In considering your approach I'd recommend that something is always better than nothing. If you have a security breach and your list of users is accessed, then that is bad, but it is much better if you are able to say that passwords, credit card information, social security numbers, and other information were not accessed due to the extra encryption on these items.

Encryption and Data Protection Regulation

One of the reasons you may be considering encryption is due to the relevant data protection regulation: either because the regulation specifies that data should be encrypted or because of the large potential penalties where there is a data breach. Some

US companies have been hit by fines in the hundreds of millions of dollars following data breaches, so we are talking large sums of money. In Europe the largest fines so far (under the GDPR) have been related to misuse of personal data or consent (750 million euros is the highest I am aware of), but there have been fines of up to 30 million euros for data breaches. In the case of a breach, you could also be sued by individuals whose data has been accessed or by class action.

I'm not aware of any fines (large ones at least), or successful lawsuits, where a hacker gained access to a company's systems but was not able to access data as it was securely encrypted. Some regulation also explicitly specifies exemptions where only encrypted data has been accessed. If you implement encryption, and do so well, you are certainly reducing your company's financial exposure in the case of an attack successfully getting through your first lines of defense. If you implement encryption poorly though, you may not be making it too hard for attackers to get around the protection you have put in place.

It's not really a point about regulation, but where you have a breach, you are also open to reputational damage, especially if you haven't followed good practice. I regularly see threads on Twitter, mocking in almost disbelief, companies who haven't protected items such as passwords in the right manner.

Most of the general regulation I'm aware of doesn't specifically require you to encrypt data, but it may recommend that you consider it. The European GDPR (General Data Protection Regulation), for instance, recommends encryption, but does not require it. Some legislation specific to particular business sectors however does specifically require encryption; in the United States, for instance, HIPAA (Health Insurance Portability and Accountability Act) does explicitly require encryption of certain healthcare data. You need to be aware of data protection regulation that applies to the industries you are working with and understand what that regulation requires you to do.

Most countries now have some sort of general data protection regulation in place. Here are a few key ones (this is by no means a comprehensive list):

- Europe has the GDPR. Note that although the UK has left the European Union since Brexit, legislation has been passed to put pretty much the same rules (known as the UK GDPR) in place.

- The United States doesn't have the same sort of regulation at the federal level, but there are many states that do have their own data-related laws and many others that are in the process of enacting them. The CCPA (California Consumer Privacy Act) is seen as a key player.

- Canada has PIPEDA (Personal Information Protection and Electronic Documents Act) which is quite similar to Europe's GDPR.

- India has the Personal Data Protection bill that also has many of the same rules as the GDPR.

- South Africa has POPIA (Protection of Personal Information Act). This doesn't align directly with the GDPR but is seen as being just as rigorous.

It's estimated that more than 120 countries have some form of data protection regulation.

In addition to general data protection regulation there may be other requirements depending on the industry you work in. We've mention HIPAA. Here are a few others:

- In the United States, there are federal laws that apply to the processing of financial data. These include Sarbanes-Oxley and FACTA (Fair and Accurate Credit Transactions Act).

- Also in the United States, there is FISMA (Federal Information Security Management Act) specific to government agencies and those who work with them.

- In the UK, the FSA (Financial Standards Authority) imposes rules regarding the processing of financial data.

Overview of the Tools Available in SQL Server

Table 1-1 shows the list of encryption features in SQL Server that we cover in this book and what each tool is intended to protect.

Table 1-1. *Encryption features available in SQL Server*

Feature	What is protected
Transparent Data Encryption (TDE)	Data saved to disk. This includes data files, transaction log files, backup files, and database snapshots
Backup Encryption	Backup files
Always Encrypted	Data stored in columns. With Always Encrypted, the data is protected on disk, in memory, and in transit across the network
Transport Layer Security (TLS)	Network traffic. TLS protects data in transit across the network as well as commands executed against the database server
Hashing and Salting	This is not strictly encryption, but we generally use it to protect passwords
Encryption Functions	Data stored in columns. Here we are referring to the encryption functions introduced in SQL 2005 that predate Always Encrypted
Extensible Key Management (EKM)	This provides extra protection and ease of management for encryption keys by enabling them to be stored with an external provider

Let's take a brief look at each of these features in turn.

TDE

TDE protects our data stored on disk, what we often refer to as "at-rest" data. It offers good protection against the scenario where the file system is accessed, and an attacker might attempt to retrieve data directly from the database files themselves or copy the backup files so they can be restored to another SQL Server to access the data. It doesn't protect us at all though where an attacker may have access to query the database directly. The "transparent" part of the name refers to the fact that TDE works transparently in the background with no impact on our queries or other application functionality. TDE protects all of the data in a database, unlike methods of column encryption which usually target specific types of information to encrypt.

Backup Encryption

Backup Encryption just encrypts our backup files. This includes full backups, differential backups, and log backups. This is particularly useful where we might store backups, possibly on tape, off-site and want to make sure they are inaccessible if stolen. TDE also does this for us, so we only consider using Backup Encryption where we can't use TDE for some reason.

Always Encrypted

Always Encrypted is a form of column encryption. It works hand in hand with the client driver that your application uses to connect to and query the database to ensure that data remains encrypted all the way to the point it reaches your application. That's what the "always" part of the name refers to. Data is protected at rest, in memory, and in transit across the network. Encryption and decryption actually take place within the client driver rather than within SQL Server.

In this book we will look in-depth at two flavors of Always Encrypted. We have the basic version that was introduced in SQL Server 2016 and Always Encrypted with Secure Enclaves that was added in SQL Server 2019. What's nice about Always Encrypted is that encryption and decryption are carried out automatically for you by the client driver, so in many cases you may not even have to make code changes. There are limitations on how you can interact with encrypted data though. The version with enclaves removes some of those restrictions by allowing certain activities to place in a secure portion of memory (called an enclave) on the database server. The use of enclaves does however come with an extra overhead in setup and management.

TLS

TLS is used to encrypt network traffic. That means that data and queries sent between the application and database server are all encrypted. This is similar to SSL, which most people are familiar with for encrypting Internet traffic (SSL in most cases actually uses the TLS protocol).

Hashing and Salting

Hashing and salting isn't actually encryption because it is a one-way process. Hashing is where we run a value through a function that produces a seemingly random output. That output will always be the same for the same input value but cannot be reverse-engineered to find the original value. Salting is a method to provide extra security for hashed values. Hashing and salting is considered the best practice for storing passwords as it means we don't even need to store actual passwords – so there should be no way for an attacker to access them.

Encryption Functions

Here we refer to the set of encryption functions that SQL Server implements to allow you to encrypt your own data. I see Always Encrypted as the successor to these functions and would recommend you use that where possible. Encryption using the functions is a bit more limiting, a bit less secure, and a bit harder to implement than with Always Encrypted. There may be some scenarios where you want to use them though, so we cover them in brief – though hopefully in enough detail that it tells you everything you need to know.

EKM

Most encryption is based on keys, and we need to think about how and where we manage them over time. EKM is functionality that allows you to store them outside of your server, either on a piece of kit that sits in a rack in your server room called a Hardware Security Module (HSM) or, more commonly these days, using a cloud service like Azure Key Vault. You don't need to use EKM in order to implement a secure encryption strategy, but it's certainly worth considering due to the ease of management that comes from having all of your keys in one place. It's also easier to manage policies such as access control when you take a centralized approach to storing your keys.

Recommended Approach to Encryption

We looked earlier at the various places our data lives – on disk, in memory, or in transit across the network. A good strategy will protect all of these locations – sometimes with multiple layers. Exactly how you go about doing that for your applications may vary – but as long as you are on SQL Server 2016 or higher, there is a default strategy that you should consider. This combines a number of the available SQL Server features to provide the best protection.

- **TDE**. For at-rest protection of all your data, though if you are on a version of SQL Server older than 2019 you will need enterprise edition to use TDE

- **Always Encrypted**. To encrypt all (or most) columns that contain personal identifiable or sensitive information

- **TLS**. To make sure network communications between the application and server are encrypted

- **Hashing and Salting of passwords**. To make sure passwords are secure and we never need to store the actual password in the database

On top of that you should definitely consider using EKM. In previous times, when we had to have dedicated hardware to support it, there was a fair barrier to entry. Now with easily usable and cost-effective cloud solutions, it's easy to get started with EKM and certainly has many advantages.

Encryption is easiest to build in "by-design" when developing new applications, but more often than not we are implementing or enhancing encryption against our existing applications. It's great if you are in that situation and have the scope to implement a full encryption strategy as outlined above. Such projects often have time and budget constraints though or need to be delivered incrementally. If that's where you are at, then you may want to focus first on where you can achieve the most with the least effort. You need to assess whether implementing any of the preceding features is going to have a performance impact that worries you, once you've dealt with that you might want to look at things in this order:

- **Hashing and Salting of passwords**. I put this item first because you should never be storing passwords in plaintext in a database. If you are encrypting passwords before storing them, then that's better than plaintext, but still you should be looking at a hashing method.

11

- **TLS**. You really should have this on for all your connections between your applications and SQL Server that could contain data or other information you care about protecting. TLS is very easy to set up and this can be done very quickly.

- **TDE**. TDE is again very easy to set up, and it comes for free with the standard edition of SQL Server 2019 onward. It used to require you to be on enterprise edition, so that was a good reason why many people didn't use it. TDE is only going to protect you against a limited number of scenarios, but you still get that for not much more than the flick of a switch.

- **Always Encrypted**. Column encryption with Always Encrypted is a little harder to understand, and there are limitations on the ways you can work with encrypted data. It is however the best tool for protecting your personal and sensitive data. If your project has limited resource (what project doesn't), focus on encrypting first the most sensitive items and those where you won't need to make code changes to work around the fact that data is encrypted. Code changes are likely to be required where you need to search against, or perform calculations on, data that you wish to encrypt.

Encryption in the Cloud

More and more SQL Server workloads are now being hosted in cloud environments, and it's common for the development of new applications to take a cloud-first approach. The key thing to understand in these cases is that SQL Server in the cloud is still SQL Server. It has most of the same features and you work with them in much the same way. Most of what we discuss in this book still applies and is valid whether you are running SQL Server on premises or on a cloud platform. It is also still valid if you are running SQL Server through a Software as a Service (SaaS) product such as Azure SQL Database, Azure SQL Managed Instance, or Amazon Web Services Relational Database Service (AWS RDS).

There will however be some differences or things you can't do. You can't, for instance, use Always Encrypted with secure enclaves on AWS RDS – though you can use the basic version of Always Encrypted. Again using Always Encrypted with enclaves as an example, you can use it with Azure SQL Database – but you use a different Attestation provider to the one we talk about in the chapters about enclaves.

We go into a bit of detail about the various encryption technologies, what is different, what is possible, and what is not, in Appendix B - Encryption in the Cloud. We'll cover all the encryption features discussed in this book and look at the main hosting options you are likely to be using if running SQL Server in the cloud:

- SQL Server in Azure running on a virtual machine

- Azure SQL Database

- Azure SQL Managed Instance

- SQL Server in AWS running on a virtual machine (EC2)

- SQL Server on AWS RDS

Summary

In this chapter we've gone over some background on why you might be wanting to encrypt data and what you might want to encrypt. We've also looked briefly at the tools available within SQL Server and where they fit in your overall encryption strategy.

Next we'll look at each tool in detail, starting with TDE.

PART II

At-Rest Encryption

CHAPTER 2

Introducing Transparent Data Encryption

In this chapter we begin to look at Transparent Data Encryption (TDE). TDE was introduced in SQL Server 2005 as a way to encrypt your data. It remains part of SQL Server and pretty much unchanged right up to the latest versions.

For a long time TDE was only available in the enterprise edition of the product, but from SQL 2019 you can use it in the standard edition also. That makes it a tool that many of us who use SQL Server can utilize without any additional price tag.

What Is TDE?

TDE is referred to as a "transparent" form of encryption. What that means is that the process of encrypting and decrypting data is fully performed in the background. The queries we write to access data are unchanged whether TDE is enabled or not. So, enabling TDE has no impact on application functionality, does not require refactoring of code, and is therefore relatively easy to implement. TDE encrypts all the data in a database, so you don't need to choose which data items to encrypt.

TDE allows us to encrypt "at-rest" data. When we talk about "at-rest" data, we are referring to data that has been written to disk. TDE works at the IO level, encrypting data automatically as it is written to disk and decrypting it as it is read from disk.

In terms of our SQL databases, the assets that are protected include the following:

- Any data files for our database

- Any log files for our database

- All backup files for the database, full, log, or differential backups

© Matthew McGiffen 2022
M. McGiffen, *Pro Encryption in SQL Server 2022*, https://doi.org/10.1007/978-1-4842-8664-7_2

- Database snapshot files

- Also the TempDB database data and log files are encrypted

The last item in that list, TempDB, needs to be encrypted for completeness of protection. Imagine that you query your database and as part of the query execution TempDB is used. If that data were written to disk, then that creates a hole in our protection, and someone could potentially read or copy the TempDB files and might see some of the data we are trying to protect. As a result, when you enable TDE against any database on your SQL Server instance, the TempDB database is automatically encrypted as well to prevent this from happening.

It's reasonably obvious to state that data "at rest" doesn't include the following things:

- Data loaded/stored in memory (buffer pool)

- Data returned from a query and being passed across the network

- Data received by a client as a result of a query

If you want to cover those scenarios as well, then you need to look at other forms of encryption such as TLS and Always Encrypted.

There are also some less obvious exceptions:

- Filestream data

- Data persisted to disk using Buffer Pool Extensions

And there are a couple of other exceptions that can occur in particular circumstances:

- Where the buffer pool gets paged to disk due to memory pressure

- SQL dump files when there is a crash

What does and doesn't get encrypted by TDE is summarized in the succeeding diagram (Figure 2-1):

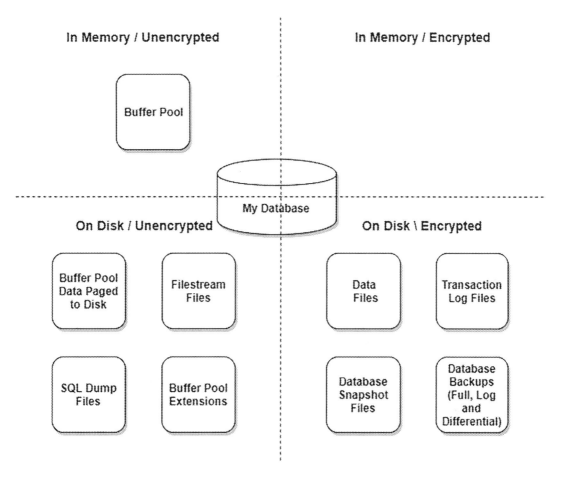

Figure 2-1. *What data does TDE encrypt?*

Let's have a look at the contents of some SQL data files so you can see the difference with and without TDE. I've created a database with a single table and inserted a row of data with the following code:

```
CREATE DATABASE TestTDE;
GO
USE TestTDE;
GO
CREATE TABLE dbo.SomeData
      (Id INT IDENTITY(1,1), SomeText VARCHAR(255));
GO
INSERT INTO dbo.SomeData (SomeText) VALUES('This is my data');
GO
```

I'll close my connection from the database and detach it so I can open the files in a Hex Editor. You can detach the database with the following SQL:

```
USE master;
GO
EXEC master.dbo.sp_detach_db @dbname = N'TestTDE';
```

Then I open the file in my Hex Editor and search for the text "This is my data" in the data file (Figure 2-2).

```
0020FFB0    F8 07 BC 07 88 07 4E 07 24 07 F6 06 DA 06 86 06    ø.¼.^.N.$.ö.Ú.†.
0020FFC0    54 06 1C 06 E0 05 A0 05 6E 05 34 05 EE 04 BE 04    T...à. .n.4.î.¾.
0020FFD0    84 04 44 04 1E 04 F4 03 BC 03 66 03 22 03 EE 02    „.D...ô.¼.f.".î.
0020FFE0    A8 02 4A 02 00 02 D4 01 AA 01 76 01 48 01 1E 01    ¨.J...Ô.ª.v.H...
0020FFF0    FC 00 CE 00 FA 1A A2 00 78 00 1A 1B D6 1A 60 00    ü.Î.ú.¢.x...Ö.`.
00210000    01 01 00 00 00 82 00 01 00 00 00 00 00 00 08 00    .....,..........
00210010    00 00 00 00 00 00 01 00 89 00 00 00 80 1F 7E 00    ........‰...€.~.
00210020    08 01 00 00 01 00 00 00 3D 00 00 00 5A 00 00 00    ........=...Z...
00210030    1C 00 00 00 00 00 00 00 00 00 00 00 24 BC 63 4D    ............$¼cM
00210040    00 00 00 00 00 00 00 00 00 00 00 00 00 00 00 00    ................
00210050    00 00 00 00 00 00 00 00 00 00 00 00 00 00 00 00    ................
00210060    30 00 08 00 01 00 00 00 02 00 00 01 00 1E 00 54    0..............T
00210070    68 69 73 20 69 73 20 6D 79 20 64 61 74 61 00 00    his is my data..
00210080    21 21 21 21 21 21 21 21 21 21 21 21 21 21 21 21    !!!!!!!!!!!!!!!!
00210090    21 21 21 21 21 21 21 21 21 21 21 21 21 21 21 21    !!!!!!!!!!!!!!!!
002100A0    21 21 21 21 21 21 21 21 21 21 21 21 21 21 21 21    !!!!!!!!!!!!!!!!
002100B0    21 21 21 21 21 21 21 21 21 21 21 21 21 21 21 21    !!!!!!!!!!!!!!!!
002100C0    21 21 21 21 21 21 21 21 21 21 21 21 21 21 21 21    !!!!!!!!!!!!!!!!
002100D0    21 21 21 21 21 21 21 21 21 21 21 21 21 21 21 21    !!!!!!!!!!!!!!!!
```

Figure 2-2. *Viewing the contents of an unencrypted database in a Hex Editor*

As you can see the data is stored as clear as day in the data file.

Now let's look at the same data file once TDE has been enabled (we will look at enabling TDE in Chapter 3). This time if I search for the same text, it's not found, and my data looks like that in Figure 2-3.

```
0020FE00  C1 44 58 84 6E C8 AC E2 81 64 1B B6 E1 BE F0 6D   ÁDX„nÈ¬â.d.¶á%õm
0020FE10  BB 3E EC B9 32 35 61 3E 26 AF BD E1 8D D0 EB CE   »>ì¹25a>&¯½á.ÐëÎ
0020FE20  7E B3 F1 8E 80 17 AA DE D0 BA 79 A0 37 EA 7F DC   ~³ñŽ€.ªÞÐºy 7ê.Ü
0020FE30  F6 F0 51 34 57 5F 89 67 44 34 ED 02 E2 70 8F CA   öðQ4W_‰gD4í.âp.Ê
0020FE40  7C E4 01 49 64 D5 D7 DE D3 CA C0 F0 31 41 D6 B3   |ä.IdÕ×ÞÓÊÀð1AÖ³
0020FE50  AA 6D ED 3D 1A 7C 5F 57 CD E7 C2 81 AE FE D5 7B   ªmí=.|_WÍçÂ.®þÕ{
0020FE60  AD 3A 8B 2D 2E B5 20 42 CF 95 FF EC F2 E7 70 70   .:‹-.µ BÏ•ÿìòçpp
0020FE70  3C E2 92 38 18 43 EC 17 89 75 E2 32 8E 22 47 8C   <â'8.Cì.‰uâ2Ž"GŒ
0020FE80  7A AF D5 27 88 83 6F F9 CC 2E 1A 11 FE 91 29 31   z¯Õ'ˆƒoùÌ...þ')1
0020FE90  33 D1 91 CB 96 D8 3A 5C 99 4E DF B1 B9 3D F1 2B   3Ñ'Ë–Ø:\™Nß±¹=ñ+
0020FEA0  B3 A5 3F 72 7B 16 D9 3B 25 9F 80 4B 7B DB 8E E0   ³¥?r{.Ù;%Ÿ€K{ÛŽà
0020FEB0  E2 91 43 15 F1 45 3A C2 43 20 DD C8 6B 27 02 52   â'C.ñE:ÂC ÝÈk'.R
0020FEC0  2D BC CF 60 27 2E B9 7D F0 05 FF F4 0D D4 C3 46   -¼Ï`'.¹}ð.ÿô.ÔÃF
0020FED0  C1 20 FE 25 98 73 73 AB 19 BE A8 92 7B 16 88 4E   Á þ%˜ss«.¾¨'{.ˆN
0020FEE0  5C F0 DB FE 41 C6 63 0F 10 BB 54 05 37 D6 D7 2F   \ðÛþAÆc..»T.7Ö×/
0020FEF0  E8 B1 41 31 DB B8 22 D9 64 30 AC 9E 5F EC 1A 31   è±A1Û¸"Ùd0¬ž_ì.1
0020FF00  6B 48 AA 9A 34 39 D5 27 58 6F 10 F4 DE B4 71 04   kHªš49Õ'Xo.ôÞ´q.
0020FF10  F5 8B 3C 46 EC C8 16 8D 84 1D ED 39 7F AD B4 83   õ‹<FìÈ..„.í9..´ƒ
```

Figure 2-3. *Viewing the contents of a TDE encrypted database in a Hex Editor*

It's interesting to also look at the end of the database file where there is free space. In the unencrypted version that free space would have simply been represented by zeros. In the encrypted version that free space too has been encrypted, so an attacker cannot even see where your data ends (Figure 2-4).

```
007FFFA0  09 AA 29 B2 35 43 2A 4B AD A0 D8 52 B0 3B 86 72   .ª)²5C*K.. ØR°;†r
007FFFB0  71 ED 2C A4 59 2E BD 2B 44 8D 7B 49 35 F6 0E 1C   qí,¤Y.½+D.{I5ö..
007FFFC0  97 36 39 56 AF F2 EC AE D0 41 F8 85 D0 80 91 09   —69V¯òì®ÐAø…Ð€'.
007FFFD0  E2 A2 8D 68 37 7D 90 50 41 95 CA 3F 87 93 EF C7   â¢.h7}.PA•Ê?‡"ïÇ
007FFFE0  41 E8 45 1D 03 76 55 18 1E 82 9B 46 BC 21 08 00   AèE..vU..,›F¼!..
007FFFF0  CE D7 64 88 CE 32 72 C0 69 24 3C 84 D5 19 4C 60   Î×dˆÎ2rÀi$<„Õ.L`
```

Figure 2-4. *Even the empty space in your database file is encrypted*

TDE works by using an encryption key that is stored in the database being encrypted – but that key is itself stored encrypted by an object outside of the database. We'll look at the various objects involved in the next section.

Understanding Keys and Certificates

When you first look at the encryption hierarchy for TDE in SQL Server, it can be a bit daunting. There seem to be a lot of objects involved, and it might not be clear why each is required. It can be tempting to skip a full understanding of all the objects and just get on with setting things up – which is relatively straightforward.

I'd encourage you not to do that and I'll explain why. There are a lot of scenarios that might crop up in the lifecycle of a TDE-protected database instance: recovering a protected database from backup, migrating database from one server to another, or managing high availability. The list goes on.

There are a lot of resources out there that will advise you on how to do these things – but many of them are inaccurate. Only by understanding how TDE works – and in particular how it uses the various encryption objects – can you be sure what approach is correct. And better than that – if you have a good understanding of the architecture of TDE, you won't need these resources; the correct approach will follow logically from your understanding of how things work.

TDE uses multiple keys and certificates in the process of protecting your database. This is something we'll see in common with other forms of encryption. The reason for that is both about providing the best level of protection and supporting ease of management for your protected databases.

Keys in SQL Server often have at least three components:

- **The Encryption Key itself** – Usually can be thought of a number expressed in binary format, long and random enough to make it difficult to guess even by brute force attempts. This is the key that is actually used to encrypt and decrypt your data.

- **Another object that's used to protect the key** – This object might be another key, it might be a certificate, or it might just be a password. This object is used to encrypt the encryption key.

- **The encrypted value of the encryption key** – Formed from the original value of the key, encrypted by the protecting object.

In SQL we rarely (maybe even never) see the actual value of the key. We have the encrypted version and we usually know what object was used to encrypt it. That second object may even be another key that is itself encrypted by a third object.

When it comes down to it though, the actual thing that is used to encrypt or decrypt data is the key itself, not the encrypted value and not the hierarchy of objects that may have been used to protect it.

So, all I really need to read your data is your key.

Let's look at that in the context of TDE. In Figure 2-5 we see the hierarchy of encryption objects supporting TDE. There are other ways of working with TDE, but the approach in Figure 2-5 is the standard.

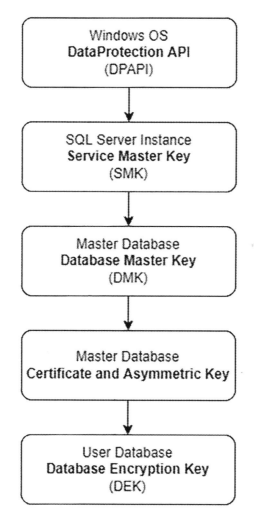

Figure 2-5. *The encryption hierarchy for TDE*

Let's look at the objects one at a time.

Database Encryption Key (DEK)

Right at the bottom of the hierarchy is the DEK. This is stored in the database itself and is what is actually used to encrypt and decrypt data in the database. The DEK is a symmetric key, which means the same key is used to both encrypt and decrypt data. Symmetric key encryption is much quicker than asymmetric key encryption which is why such a key is used in this case. We want the "transparent" encryption activities to have as little overhead as possible while keeping things secure.

The DEK is actually stored encrypted in the database. Encryption wouldn't be very effective if the key was stored in plain sight for anyone to access and use. As it is stored encrypted, even if someone has your files, there is no way for them to access the unencrypted version of the DEK and use it to read your data.

The encrypted DEK is also stored in any database backups.

Certificate and Associated Asymmetric Key Pair

At the next level up we have the certificate, which contains a public key which can be used to encrypt data and has a reference to a private key which must be used to decrypt data. The two keys together are known as a public/private key pair and are used to encrypt the DEK using asymmetric encryption.

The public key can be held in plain sight as it can only be used to encrypt data. The private key is required to decrypt data. The private key is in turn encrypted to make sure it is protected.

There are other options for protecting your DEK which include using an asymmetric key that is stored externally to your SQL Server. This is managed through something called Extensible Key Management (EKM), and we look at that in Chapter 20.

Database Master Key (DMK)

The DMK is stored in the Master database and is what's used to encrypt the private key. However, the DMK isn't just used for your database and indeed isn't just used for TDE. It can support a number of activities. There can be only one DMK for your SQL instance. The DMK is in turn encrypted.

Service Master Key (SMK)

The SMK is created when you first install your SQL Server instance and is unique to the instance. The SMK is used to protect your DMK. It is in turn protected by the operating system Data Protection API (DPAPI).

Understanding the Need for the Hierarchy

That's a lot of layers of encryption to deal with. It can be difficult to understand why we need so many.

Let's look at one scenario to aid our understanding. We'll look at how it works in practice and what the vulnerabilities might be if we didn't have all these different levels of encryption.

Let's say you want to restore a TDE-protected database to another server – a common requirement. The encrypted DEK is already stored in your backup file – so we have that. You would be forgiven however in thinking that we need to migrate copies of all the layers above it in order to be able to read our protected database.

We run into problems however as soon as we think about migrating the DMK. Remember there can only be one DMK per instance: what if the instance we are restoring to already has a DMK and that DMK is already used to protect other objects. We can't just replace it. That is why it is critical that there must be an object between the DMK and the DEK; the DMK cannot be used to encrypt the DEK directly.

However, we still need the DMK to read the private key associated with the certificate. Don't we?

In practice you are able – and pretty much required – to back up the certificate to disk and also the private key associated with it. If you don't do this and it is lost (for instance, if the server crashes and is unrecoverable), then your data is pretty much lost.

The command for backing up the certificate looks something like this (though note you will not be able to execute it until you follow the steps for setting TDE up in Chapter 3 where we will look at the command again):

```
USE master;
GO
BACKUP CERTIFICATE MyTDECert
    TO FILE = 'C:\Test\MyTDECert.cer'
```

```
WITH PRIVATE KEY(
   FILE = 'C:\Test\MyTDECert_PrivateKeyFile.pvk',
   ENCRYPTION BY PASSWORD = 'C0rrecth0rserbatterystab1e'
);
```

As mentioned previously, code samples for this book can be found at
www.github.com/apress/pro-encryption-sql-server-2022

You can see that when we backup the certificate, we specify a password to encrypt the private key. Remember that the private key was already encrypted by the DMK? This BACKUP CERTIFICATE command doesn't just encrypt it a second time – what would be the point of that? No, the reason we need to supply a password is that the command retrieves the unencrypted version of the private key and re-encrypts it with the password INSTEAD and then that is what gets saved to disk.

Remember that at the point I run the command, SQL has access to all the objects, all the way up the chain, that are used for the encryption. So, it has no problem getting the actual value for the private key.

Now, when I restore that certificate to – let's say – another instance of SQL Server, the command looks like this (again this is just an example for discussion purposes, we will look at this command again in Chapter 3 once the actual objects are created):

```
USE master;
GO
CREATE CERTIFICATE MyTDECert
FROM FILE = 'C:\Test\MyTDECert.cer'
WITH PRIVATE KEY(
   FILE = 'C:\Test\MyTDECert_PrivateKeyFile.pvk',
   DECRYPTION BY PASSWORD = 'C0rrecth0rserbatterystab1e'
);
```

Considering what the BACKUP command did, you can figure out that the preceding command will do the opposite. It first of all decrypts the private key using the password supplied. Then it encrypts it again using the DMK for the local instance before saving it in the master database locally.

Remember it is the actual values of keys that get used for encryption – not their encrypted value. So, the private key for this certificate is exactly the same as it was where we backed it up from – though the encrypted value will be different as it is protected by a different DMK.

If I now go to restore a copy of a database whose DEK has been encrypted with this certificate onto the new instance, I can do so without any problem.

Many articles will tell you that you also need to migrate the DMK from your old instance, and some will say that you also need the SMK. This is simply not correct – I mean, it will work if you do that, in the right order, but it isn't necessary.

So all you need to have to restore a database protected by TDE is the database backup, the certificate/private key backups, and the password specified when the certificate and key were backed up.

Equally that's all someone else needs too, so make sure those things are protected.

There are other reasons it would not be desirable to have the DEK directly protected by the DMK. We can have a separate certificate for each database protected by TDE if we wish – and I would suggest that is good practice. Someone could steal the backup of that, not a big deal unless they have the password used to protect it also. If they do, then they can access our data. That's not good, but at least we have minimized the attack surface and they have only accessed one database. If the DMK was used to protect the DEK directly, then we would need to back that up in a similar manner – and if that was stolen in the same way, then protection for all objects and databases protected by the DMK would be breached.

We'll see other scenarios where the multiple levels in the encryption hierarchy for TDE help us in the later chapters in this section around managing TDE and its lifecycle with your databases.

How Secure Is TDE?

When we consider how secure a form of encryption is, there are two things we want to consider.

- What threat scenarios we are protected from.

- How easy is it to break down the encryption.

Let's discuss each of these in turn.

What Are We Protected From?

TDE encrypts data stored on the file system, so it should be pretty clear that we are trying to protect ourselves from an attacker who gets access to our files. You would be right in suggesting that shouldn't be allowed to happen. Access controls should be in place to prevent inappropriate access. The reality though is that sometimes we get hacked and someone is able to work around our access controls. Sometimes backup files are stored offsite with a different organization where we do not control the access. That is why we have encryption – encryption is an extra line of defense. TDE offers no protection however against individuals who have direct access to query the database.

Let's say someone does get access to our files – does TDE mean we are still sufficiently protected?

The answer unfortunately is that it depends. If someone has managed to get admin access to your database server, then if they are sufficiently motivated, they will be able to read your data. TDE only protects you against lower levels of access.

The fact that an admin can get around the protection is an inevitability of many forms of encryption. TDE is managed by an administrator who has the sysadmin permissions on the database instance. They can enable TDE, and they can disable TDE. They can change keys or export existing ones with their own password – but also they have direct access to the data anyway, so they can just run queries to view data.

Not all users who have admin rights over the box will have admin rights over the SQL instance, but anyone who has admin rights over the box can add themselves as an admin of the instance – though that usually requires restarting the SQL instance.

There are also other ways an admin can extract the keys from the file system – this is more complicated but can be done if someone is knowledgeable enough.

So TDE only offers a very specific but still very important protection. If you need more, then you will have to consider other forms of protection – such as Always Encrypted – possibly in conjunction with TDE.

How Easy Is It to Break Down the Encryption?

TDE implements symmetric key encryption using standard encryption algorithms based on AES (Advanced Encryption Standard). When you set up TDE, you can specify which AES algorithm you wish to use, AES_128, AES_192, or AES_256. In each case, the number specifies the length of the key to be used for encryption in bits. Currently the only known way to crack such encryption is by brute force, that is, try all the possible keys until you get lucky.

Obviously the longer your key, the harder the encryption should be to break; however, even for AES_128, estimations of how long it would take to break down the key by brute force vary between a thousand years and numbers many times greater than the age of the universe – trillions of years.

The difference in those estimates is based on how we anticipate processing power to grow in the future, in particular, whether the development of quantum computing might allow such activities to be carried out millions or billions of times faster than with conventional processors.

Even with the lowest estimates, AES_128 should theoretically be sufficient in most scenarios, but most people go for AES-256 which requires the same number of operations squared to crack. I recommend using AES-256 which should remain safe even if we see a quantum leap in processing power that exceeds all current expectations.

Up to 2016, SQL also supported the TRIPLE_DES_3KEY encryption protocol. This is now generally not considered to be as secure as AES, and from SQL 2016, its use is deprecated. So, it is best if you stick to AES even if you are on an older version of SQL Server.

Summary

TDE is a form of encryption for your databases that can be implemented easily and without impacting the existing functionality of your code. What is encrypted – data at rest – gives us protection against a number of scenarios where our files may be stolen or accessed inappropriately. It will not however protect us in the scenario where an attacker has gained admin level privileges against our servers. It also doesn't protect us from users who have direct access to query the database.

Up until SQL Server 2019 TDE was only available in enterprise edition, which means implementing it would have a heavy price tag for those using standard edition. However, from 2019 it was made available in the standard edition of the product, making it available at no cost to a much wider user base. There's an argument that if you are already on an edition of SQL Server that supports TDE, then it should almost be considered to turn it on by default as the protection it offers comes at little cost of ownership.

In the next chapters we'll look at setting up TDE and ongoing considerations for managing your TDE-protected databases.

CHAPTER 3

Setting Up TDE

Transparent Data Encryption (TDE) is one of the easiest ways of encrypting your data at rest. In the previous chapter we looked at what TDE is and how it works.

In this chapter we go through the steps of setting TDE up. You can set up TDE when you first create a database, or you can apply it to an existing database. In the latter case, once TDE has been enabled, it will encrypt your existing data in the background. In either case the steps are the same.

Creating the Keys and Certificate

The first step in setting up TDE is to create the required keys and certificate. We're going to focus on the default encryption hierarchy we looked at in the last chapter where we have the Service Master Key (SMK) at the top level, which protects the Database Master Key (DMK) in the master database, in turn protecting a certificate and associated asymmetric key pair, also in the master database. Finally, at the bottom we have the Database Encryption Key (DEK) in the user database which is protected by the certificate's asymmetric key.

The SMK always exists for a SQL Server instance, so we just need to create the objects underneath it in the hierarchy. If you are planning on using Extensible Key Management (EKM) for managing your keys, then some of these steps are unnecessary. We cover EKM in Chapter 20.

© Matthew McGiffen 2022
M. McGiffen, *Pro Encryption in SQL Server 2022*, https://doi.org/10.1007/978-1-4842-8664-7_3

Creating the Database Master Key (DMK)

First of all you must have a DMK. This lives in the master database and you can only have one per instance of SQL Server. You can create a DMK with the following SQL command (substitute your own password):

```
USE master;
GO
CREATE MASTER KEY
ENCRYPTION BY PASSWORD = 'UseAStrongPasswordHere!£$7';
```

We've already mentioned that the DMK is encrypted by the SMK, so it's reasonable to ask why in this command we must also specify encryption by a password. What happens when you create the DMK is that a key is generated and two encrypted copies of that key are then created and stored in the master database, one encrypted by the SMK and one by the password specified (both encrypted using the AES_256 algorithm). Having the copy encrypted by the password is necessary where you might need to restore a backup of the master database (including the DMK) to a separate SQL Server instance where the original SMK will not be available. In general, you don't need to do this to recover a TDE enabled database to a separate SQL Server instance as long as you have backups of the certificate and private key; however, you may use the DMK for purposes other than TDE.

It is recommended you back up the DMK. In most cases this backup is not useful in the context of TDE, but as mentioned you may have other objects not related to TDE that depend on the DMK so it is good practice. Backing up the DMK is a single command:

```
BACKUP MASTER KEY TO FILE = 'C:\Test\MyDMK'
ENCRYPTION BY PASSWORD = 'UseAnotherStrongPasswordHere!£$7';
```

I've saved my DMK backup to my C:\Test folder and will use that location for other objects in the rest of this book. If you want to execute the examples, then you should make sure the folder exists and that the SQL Server service account has access to it. Or you can substitute the file path with one you prefer to use.

Creating the Certificate

Next, we need to create a certificate for use by TDE. We do that with the following code:

```
USE master;
GO
CREATE CERTIFICATE MyTDECert
WITH SUBJECT = 'Certificate used for TDE in the TestTDE database';
```

This command tells SQL Server to generate a self-signed certificate and associated public\private key pair which can be used for asymmetric encryption. The private key will automatically be encrypted by the DMK. As mentioned previously, you can create a separate certificate for each database you wish to protect with TDE – or you could share the certificate between multiple databases. Having a separate certificate for each database minimizes the attack area if someone gets access to one of them, but you may choose to share the certificate between multiple databases on the same instance for ease of management. Make sure you give your certificate a meaningful and unique name as you may want at some point to migrate it to another server which might already have other certificates used for TDE. You wouldn't want them to have the same name, and it is useful to easily be able to identify what each is for – for instance, you may want to include a suffix to represent the environment the certificate belongs to.

These objects are absolutely critical in being able to encrypt and decrypt your data, so it is essential that you back them up. That can be achieved with the following SQL:

```
USE master;
GO
BACKUP CERTIFICATE MyTDECert
TO FILE = 'C:\Test\MyTDECert.cer'
WITH PRIVATE KEY
(
    FILE = 'C:\Test\MyTDECert_PrivateKeyFile.pvk',
    ENCRYPTION BY PASSWORD = 'UseAStrongPasswordHereToo!£$7'
);
```

This creates two backup files, one for the certificate and one for the private key. The private key is backed up encrypted by the password supplied. These files, and the password used to protect the private key, need to be stored securely. It is impossible to overstress how important this is. The most common pitfall people fall into with TDE is needing to recover or restore a TDE-protected database and not knowing where to find these backups or what the password is, particularly where the person who set TDE has left the organization. If the backup has not been taken or cannot be found or you don't have the password it was protected with, then you have the potential to permanently lose all data that has been protected by TDE. If you enter a new organization or role where you are responsible for TDE-protected databases, you should make sure you know where these items are stored or take your own backups if they can't be produced.

We have seen a few cases in this chapter where we need to use a password to protect an object. If your organization doesn't already use one, then you should consider using a password manager such as KeePass (many others exist) to manage your passwords securely and safely.

Creating the Database Encryption Key (DEK)

The DEK is what is actually used to encrypt and decrypt data stored in your TDE-protected database. The DEK is stored in the database itself (in the database root record) but is stored encrypted by the private key we created in the previous step. The DEK is a single key used for symmetric encryption; the same key is used to both encrypt and decrypt data. A symmetric key is used in this case as symmetric encryption is much faster than asymmetric, and we want our transparent encryption activities to occur with a minimum of overhead and latency.

Before we create the DEK we need a database we are going to protect with TDE. If you haven't already created the TestTDE database, then you can do so with the following SQL:

```
CREATE DATABASE TestTDE;
```

Now we can go ahead and create the DEK.

```
USE TestTDE;
GO
CREATE DATABASE ENCRYPTION KEY WITH ALGORITHM = AES_256
ENCRYPTION BY SERVER CERTIFICATE MyTDECert;
```

You can see we specify the algorithm – AES (Advanced Encryption Standard) with a 256-bit key is recommended. We also specify the certificate to be used which will identify the public/private key pair to be used to encrypt the DEK.

Unlike the other keys, you don't need to back up the DEK as it is automatically included in any backups you take of the database itself.

Encrypting the Database

Encrypting the database is the simple action of turning encryption on for the database.

```
ALTER DATABASE TestTDE SET ENCRYPTION ON;
```

In this case we have just created a new empty database, so there is no data to encrypt and the action is instantaneous. As we then start to add tables and data, the data will be automatically encrypted as it is written to disk for the first time. Similarly, any backups taken, full, log, or differential, will automatically be encrypted as they are written to disk.

In *sys.databases* you can see which databases have TDE turned on by looking at the *is_encrypted* column; you can query that as follows:

```
SELECT name
FROM sys.databases
WHERE is_encrypted = 1;
```

We can see the results of this query in Figure 3-1:

	name
1	tempdb
2	TestTDE

Figure 3-1. *Viewing the list of encrypted databases from sys.databases*

We can see that both our TestTDE database and tempdb get encrypted. As discussed previously tempdb gets encrypted when any other database uses TDE. We can view more details about our TDE encrypted databases by looking at the *sys.dm_database_encryption_keys* view. Let's query that view and look at some columns of interest.

```
SELECT
    d.name,
    k.encryption_state,
```

```
    k.encryptor_type,
    k.key_algorithm,
    k.key_length,
    k.percent_complete
FROM sys.dm_database_encryption_keys k
INNER JOIN sys.databases d
    ON k.database_id = d.database_id;
```

Figure 3-2 shows what I see if I executed this query before I turned encryption on.

	name	encryption_state	encryptor_type	key_algorithm	key_length	percent_complete
1	TestTDE	1	CERTIFICATE	AES	256	0

Figure 3-2. *Viewing details about our encrypted databases before turning encryption on*

We can see information about the DEK. We also see the *encryption_state* column which describes the current state of the database. The possible values you'll see are:

1. Unencrypted

2. Encryption in progress

3. Encrypted

4. Key change in progress

5. Decryption in progress

6. Protection change in progress (this occurs where the object protecting the DEK is being changed)

Figure 3-3 shows what we see if we execute the query after encryption has been enabled:

	name	encryption_state	encryptor_type	key_algorithm	key_length	percent_complete
1	tempdb	3	ASYMMETRIC KEY	AES	256	0
2	TestTDE	3	CERTIFICATE	AES	256	0

Figure 3-3. *Viewing details about our encrypted databases after turning encryption on*

We see that both my database and the *tempdb* database are now encrypted. We also see the *percent_complete* column, which confusingly says zero. This column only has meaning when an encryption state change is occurring. So, if the encryption state was 2 (encryption in progress) – then we would see a value here while the database was in the process of being encrypted. Here my database contained no data, so it was instantaneous to flip encryption on. This column becomes relevant when we are encrypting an existing database that has a reasonable amount of data; we'll look at that shortly.

The query we've just looked at will work on all versions of SQL Server. From SQL 2019, however, we have a few extra columns of information available to us in the *sys.dm_database_encryption_keys* view. In particular there is the column *encryption_state_desc* that gives us a plaintext description of the encryption state.

Securing the Root Keys

Here we're going to look at an additional step you should take to secure your TDE databases. This is a step you won't find in any other documentation on setting up TDE in SQL Server that I've seen, so it probably bears a little explaining.

We looked at the encryption hierarchy in Chapter 2. Let's look at that again to give us context for what we are about to discuss (Figure 3-4).

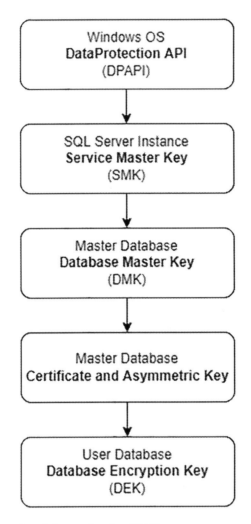

Figure 3-4. *The encryption hierarchy for TDE*

At every level in the diagram, the keys are securely encrypted by the level above. What concerns us here is the very top level in the diagram, the keys used by the DPAPI. These keys are unique to your server, but as they sit at the root level, there is nothing left to encrypt them, so they have to be stored unencrypted somewhere.

The keys are held in the following directory on most Windows systems: C:\Windows\ System32\Microsoft\Protect\S-1-5-18

It's not a trivial technical task, but if someone can access these keys as well as a copy of your database files (including the master database) – or a copy of your database backups including master – then it is possible for them to decrypt the chain of keys working from the SMK down and eventually be able to decrypt your TDE-protected data.

That means if someone has read access to the DPAPI keys, then they could access your data. However, this is easy to protect against. You just need to secure the preceding directory to ensure that only Local Administrators, the LOCAL SYSTEM account, and the SQL Server service account can read anything within it. You can do that by applying the appropriate file system permissions if they are not already in place.

Encrypting Existing Data with TDE

As we've seen, the process of turning TDE on for an empty database with no data is instantaneous. Most of the time though you'll be applying TDE to an existing system where you may have a large amount of data that needs to be encrypted.

The process of setting up TDE is the same whether you've just set up a new database or whether you're working with a live database. Once you turn encryption on, SQL Server will automatically begin the process of encrypting any data in your database: be that one row or terabytes of data.

There is nothing extra you need to do to make that happen. However, there are some questions you should be asking. How long will it take to encrypt your database? What sort of overhead is that going to put on your server – particularly for a live system? What should you do if you run into any issues?

We'll look at answers to those questions in this section. The answers to questions of performance are very much going to depend on your hardware and other configuration, so I can't give you fixed numbers. I can however help you understand some ballpark figures and demonstrate how to benchmark against your servers to gain a better estimate.

Benchmarking TDE Performance on Your Server

I'm going to load up my previously created TestTDE database with about 10GB of data, so we can see how the encryption process performs. We'll do this with TDE turned off and then turn it on once the data is loaded. I'm running this on a reasonably quick laptop, and it takes a couple of minutes to load the data. If you've been following through these examples on your own SQL Server, then first you'll need to turn TDE off with the following SQL:

```
ALTER DATABASE TestTDE SET ENCRYPTION OFF;
```

Then we can load the dummy data with the following code:

```
USE TestTDE;
CREATE TABLE dbo.SomeData(Id INT IDENTITY(1,1), SomeText VARCHAR(255));
GO

INSERT INTO dbo.SomeData (SomeText)
SELECT TOP 1000000
('XXXXXXXXXXXXXXXXXXXXXXXXXXXXXXXXXXXXXXXXXXXXXXXXXXXXXXXXXXXXXXXXXXXX
XXXXXXX')
FROM sys.objects a
CROSS JOIN sys.objects b
CROSS JOIN sys.objects c
CROSS JOIN sys.objects d;
GO 100
```

After I turn encryption on again, I'm going to run a query to monitor the progress of encryption – polling every 5 seconds. If you're working through this example on your own machine, you'll want to have the query ready to go before you turn encryption on.

The command to turn TDE on is as previously stated.

```
ALTER DATABASE TestTDE SET ENCRYPTION ON;
```

Then you can immediately execute this query to report the progress.

```
DECLARE @state tinyint;
DECLARE @encyrption_progress
    TABLE(sample_time DATETIME, percent_complete DECIMAL(5,2))

SELECT @state = k.encryption_state
FROM sys.dm_database_encryption_keys k
INNER JOIN sys.databases d
   ON k.database_id = d.database_id
WHERE d.name = 'TestTDE';

WHILE @state != 3
BEGIN
   INSERT INTO @encyrption_progress(sample_time, percent_complete)
   SELECT GETDATE(), percent_complete
```

```
FROM sys.dm_database_encryption_keys k
INNER JOIN sys.databases d
    ON k.database_id = d.database_id
WHERE d.name = 'TestTDE';

WAITFOR delay '00:00:05';

SELECT @state = k.encryption_state
FROM sys.dm_database_encryption_keys k
INNER JOIN sys.databases d
    ON k.database_id = d.database_id
WHERE d.name = 'TestTDE';
END

SELECT * FROM @encyrption_progress;
```

Figure 3-5 shows the results from running this test on my laptop.

	sample_time	percent_complete
1	2021-10-18 15:23:39.240	0.09
2	2021-10-18 15:23:44.257	9.16
3	2021-10-18 15:23:49.270	18.23
4	2021-10-18 15:23:54.280	27.30
5	2021-10-18 15:23:59.297	36.37
6	2021-10-18 15:24:04.310	45.44
7	2021-10-18 15:24:09.320	54.52
8	2021-10-18 15:24:14.330	63.59
9	2021-10-18 15:24:19.340	72.66
10	2021-10-18 15:24:24.347	81.69
11	2021-10-18 15:24:29.350	90.80
12	2021-10-18 15:24:34.367	99.88
13	2021-10-18 15:24:39.383	100.00
14	2021-10-18 15:24:44.390	100.00

Figure 3-5. *Viewing the progress of TDE encryption*

You can see it took about a minute to encrypt 10GB of data. Figures will be different on your hardware, but that gives us an idea of the order of magnitude involved. If that scaled up linearly, then it might take between 1 and 2 hours to encrypt a terabyte of data. I'm working here with data on an SSD; if you're using older-style disks, then it would take considerably longer. I'd recommend using this technique to benchmark how your hardware will perform before you turn encryption on for your production databases.

Monitoring for Problems

The encryption occurs as a background process referred to as the encryption scan, but it will consume resources while it runs, so if you are implementing this against a system with large databases where performance is critical, then you will want to either run it in a period of quiet (or downtime), or you will want to monitor to check that encryption isn't impacting your system too much. Experience suggests that it shouldn't be a problem unless your server is already under strain.

There are a few things to look out for if you are monitoring during the encryption scan:

- CPU and IO, both these could take a hit.

- You may want to look out for blocking caused by encryption; you can do this by checking the *sys.dm_tran_locks* view where the *resource_subtype* is "ENCRYPTION_SCAN". Here is an example of the SQL for that:

```
SELECT *
FROM sys.dm_tran_locks
WHERE resource_type = 'ENCRYPTION_SCAN';
```

- Monitor transaction log usage with DBCC LOGINFO. While the encryption scanner is running, the transaction log can't be truncated and VLFs marked for reuse. This could mean the transaction log might grow larger than normal, so you need to watch out if you are constrained for disk space.

- If your database is synched to a secondary in an HA scenario, for example, as part of an Availability Group or through log shipping, you may want to check your synch process remains healthy during the encryption scan. We talk a little bit about working with TDE and HA in the next chapter.

What If You Run into Any Performance Problems During the Scan?

First things first – don't turn encryption off.

```
ALTER DATABASE TestTDE SET ENCRYPTION OFF;
```

This isn't going to stop the encryption scan; rather it's just going to change direction. So now it will begin decrypting everything it's just encrypted, that's likely to have just as much impact; then sooner or later, you're going to have to start again.

What we want to do is to pause the encryption scan. Prior to SQL Server 2019, there was no direct command to achieve this; however, there was a trace flag that could be used to achieve much the same thing. Let's look at both methods. First, if you are on SQL Server 2017 or lower, you can pause the encryption scan with the following command:

```
DBCC TRACEON(5004);
```

When you do this, if you then query *dm_database_encryption_keys*, you will see the database is set to a state of 2 (encryption in progress), and the *percent_complete* column will show zero – as nothing is currently in progress.

When you wish to begin the scan again, you need to disable the trace flag and then set encryption on again (even though it's not technically off):

```
DBCC TRACEOFF(5004,-1);
ALTER DATABASE TestTDE SET ENCRYPTION ON;
```

When you do this, the scanner will pick up where it left off, for instance, if it had got to 50%, then it will then continue from there.

It's important to note that the trace flag doesn't actually turn TDE off. In fact, if you add new data or update data and it gets written to disk while the trace flag is enabled, the data will still become encrypted. The trace flag just pauses the background process of converting all the data already on disk.

Note that this method will pause the encryption scan for all databases that are in the process of being encrypted. The SQL 2019 method is better as it gives us the control to pause the scan for a specific database using the following code:

```
ALTER DATABASE TestTDE SET ENCRYPTION SUSPEND;
```

To set the encryption running again from where it left off, we just use the following command:

```
ALTER DATABASE TestTDE SET ENCRYPTION RESUME;
```

Just like with the trace flag, this method doesn't turn TDE off, it just pauses the background process of encrypting existing data. New data will still be written to disk encrypted.

Along with this new functionality, SQL 2019 also added extra columns to the *dm_database_encryption_keys* view to help you manage the process of pausing and resuming the encryption scan. These columns include *encryption_scan_state_desc* which will tell us the state of the scan, for instance, if it is running or suspended. We also have *encryption_scan_modify_date* which tells us when the scan was last modified, we can use that to tell when a scan was suspended or resumed.

If performance impact is an issue for you with the scanning process, you can use one of these methods to incrementally run the scan out of hours, pausing it when you want to ensure maximum performance of your systems.

What If the Encryption Scan Fails?

It is possible for the encryption scan to fail. The most likely scenario is a failure due to corruption in your database. Because the scan is a background process you won't get an error message telling you that it has stopped, so it is good to use the methods we've looked at in this chapter to check when the scan is complete.

Prior to SQL 2019 a failure would exhibit itself by the *encryption_state* column showing as 2 (in progress) in *dm_database_encryption_keys* and the *percent_complete* column showing as zero. Usually the 5004 trace flag would also have been enabled to prevent the scan from resuming.

From SQL 2019 we have a little more information and can see in *dm_database_ encryption_keys* that *encryption_scan_state_desc* is set to aborted and can tell when that happened.

In either case your first action should be to check the database for corruption and resolve that if there are any issues. After that you can attempt to restart the encryption scan using the methods we've just looked at. If you have no corruption, and the scan still fails, then you'll need to reach out to Microsoft for support, but that's an unlikely scenario.

Taking Backups While Encryption Is in Progress

You can continue to take backups while the scanner is running to encrypt your existing data. However, it is important to understand that until that process is complete your backups will not be fully encrypted.

What will happen in the meantime is that a mixture of encrypted and unencrypted data will get written to your backup files. Only backups taken after the TDE encryption scan is complete will be fully protected.

Summary

TDE is very quick and easy to set up, but you absolutely must make sure the certificate and private key are backed up and stored securely and safely along with any passwords used to protect them and that you have a process in place for managing that. If you lose those items, then you have the potential to lose all your data. It's also not great if the knowledge of where to find them is locked up in one person's head.

Existing data is encrypted automatically but it may take some time. You can benchmark to get an idea of how long that will be. During the encryption process there may be overhead which you can monitor, and you can pause the encryption scan if there are any problems.

In the next chapter we'll look at aspects of managing TDE once it is set up and running. This includes performance and the recovery or migration of TDE-protected databases.

CHAPTER 4

Managing TDE

In the previous chapters, we've looked at how TDE works and how simple it is to set up. In this chapter, we're going to look at various scenarios that are likely to come up over the lifecycle of your TDE-protected databases, such as migrating or recovering a database to another SQL Server instance. We'll also look at some issues you should be aware of in regards to the day-to-day running of TDE, such as the impact on performance.

Migrating or Recovering a TDE-Protected Database

When encrypting a database with Transparent Data Encryption (TDE), a vital consideration is to make sure we are prepared for the scenario where something goes wrong. For instance, if the server hosting our SQL instance goes belly-up, can we recover the data that we have encrypted with TDE?

In the ordinary recovery scenario, we would make sure that we have appropriate backups of our database and that they (or copies of them) are stored off the server itself so that we can access them in case of a failure.

If you have followed the instructions in the previous chapter, then you will also have taken a backup of the certificate and private key via the following command:

```
BACKUP CERTIFICATE MyTDECert
TO FILE = 'C:\Test\MyTDECert.cer'
WITH PRIVATE KEY
(
    FILE = 'C:\Test\MyTDECert_PrivateKeyFile.pvk',
    ENCRYPTION BY PASSWORD = 'UseAStrongPasswordHereToo!£$7'
);
```

© Matthew McGiffen 2022
M. McGiffen, *Pro Encryption in SQL Server 2022*, https://doi.org/10.1007/978-1-4842-8664-7_4

You need to make sure that these are also stored securely off the server and that you have kept the password you used somewhere you can access it – but not so accessible that unauthorized users can read it.

In summary you need:

- The database backup file

- The backup of the certificate

- The backup of the private key

- The password used to encrypt the private key

Armed with those objects, you are equipped to restore your database to another SQL instance. Working on the new SQL instance, the steps are straightforward.

Create a Database Master Key (DMK) If One Doesn't Exist

The new SQL instance will need a DMK if one doesn't already exist. You can create one with the following code:

```
USE master;
CREATE MASTER KEY
ENCRYPTION BY PASSWORD = 'UseAStrongPasswordHere!£$7';
```

Note that this will be a new and unique DMK; it will not be the same as the one you had on your old instance – and you don't need to use the same password to protect it.

Restore the Certificate and Private Key

On the new SQL instance, you need to restore the certificate and private key into the master database with the following SQL:

```
USE master;
CREATE CERTIFICATE MyTDECert
FROM FILE = 'C:\Test\MyTDECert.cer'
WITH PRIVATE KEY
(
    FILE = 'C:\Test\MyTDECert_PrivateKeyFile.pvk',
    DECRYPTION BY PASSWORD = 'UseAStrongPasswordHereToo!£$7'
);
```

This will decrypt your key using the password supplied and then re-encrypt it using the DMK you created. Then the certificate and its key will be stored in the master database on your new SQL instance.

If you've done something wrong, it's entirely possible you may get an error at this stage, commonly:

```
Msg 15208, Level 16, State 6, Line 56
The certificate, asymmetric key, or private key file is not valid or does
not exist; or you do not have permissions for it.
```

If you're confident that all details specified are correct and that the certificate and private key were backed up properly, then the most likely issue is that the current SQL instance doesn't have access to the file path you've placed the files in.

Another possible issue is that you receive an error telling you the certificate already exists. If you have checked and verified that a certificate with the same name doesn't exist, then the most probable cause is that you have another certificate with the same thumbprint. The thumbprint is the actual identifier for the certificate (the name we give it is more of a friendly name).

Restore the Database

Once you've completed the previous steps, you are ready to restore the database from the backup. You do that as you would restore any other database. Potentially as simply as with the following command:

```
RESTORE DATABASE TestTDE FROM DISK = 'C:\Test\TestTDE.bak';
```

Then you'll find you can access your database and view data without any issues. At this point you can celebrate – you are done. You only get a problem if you haven't set up the certificate and key correctly or you have the wrong one, in which case you get an error like the following:

```
Msg 33111, Level 16, State 3, Line 2
Cannot find server certificate with thumbprint
'0x682C8797633B9AD8875967502861CCAE33ECAD66'.
Msg 3013, Level 16, State 1, Line 2
RESTORE DATABASE is terminating abnormally.
```

Recovering a TDE Database Without the Certificate

If you don't have the backups of the certificate and private key from the old server, as well as the password used to encrypt the private key backup, then you could be in a lot of trouble. There is one scenario where you have a way out. I'm going to assume you don't have the possibility to recover your old server from a complete file system backup – if you do, then you can do that and access all the keys you require. If the two following things are true though, then you can still recover your database:

- You have a backup of the master database from the previous instance.

- The previous instance used a domain account as its service account.

The reason you are going to be okay is that all the objects in the SQL Server Encryption Hierarchy that sit above the Database Encryption Key (that exists in your TDE database) are stored in the master database. That includes the certificate and associated keys, the Database Master Key (DMK) and the Service Master Key (SMK). There are two copies of the SMK:

- One encrypted by the keys associated with the machine account

- One encrypted by the keys associated with the SQL Server
  service account

The first copy is only going to be of any use to us if we can recover the old machine (and its account) directly from backups, but we've already ruled that out.

If the service account is a domain account though, then we should be able to use it. The method is going to involve:

- Setting up a new SQL instance using the same service account as the
  old instance.

- Restoring your backup of master from the old instance onto the new
  instance.

- Rebooting your new server – that's the whole server, not just SQL.

- Backing up your certificate and private key – and don't lose them
  this time!

My personal opinion is that it's not the greatest of ideas to restore the master database from one instance onto a new one and expect everything to work okay. So, I'm only suggesting you use this so you can recover the certificate. Once you've got that, I would go back to the steps in the previous section on recovering your TDE-protected database(s).

Let's go into each of these steps in a little more detail.

Setting Up a New SQL Instance Using the Same Service Account as the Old Instance

What this obviously means is that your server must be on the same domain as the old server (or at least another domain that is trusted). You also must have the credentials for the service account.

You can't fake this, for example, setting up a new account on another domain called the same thing as the old one. The new account won't have the same keys associated with it as the ones used to encrypt your SMK, so you will achieve nothing.

Restore Your Backup of Master from the Old Instance onto the New Instance

There are a lot of resources available on the Internet that tell you how to do this in detail and will give you a number of methods you can use. In short you need to first stop your new SQL Server instance and then from a command prompt start it in single user mode with the following command:

```
sqlservr.exe -c -m -s {InstanceName}
```

Then you need to (again from a command line) issue the command to restore/overwrite the master database. First start SQLCMD with this command:

```
sqlcmd -s {InstanceName}
```

Then at the prompt that opens up within your command window you can execute the following SQL:

```
RESTORE DATABASE master FROM DISK = 'C:\Test\master.bak' WITH REPLACE;
GO
```

Reboot Your New Server: The Whole Server, Not Just SQL

If you restart the SQL Server service, rather than the machine itself, you can still go in and everything looks okay. You can even restore a TDE database from your old instance, and you'll find you can access the data.

Everything is not okay though, and if you tried to back up your certificate and private key, you would get an error like the following:

```
Msg 15151, Level 16, State 1, Line 7
Cannot find the certificate 'MyTDECert', because it does not exist or you
do not have permission.
```

The reason for this error is that the SMK isn't in the correct state. The copy that is encrypted by the service account is fine, but the copy that is encrypted by the machine account is currently using the wrong machine account. You need to reboot the whole server to fix this; just restarting SQL doesn't do it. On a full restart the SMK is retrieved from the copy encrypted by the service account and then encrypted with the current machine account. That version then replaces the one using the wrong machine account.

Once that's done, the encryption hierarchy is fully fixed, and the certificate becomes accessible for a backup command.

Backup Your Certificate and Private Key – and Don't Lose Them This Time

I've given the command to back up these a few times, but here it is again:

```
BACKUP CERTIFICATE MyTDECert
TO FILE = 'C:\Test\MyTDECert.cer'
WITH PRIVATE KEY
(
    FILE = 'C:\Test\MyTDECert_PrivateKeyFile.pvk',
    ENCRYPTION BY PASSWORD = 'UseAStrongPasswordHereToo!£$7'
);
GO
```

You can now take those backup files and use them to restore the certificate and key to the SQL Server instance of your choice and then restore the backups of your TDE-protected database(s).

This has been mentioned a few times, but I'll reiterate once more as it is the most important issue to consider when managing TDE. Making sure you don't lose these backups – or the password – is a vital consideration. If you're responsible for setting up any form of encryption, you need to think about the process that's going to manage the objects used to protect your data. People move from one role to another, from one company to another, and often things tick along happily for many years before a failure happens. You need to be confident that come next year, or in 5 or 10 years, whoever is responsible for the data will be able to recover it if the worst happens.

Key Rotation

In terms of encryption, key rotation is the process of replacing your encryption keys on a periodic basis. This is considered good practice and is required by many security certifications.

In practice, if you had to rotate/replace the key that is used to encrypt your data, then that would be an intensive activity requiring all your data to be decrypted with the old key before being re-encrypted with the new key. This could also create a vulnerability where data sits in an unencrypted state during the process.

This is a reason why many forms of encryption maintain a separation between the actual key used to protect the data and a second key used to protect the encryption key. In terms of TDE, we have the DEK which is protected by the certificate and associated key pair. In general with TDE, when we talk about rotation, we just rotate the certificate. This means the activity can be done without changing the underlying DEK, so the data does not need to be decrypted and re-encrypted. Thus, there is minimal overhead and the process is quick and secure.

Many sources will tell you that this process DOES decrypt and re-encrypt your data. This is not correct and can be demonstrated with a simple test.

The DEK used by TDE is held securely. It is only stored encrypted in the database, and we never see the unencrypted value of the key. The certificate however is a little more public, and we must back up it and the private key outside of the database. This makes it a little more vulnerable, and so it makes sense that we would want to rotate it periodically. Due to that consideration certificates have an expiry date. This date is a reminder to us that, as a good practice, we should create a new certificate and use that going forward before the existing one expires.

TDE doesn't stop working if the certificate expires; it is up to you to monitor your certificates and replace them when they come to the end of their life. One option is to monitor them using Policy Based Management.

Creating a New Certificate

If we query the *sys.certificates* view with the following SQL, we can find our TDE certificate and examine the expiry date:

```
USE master;
SELECT name, subject, expiry_date
FROM sys.certificates
WHERE name = 'MyTDECert';
```

Here is the output (Figure 4-1):

	name	subject	expiry_date
1	MyTDECert	Certificate used for TDE in the TestTDE database	2022-09-13 10:55:50.000

Figure 4-1. *Viewing the expiry date for our certificate*

I didn't specify an expiry date for this certificate when I created it, so it was automatically given one that was a year in the future. Let's create a new certificate, and this time we'll specify a longer expiry. Then we will rotate the encryption to use that one. Here's the code to create a new certificate and specify the expiry date:

```
USE master;
CREATE CERTIFICATE MyTDECert_with_longevity
WITH SUBJECT = 'Certificate used for TDE in the TestTDE database for years
to come',
EXPIRY_DATE = '20251231';
```

Let's have a look at the values that are in the *sys.certificates* view using the same query given earlier (Figure 4-2):

	name	subject	expiry_date
1	MyTDECert_with_longevity	Certificate used for TDE in the TestTDE databas...	2025-12-31 00:00:00.000

Figure 4-2.   *Viewing the expiry date for our new certificate*

We're now ready to "rotate" from the old certificate to the new one.

Rotating the Certificate

Rotation is the process of moving from the old certificate to the new one. In this case all that happens is that the encrypted value of the database encryption key (stored in our TDE-protected database) is decrypted with the old certificate and re-encrypted with the new certificate, and that new encrypted value is stored in the database, overwriting the old one.

The key value itself hasn't changed, just the object protecting it, and as such we can still read/write data from the database without any change to the encryption of the underlying data. It is a simple command to rotate the certificate:

```
USE TestTDE;
ALTER DATABASE ENCRYPTION KEY
ENCRYPTION BY SERVER CERTIFICATE MyTDECert_with_longevity;
```

The operation is almost instantaneous, shouldn't require any database downtime, or create additional overhead on your server. Though in production I'd still do it when things are quiet just in case anything goes wrong!

Impact of TDE on Performance

Microsoft states that enabling TDE usually has a performance overhead of 2–4%. That doesn't sound like very much, and personally I wouldn't let it bother me if I want to make sure my data is encrypted at rest. However, you may have heard other sources saying that it's actually a lot more than that – and the performance impact is a high price to pay for the level of protection offered. So, what's the truth?

Where Do We See an Overhead?

When we talk about performance, we are likely to be concerned about two things. One is the impact on query performance. Are my queries going to execute slower with TDE enabled? The other is what overall pressure is going to be added to the server.

The important point to start with is in understanding where and how TDE adds overhead. Encryption occurs as data is written to disk, and decryption occurs as data is read from disk. Each of those activities uses CPU. So, the CPU overhead added by TDE is going to be in proportion to your disk activity. If you have a system that is heavy on IO, then there is going to be more CPU overhead.

SQL Server tries to keep data that is referenced repeatedly in memory (the buffer pool). So, if your SQL instance is provisioned with enough memory, a lot of your read queries can access the buffer pool and don't have to go out to disk. Such queries should not be affected performance-wise by TDE. There may be other read queries however that access older data that hasn't been read for a while, and these queries would need to retrieve that data from disk and so there would be an overhead from TDE.

Any queries that modify data will need the outcome to be written to disk, so in these cases we will see an overhead. This overhead is likely to come in two parts: first when the transaction is written to the log file before committing and then later as the updated data gets written to the data file as part of a checkpoint operation.

We also have other operations that write or update encrypted data on disk, so we would also expect these to have some overhead. This would include operations such as index rebuild operations.

You can see from this that the overhead will very much depend on how your application interacts with your data. At one extreme, if you have a set of static data that is small enough to be held in memory and is queried regularly, then there should be no overhead. At the other end of the spectrum, if you have an application that writes to the database a lot and reads less often, then the overhead will be higher.

How to Estimate the Performance Impact for Your Server?

Performance impact for your queries is going to be very much on a case-by-case basis, but in reality, it's generally likely to be quite small. The reason for that is that, as discussed, we're only going to see extra CPU requirements when our query needs to access the disk. Reading from and writing to disk is itself an activity that takes time, and even with the fastest disks, encryption/decryption is likely to take no longer than the disk access time. The encryption activities can usually be carried out in parallel to the disk activity, so you don't see much increased time to read or write data. We'll see an example of that shortly when we look at how you can get an idea of likely overhead on your server.

In terms of estimating overall overhead on your server, you need to understand the level of IO on the server as well as how well encryption will perform on the box.

Let's work through an exercise to get an idea of the sort of numbers we might be talking about. For this, we're going to need the database we created in Chapter 3 that has about 10GB of data in a single table. We'll also need a database that has the same set of data but without encryption turned on so we can get comparison figures. You can create that using the same scripts – just don't run the final step of turning encryption on. We'll call that database TestTDEOff.

We're first going to run a query that will force SQL Server to read all the data in a table. We'll repeat that across four scenarios:

- TDE-protected database where the buffer cache is empty, so all data has to be read from disk

- TDE-protected database where all the data for the table is in the buffer cache, so no data has to be read from disk

- Database without TDE where the buffer cache is empty, so all data has to be read from disk

- Database without TDE where all the data for the table is in the buffer cache, so no data has to be read from disk

Here is our query:

```
DBCC DROPCLEANBUFFERS;
SET STATISTICS IO, TIME ON;
SELECT *
FROM dbo.SomeData
WHERE Id = 100000000;

SELECT *
FROM dbo.SomeData
WHERE Id = 100000000;
```

The DBCC DROPCLEANBUFFERS command flushes all data held in the buffer cache. You won't want to do this on a live system as it will affect performance, but if you have a server with similar hardware, you can run this to get an idea of how encryption performs.

The test runs the same select statement twice, once with no data loaded into memory and a second time once data has been loaded by the first run. We use the SET STATISTICS command to output information about performance to the messages tab in SSMS. The table we are querying from is a heap and has no indexes defined, so SQL Server has no option but to scan the whole table in order to generate the result set.

Let's look at an extract of the information outputted by STATISICS IO, TIME to see what we're getting. This is for the database with TDE enabled:

```
Table 'SomeData'. Scan count 13, logical reads 1204820, physical reads 0,
page server reads 0, read-ahead reads 1203777, page server read-ahead reads
0, lob logical reads 0, lob physical reads 0, lob page server reads 0, lob
read-ahead reads 0, lob page server read-ahead reads 0.
 SQL Server Execution Times:
   CPU time = 10046 ms,  elapsed time = 5580 ms.

Table 'SomeData'. Scan count 13, logical reads 1204820, physical reads 0,
page server reads 0, read-ahead reads 0, page server read-ahead reads 0,
lob logical reads 0, lob physical reads 0, lob page server reads 0, lob
read-ahead reads 0, lob page server read-ahead reads 0.
 SQL Server Execution Times:
   CPU time = 12407 ms,  elapsed time = 1050 ms.
```

We have two sets of output here: one for the first run where there was no data loaded into memory and one for the second once the data was loaded. The key difference is that in the first we have a large number of "read-ahead" reads, which are where data is read from disk. Read-ahead refers to the fact that they are read in parallel with the processing, rather than all needing to be read before the CPU can get to work. In the second output we only have "logical" reads where data is read from memory.

You get a reasonable amount of variance in the CPU and elapsed times when running such tests, so I executed the query five times against each database, averaged the results, and rounded off to the nearest 100ms. The figures are shown in Table 4-1.

Table 4-1. *Performance comparison with and without TDE enabled*

Test	CPU time (ms)	Elapsed time (ms)
TDE with all data read from disk	10,600	5,600
No TDE with all data read from disk	7,600	5,700
TDE with all data read from memory	12,400	1,100
No TDE with all data read from memory	12,200	1,100

Due to the variance between test runs, we'll ignore small differences. There are a few key takeaways:

- The elapsed time was about the same with and without TDE.

- The CPU consumption was about the same where data was read from memory.

- When reading from disk, there was a higher CPU consumption when TDE was enabled.

That is about what we would expect; TDE only adds overhead when reading or writing to disk. When we were reading from disk, my disk was being accessed at full speed and the disk access time was the bottleneck, so the decryption required by TDE was easily able to complete while that was occurring.

In terms of what this shows regarding the performance impact on a production server, there are a few ways you can think about the data.

The scariest way of looking at it – and not necessarily the correct one – is to focus on the fact that when reading from disk TDE added about 3 seconds of CPU. That was about a 40% increase. The reason that's not going to be the impact you see in live though is that (hopefully) most of the data accessed by SQL Server is already going to be sitting in memory and so will not be affected. Still, I might envision that I'm going to see between a zero and 40% impact.

Another way to look at it is to realize that my disk was maxed out during this test, loading about 2GB of data per second (actually slightly less but we'll stick with round numbers). I can calculate that during every second of execution about an extra half a second of CPU, power was consumed by the TDE decryption. That equates to half a CPU core being busy. My machine has 12 cores so that's about 4% of physical CPU overhead added. Running the Windows Performance Monitor (perfmon) during the tests, I can see that is about right. If I only had four cores in this box, I'd be using the same half a core, so that would be about 12.5%. It couldn't go any higher though because my disks are already maxed out. I'd have to be able to physically read data from disk quicker in order to create more TDE overhead. On this box, I can see that decrypting data with TDE costs me about 0.3 seconds of CPU per GB of data.

Where this leaves us is that the best way to get an idea on TDE impact on a particular server is to look at the level of disk access and the number of CPU cores. You can look at how much disk access you have (to the relevant database data and log files only) at peak times and get an idea from there. Hopefully you can see that to add a significant percentage of CPU overhead with TDE, you're going to need to be reading a huge amount of data from disk, have superfast disks, and not have a lot of CPU power.

If you are able to run through something similar to this exercise to benchmark a production system – and you come up with numbers that worry you – I'm going to suggest that you might have an excessive amount of disk access, and that might be indicative of a problem. In particular, you may want to consider if the server would benefit from having more memory so that data can be held in the buffer cache for longer – and not read from disk so often. Also, are queries being forced to scan whole tables due to a lack of adequate indexes – or because they are poorly written.

TDE and Backups

Database backups continue to work without change when you have TDE enabled. The only difference is that the backups contain encrypted data that cannot be read without the certificate and private key. There are a couple of points that are worth discussing though.

Backup Performance

Following on from general questions of TDE performance, it's sensible that you might also be concerned whether TDE has an impact on backup times. You may also have read of people complaining about long backup times with TDE.

It's not necessarily true that TDE has much of an impact on backup performance. The reason is that when a backup is performed, SQL Server does not have to encrypt the data. The data already sits encrypted on disk in the data and log files, and those copies of the data are what are used for performing the backup. In practice there may be some data in memory that has yet to be encrypted and written to disk, but in general, that is not going to be large enough to cause significant overhead.

When people talk about issues with backup performance and TDE, they are likely to be talking about the case involving backup compression.

Backup Compression

Many people use backup compression with database backups in SQL Server. It is simple functionality to use as shown in this code example:

```
BACKUP DATABASE [TestTDE] TO DISK = 'C:\Test\TestTDE_Compressed.bak' WITH
COMPRESSION;
```

The benefit of backup compression isn't just about having smaller backup files but also in the time taken to perform a backup. The biggest bottleneck involved in taking a backup is usually the time it takes to write it to disk. By taking compressed backups you can significantly reduce backup takes. This comes at the cost of some extra CPU overhead to perform the compression, but unless your CPU is under pressure, it's often worthwhile.

Up until the 2016 version, SQL Server did not support backup compression on TDE enabled databases. One reason for this may be that most compression algorithms work best where there is some repetition in the data to be compressed, but encrypted data looks pretty much random. What this meant in practice was that you might specify the WITH COMPRESSION option when backing up your TDE-protected databases but you wouldn't see much difference in the file size or backup times. This changed from SQL 2016 and was a welcome improvement.

To use backup compression with TDE, however, you needed to specify an additional parameter MAXTRANSFERSIZE. This parameter specifies the largest unit of transfer in bytes used between SQL Server and the backup media. If you're interested in fine-tuning your backup performance, this is one value you can play with. Backup compression with TDE doesn't kick in unless your MAXTRANSFERSIZE is greater than 64kb (65536). As long as the value you specify is at least one greater than 64k, then an optimized algorithm for compression of TDE encrypted databases is enabled. Commonly people use the value of 128kb. The command looks like this:

```
BACKUP DATABASE TestTDE TO DISK = 'C:\Test\TestTDE_Compressed.bak'
WITH COMPRESSION, MAXTRANSFERSIZE = 131072;
```

This extra parameter becomes unnecessary if you are on SQL Server 2019 Cumulative Update 5 or higher. With that release, if you specify `WITH COMPRESSION` for a backup taken for a TDE-protected database and you don't specify `MAXTRANSFERSIZE`, then `MAXTRANSFERSIZE` will automatically be increased to 128kb, and your backup will be compressed.

Backup Compression Issues

The introduction of backup compression for TDE-protected databases has however not been without problems, and this is something you really need to be aware of. There have been a number of bugs discovered where a compressed backup of a TDE database was found to be unrecoverable. Some people have also reported that restore times were massively increased in some cases.

If you're on a version of SQL Server higher than 2016 CU 7 or 2016 SP1 CU4, then you should be fine, but I would stress the importance of regularly testing your backups by restoring them. A few days before writing this, I came across the term Schrodinger's Backup – the condition of any backup is unknown until a restore is attempted. When it comes to TDE and backup compression, you should consider that as a very true statement.

TDE and High Availability

In general, TDE plays nicely with any of the built-in features that SQL Server has for high availability (HA). That includes:

- Availability Groups

- Log Shipping

- Database Mirroring

In theory, in all cases, the actions you need to take to support TDE are the same. You just need to ensure that the secondary server has a Database Master Key (DMK). Then you need to ensure that copies of your certificate and private key have been restored to the secondary before you turn encryption on. This is the same step you would take if you were attempting to restore a TDE-protected database to a different server. We covered that in the previous section in this chapter "Migrating or Recovering a TDE-Protected Database."

As long as that is done, then whichever HA tool you use should take care of the rest.

In practice, we DBAs are cautious folk, and you don't want to risk anything going wrong when you are dealing with a live system. As such you may want to take the following steps:

1. Remove the database from HA.

2. Set up TDE for the database and turn on.

3. Set up the keys and certificate on the secondary.

4. Add the database back into HA.

Summary

Overall, TDE is fairly easy to manage. The key items to remember are how you restore a TDE-protected database to another server and how you go about key rotation. As stressed many times, you should make sure you have a process for managing the backups of the certificate and private key so these are accessible when required but kept securely nonetheless.

Performance impact of TDE in most cases is pretty minimal though it will vary according to workload and server configuration. You can however perform testing to get an idea of the order of magnitude of that overhead. It's key to understand that the overhead only occurs when writing to and reading from disk.

TDE also works well with database backups. There have however been some issues with the combination of TDE and backup compression. You should be aware of that and make sure that you test your restores.

TDE also works well with HA. In general, you can have confidence that you set up TDE first, and then add it to the HA tool; it will work seamlessly as long as the private key and certificate exist on the secondary server.

This brings us to the end of the section on TDE. In the next chapter, we'll have a look at Backup Encryption.

CHAPTER 5

Backup Encryption

We've seen in the previous chapters that TDE is a simple way of protecting your at-rest data. There may however be times where you can't or don't want to use TDE. The main scenario for this is where you are on a version of SQL Server before 2019 (when TDE was made available in standard edition) and you don't want to pay for the enterprise version which has a high price tag associated with it.

When we talk about protecting our at-rest data, the item that we are likely to be most concerned about is the security of our backups. Backups are generally – and should be – stored off the server itself, and often we will ship copies offsite to a third party where we don't have control over who can access the data, even if we trust that that will be well managed.

From SQL Server 2014 the product has included the ability to encrypt data while creating a backup. This feature is available in both the standard and enterprise editions of SQL Server, so it is something you can use even when TDE may not be a feature that is available to you.

Backup Encryption has a lot in common with TDE in terms of the objects required. The encryption hierarchy is the same; you require a DMK and a certificate with a public/private key pair. In theory you can use an asymmetric key instead of a certificate, but this has the disadvantage that you can't export the asymmetric key – which means you will struggle to restore your database backup to a different server. As such, for the sake of the examples that follow, we'll just look at the certificate option.

You may however choose to use an asymmetric key if you wish to use Extensible Key Management (EKM) and store the key externally to your SQL Server. We look at EKM in Chapter 20.

© Matthew McGiffen 2022
M. McGiffen, *Pro Encryption in SQL Server 2022*, https://doi.org/10.1007/978-1-4842-8664-7_5

Setting Up Backup Encryption

As mentioned, the prerequisites for Backup Encryption are the same as for TDE. We'll go over creating them again here, but a little more briefly this time. Refer to Chapter 3 for more information.

Creating a Test Database

We'll start with creating a sample database that we want to backup. You can skip this step if you just want to work with an existing database. We'll use basically the same database we used for the TDE examples, just with a different name. The following SQL creates the database and populates it with test data:

```
CREATE DATABASE TestBackupEncryption;
GO

USE TestBackupEncryption;
CREATE TABLE dbo.SomeData(Id INT IDENTITY(1,1), SomeText VARCHAR(255));
GO

INSERT INTO dbo.SomeData (SomeText)
SELECT TOP 1000000
('XXXXXXXXXXXXXXXXXXXXXXXXXXXXXXXXXXXXXXXXXXXXXXXXXXXXXXXXXXXXXXXXXXXXXXX')
FROM sys.objects a
CROSS JOIN sys.objects b
CROSS JOIN sys.objects c
CROSS JOIN sys.objects d;
GO 100
```

Create the Database Master Key (DMK)

You must have a DMK, which resides in the master database, and you can create it with the following code:

```
USE master;
CREATE MASTER KEY
ENCRYPTION BY PASSWORD = 'UseAStrongPasswordHere!£$7';
```

You should also backup the DMK using the following command:

```
BACKUP MASTER KEY TO FILE = 'C:\Test\MyDMK'
ENCRYPTION BY PASSWORD = 'UseAnotherStrongPasswordHere!£$7';
```

Creating the Certificate

You also require a certificate in the master database which has an associated public/ private key pair. Unlike TDE, in the case of Backup Encryption, this key pair will be used to directly encrypt the backup using asymmetric encryption. There is no separate Database Encryption Key required. You create the certificate with this SQL:

```
USE master;
CREATE CERTIFICATE BackupEncryptionCert
WITH SUBJECT = 'Certificate used for backup encryption';
```

You should take backups of the certificate and private key and keep them safe if you ever want to be able to restore your backups to another server. Here is the SQL to backup these objects:

```
BACKUP CERTIFICATE BackupEncryptionCert
TO FILE = 'C:\Test\BackupEncryptionCert.cer'
WITH PRIVATE KEY
(
    FILE = 'C:\Test\BackupEncryptionCert_PrivateKeyFile.pvk',
    ENCRYPTION BY PASSWORD = 'UseAStrongPasswordHereToo!£$7'
);
```

Permissions

It's possible that the account you generally use for taking backups doesn't have sysadmin permissions on the server. If that is the case, then there are some additional permissions required. The account needs the db_backupoperator role in each database being backed up, but that should already be in place. The only additional permission required is that the account must have the VIEW DEFINITION permission on the certificate. You can assign that permission with this SQL:

```
USE master;
GRANT VIEW DEFINITION ON CERTIFICATE::BackupEncryptionCert
TO [MyBackupAccount];
```

That's all we need to do before we are ready to start encrypting our backups.

Working with Encrypted Backups

Now that we have all the objects in place to encrypt our backups, we can look at how you take a backup with encryption enabled and how you restore an encrypted backup.

Taking an Encrypted Backup

It is possible to encrypt any of the backup types – FULL, DIFFERENTIAL, or LOG. In practice if you are using Backup Encryption, you are likely to want to make sure all are encrypted. The syntax is the same in each case though, so we'll just look at FULL backups. This is the backup command with encryption specified:

```
BACKUP DATABASE TestBackupEncryption
TO DISK = 'C:\Test\TestBackupEncryption_Encrypted.bak'
WITH ENCRYPTION(ALGORITHM = AES_256, SERVER CERTIFICATE =
BackupEncryptionCert);
```

You can see we specify the algorithm. As with TDE, AES_256 is recommended (Advanced Encryption Standard with a 256-bit key). We also specify which certificate to use.

We can view data about the backup using the RESTORE HEADERONLY command, which will include information about encryption. Here is the code for that:

```
RESTORE HEADERONLY
FROM DISK = 'C:\Test\TestBackupEncryption_Encrypted.bak';
```

This returns us a lot of information, so I won't include the full set of columns. Relevant to encryption though, we will see the following:

```
KeyAlgorithm - aes_256
EncryptorThumbprint - 0xA2E4A2A29182054B2F97FCD9954FA9349B4351EC
EncryptorType – CERTIFICATE
```

You can use this if you need to be able to check whether a particular backup is encrypted or not.

Restoring an Encrypted Backup

Restoring an encrypted backup is the same as restoring any other backup – as long as the certificate used to encrypt the backup exists on the server.

If you are restoring to a different server, you will need to restore a copy of the certificate and private key from the backup taken before you can restore the encrypted database (the server must also have a DMK before you can do this). This is the same command we covered in Chapter 4:

```
USE master;
CREATE CERTIFICATE BackupEncryptionCert
FROM FILE = 'C:\Test\BackupEncryptionCert.cer'
WITH PRIVATE KEY
(
    FILE = 'C:\Test\BackupEncryptionCert_PrivateKeyFile.pvk',
    DECRYPTION BY PASSWORD = 'UseAStrongPasswordHereToo!£$7'
);
```

Then you can simply restore the database as normal with the following command:

```
RESTORE DATABASE  TestBackupEncryption
FROM DISK = 'C:\Test\TestBackupEncryption_Encrypted.bak';
```

If you get an error, it is likely to be because the certificate doesn't exist – for instance, if you have restored the wrong one:

```
Msg 33111, Level 16, State 3, Line 25 Cannot find server certificate with
thumbprint '0xA2E4A2A29182054B2F97FCD9954FA9349B4351EC'. Msg 3013, Level
16, State 1, Line 25
RESTORE DATABASE is terminating abnormally.
```

Backup Encryption Performance

Unlike TDE, there is some extra CPU overhead when you take an encrypted backup as the data has to be encrypted before being written to disk – whereas with TDE the data is already encrypted. Backup times however are unlikely to be affected significantly as the bottleneck is usually going to be the time it takes to physically write the data to disk. The CPU processing should take a fraction of that time.

We can run a quick test with our database to show how backup performs with and without encryption. If you're running this test yourself, then make sure the previous backup files are removed before executing the below script.

```
BACKUP DATABASE TestBackupEncryption
TO DISK = 'C:\Test\TestBackupEncryption_Unencrypted.bak';

BACKUP DATABASE TestBackupEncryption
TO DISK = 'C:\Test\TestBackupEncryption_Encrypted.bak'
WITH ENCRYPTION(ALGORITHM = AES_256, SERVER CERTIFICATE =
BackupEncryptionCert);
```

Here is the output for the unencrypted backup:

```
Processed 1205416 pages for database 'TestBackupEncryption', file
'TestBackupEncryption' on file 1.
Processed 1 pages for database 'TestBackupEncryption', file
'TestBackupEncryption_log' on file 1.
BACKUP DATABASE successfully processed 1205417 pages in 17.428 seconds
(540.355 MB/sec).
```

And here is the output for the encrypted backup:

```
Processed 1205416 pages for database 'TestBackupEncryption', file
'TestBackupEncryption' on file 1.
Processed 1 pages for database 'TestBackupEncryption', file
'TestBackupEncryption_log' on file 1.
BACKUP DATABASE successfully processed 1205417 pages in 19.631 seconds
(479.716 MB/sec).
```

You can see the backup with encryption did take a bit longer, about 2 seconds, a little over a 10% increase which seems not too bad.

With backup performance, it's also worth considering how long it takes to restore a database from a backup. Let's take a quick look at that. We'll drop the database, restore the unencrypted backup, then drop it again, and restore from the encrypted backup. Then we can compare the performance. We do all that with the following code:

```
DROP DATABASE TestBackupEncryption;
GO

RESTORE DATABASE TestBackupEncryption
FROM DISK = 'C:\Test\TestBackupEncryption_Unencrypted.bak';

DROP DATABASE TestBackupEncryption;
GO

RESTORE DATABASE TestBackupEncryption
FROM DISK = 'C:\Test\TestBackupEncryption_Encrypted.bak';
```

Here is the output for restoring from the unencrypted backup:

```
Processed 1205416 pages for database 'TestBackupEncryption', file
'TestBackupEncryption' on file 1.
Processed 1 pages for database 'TestBackupEncryption', file
'TestBackupEncryption_log' on file 1.
RESTORE DATABASE successfully processed 1205417 pages in 17.979 seconds
(523.795 MB/sec).
```

And here is the output with the encrypted backup:

```
Processed 1205416 pages for database 'TestBackupEncryption', file
'TestBackupEncryption' on file 1.
Processed 1 pages for database 'TestBackupEncryption', file
'TestBackupEncryption_log' on file 1.
RESTORE DATABASE successfully processed 1205417 pages in 20.794 seconds
(452.886 MB/sec).
```

You can see that like the backup itself, the restore from the encrypted backup took slightly longer – in this case about 3 seconds or 15%. It's not too bad, but it's good to be aware that you may see some impact.

Backup Encryption and Compression

You can also compress your encrypted backups. Unlike TDE this has been possible with Backup Encryption since the feature was first made available, and there have been no issues that have required fixing – though as always you should still test that restores work correctly. As mentioned in the section on TDE, compressing backups has benefits not just in terms of file size but potentially also in reduced backup times as the time taken to write to disk is smaller.

Compressing an encrypted backup is the same as compressing a regular backup; you just need to specify WITH COMPRESSION as shown in the following SQL:

```
BACKUP DATABASE TestBackupEncryption
TO DISK = 'C:\Test\TestBackupEncryption_EncryptedAndCompressed.bak'
WITH ENCRYPTION(ALGORITHM = AES_256, SERVER CERTIFICATE =
BackupEncryptionCert),
COMPRESSION;
```

We can run a quick test to see how compression performs against the same functionality with an unencrypted backup taken by executing this backup command:

```
BACKUP DATABASE TestBackupEncryption
TO DISK = 'C:\Test\TestBackupEncryption_UnencryptedAndCompressed.bak'
WITH COMPRESSION;
```

In Figure 5-1 we can see both backups:

Name	Date modified	Type	Size
TestBackupEncryption_EncryptedAndCompressed.bak	17/01/2022 13:58	BAK File	404,307 KB
TestBackupEncryption_UnencryptedAndCompressed.bak	17/01/2022 13:56	BAK File	403,166 KB

Figure 5-1. *Comparing compressed backup sizes with and without encryption*

Both backups are a fairly similar size. The encrypted one seems to be very slightly bigger, and I'd say this is the pattern I usually see, not enough that we are likely to be bothered with it. Compression is usually just as effective with encrypted backups as with unencrypted.

Summary

Backup Encryption is a form of at-rest encryption we can use for protecting our database backups. It is available from SQL Server 2014 onward in both the standard and enterprise editions of the product – that means it may be available to use even if you are on an edition that doesn't support TDE.

Backup Encryption is simple to work with and has little downside in terms of performance. You can also compress your encrypted backups to gain potential savings in terms of both disk space and backup times.

That brings us to the end of this chapter on Backup Encryption, and with that we have covered the tools available for at-rest encryption in SQL Server. In the next chapter we start to look at Always Encrypted, an exciting new way of protecting your data that was added in SQL Server 2016.

PART III

Column Encryption using Always Encrypted

CHAPTER 6

Introducing Always Encrypted

Always Encrypted was a new encryption feature added to SQL Server with the 2016 version of the product. Initially it was just available in enterprise edition, but from SQL Server 2016, SP1 was made available in standard edition also.

Unlike TDE which encrypts the whole database, Always Encrypted is a form of column encryption that means you choose which columns of data you want to encrypt. The "Always" part of Always Encrypted refers to the fact that data is encrypted at rest, in memory, and as it is transmitted across the network. That means that it provides the highest level of protection possible for your data.

The beauty of Always Encrypted, and what makes it a great feature, is that you don't necessarily need to make any code changes to use it. Neither your application side code nor your database side code – stored procedures/functions – needs to know which columns are encrypted or not. Encryption and decryption of data is carried out automatically for you. It does however come with limitations on how you can interact with data.

A key difference between Always Encrypted and existing forms of column encryption available in SQL Server is the encryption hierarchy used. Previous methods would rely on the encryption hierarchy within SQL Server. That would mean that a user with elevated permissions on the database server would be able to read encrypted data. Always Encrypted relies on a key stored in the database server as well as a certificate and associated asymmetric key pair that are only stored on the application server. That means you need elevated access on both servers to be able to read encrypted data.

A key concept with Always Encrypted is the idea of role separation. That refers to the idea that you should ensure there is a separation of roles between your system administrators. If different individuals (or teams) manage your application and database servers, and no individuals have admin rights on both, then no one can access encrypted

© Matthew McGiffen 2022
M. McGiffen, *Pro Encryption in SQL Server 2022*, https://doi.org/10.1007/978-1-4842-8664-7_6

data outside of the context it should be accessed. Even without role separation, the access requirements to read encrypted data make it much harder for an external attacker.

SQL Server 2016 vs. SQL Server 2019 and Beyond

In SQL Server 2019 new functionality was added to Always Encrypted that addressed many of the limitations in the previous version. To access the extra functionality however requires additional setup and management. I find it's worth thinking about these as almost two separate versions of the same feature, and you may choose which to use depending on your requirements and circumstances. We can think of these as "Basic Always Encrypted" which is mainly what we got with SQL 2016 and "Always Encrypted with Enclaves" which was the main addition with SQL 2019.

The difference arises from the reason why we have limitations with Always Encrypted at all. A key thing to understand is the "Always" part. SQL Server never sees the unencrypted value of your data; encryption and decryption is actually carried out on the client side – on the application servers. As SQL Server is unaware of the unencrypted values of data, it is limited in the questions it can answer about your data.

With SQL 2019 the use of enclaves was added. An enclave is a secure partition within memory where protected operations can take place securely. Always Encrypted with Enclaves allows for decryption and encryption of data within a secure enclave on the SQL Server box which can therefore support a wider range of functionality.

In this chapter and the following ones, we're going to first focus on basic Always Encrypted and then move onto the version with enclaves in later chapters.

How Does Always Encrypted Work?

As mentioned, we're going to focus on the basic version to begin with. The concepts around Always Encrypted are reasonably straightforward, but you'll find yourself asking questions that seem tricky. Will Always Encrypted work if I try to do this or that? Why are you getting a particular error? I've blogged about Always Encrypted and some of the specific questions readers ask me aren't covered in the documentation; having a knowledge of how it all works generally enables me to answer those questions. If you understand the mechanics of encrypting and decrypting data, then any limitations make sense. As such, I'm going to spend quite a bit of time in this chapter explaining how it all works.

Encryption Hierarchy

SQL Server has a standard encryption hierarchy that we've seen when we looked at TDE and Backup Encryption. Always Encrypted doesn't use that, mainly because the encryption activities don't occur on the database server, as they are done on the client machine.

On the SQL Server side we have a Column Encryption Key (CEK) that is used to encrypt and decrypt data. That is stored encrypted in the database. The CEK is encrypted by the Column Master Key (CMK) which is actually a certificate and key pair that commonly sit on the client machine – usually an application server.

On SQL Server we do have a CMK object, but this is just a pointer to the location of the actual CMK.

You can have one CEK for all the encrypted columns in your database, or you could have one for each separate column – or something in between. The CMK can be shared by multiple CEKs so again you could have one or multiple CMKs.

Encryption in Practice

Let's go through the process of how Always Encrypted works. Figure 6-1 shows all the steps that occur when you issue a query.

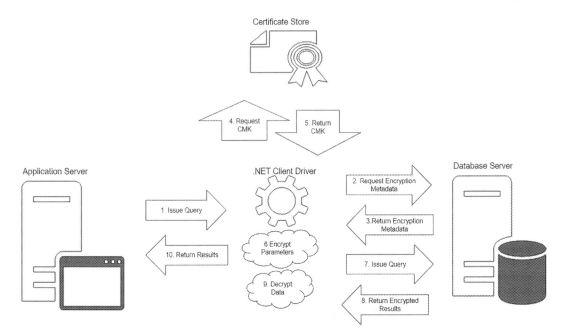

Figure 6-1. *How Always Encrypted works*

At first glance it seems like a lot is going on, but we'll go through each step in turn and you'll see it is quite simple.

1. **Issue Query**

   The application will have created a connection to the database server. It has to specify that the connection will use Always Encrypted. Potentially, that is the only change you need to make to your application – if you're lucky. It depends whether you end up needing to do work to get around the natural limitations of the technology – but we'll get to that later. Once the connection is in place, then the application simply issues the query in the normal manner.

2. **Request Encryption Metadata**

   When issuing a query, any plaintext values that target encrypted columns must be passed as parameters and must be encrypted before being sent to the database. Where such a parameterized query is being executed, the client driver requests the relevant encryption metadata from SQL Server to understand what encryption activities must be carried out before the query is sent to be executed.

3. **Return Encryption Metadata**

   SQL Server parses the query text and identifies if there are any
   columns targeted by parameters that are the subject of column
   encryption using Always Encrypted. This information is sent
   back to the client, along with the encrypted values of any Column
   Encryption Keys (CEKs) used and in each case the location of the
   Column Master Key (CMK). This encryption metadata is cached
   locally on the client machine so that repeated calls to get the
   metadata do not need to be made for the same query.

4. **Request CMK**

   Using the details provided in the encryption metadata, the client
   driver makes calls to access the certificates and keys for the CMKs
   it requires. Usually these are stored in the certificate store on the
   application server. Where there are multiple application servers,
   then they need to be stored on each. You can also store your CMKs
   in an external store such as Azure Key Vault; we cover that in
   Chapter 20.

5. **Return CMK**

   The CMKs are received by the client driver.

6. **Encrypt Parameters**

   Any parameters that target encrypted columns need to be
   encrypted. The CEK that was returned by SQL Server for a given
   column is decrypted using the associated CMK; the parameter
   value can then be encrypted using the underlying key value.
   Only parameters will be encrypted, so if you have literal values in
   your query, then these will be a problem if they target encrypted
   columns. Update and insert queries must specify the values
   using parameters for them to function when targeting tables with
   Always Encrypted columns.

7. **Issue Query**

   The query with its parameters encrypted by the last step is sent to
   SQL Server to be executed.

8. **Return Encrypted Results**

   Where the query has results, such as with a select query, the results are returned. Where these include encrypted columns, then it is the encrypted values that get passed back. Encryption metadata is sent back alongside the result set which supplies the encrypted CEKs and CMK locations for any encrypted columns in the results.

9. **Decrypt Data**

   Where we have results containing encrypted columns, these are decrypted by the client driver before being returned to the application. This is done using the encryption metadata supplied alongside the results. As with the parameters, the CEK is decrypted using the associated CMK – sometimes this has already retrieved from the certificate store, and if not then there is an additional step to retrieve the CMKs. The unencrypted value of the CEK can then be used to decrypt the data in the column or columns that it is related to.

10. **Return Results**

   Finally, the results are returned to the application with values that were stored encrypted returned as the plain text version.

Summary

That can feel like a lot of steps to get to your data, but it all happens in the background and generally with little overhead. Each step is itself quite simple. It's good to understand the overall flow so you can understand what will happen in different querying scenarios.

We'll go over some of this again in a bit more detail when we have Always Encrypted set up and start looking at how you execute queries. Having seen the process though, we can now start to understand some of the key things about Always Encrypted.

- Data only exists unencrypted after it hits the client.

- SQL Server does not encrypt or decrypt data. That is all handled in the client driver. As such there is no way for SQL to know what the unencrypted values of your data are – it just sees an encrypted string.

That is key for understanding why there are limitations on the sort of queries you can execute and on things like indexing.

- We need both the CEK – stored encrypted on the SQL box – and the CMK stored on the client to access encrypted data. As such, you need access over both. Someone with access to just one side of the equation will not be able to read encrypted data.

- Plaintext values that target encrypted columns must be passed as parameters which can be encrypted before being sent to the database server.

In the next chapter, we'll look at how you set up Always Encrypted. Don't worry if the complexity seems confusing now; as we start to work through a few demos, it will all become clear.

CHAPTER 7

Setting Up Always Encrypted

It is a straightforward process to set up everything required for Always Encrypted. In fact, there is a wizard provided in SQL Server Management Studio (SSMS) that will do it all for you. In these examples, however, we will focus on performing the individual steps manually as that gives you a better view of what is going on. For all the objects involved we'll look in detail at what is created so that you have a good level of understanding.

Before starting it is best to make sure that the version of SSMS you are using is up to date so that it has the full support for Always Encrypted. Anything above version 18 is fine.

Create Keys and Certificates

Before we start, we need a database we're going to work in. We'll call it TestAlwaysEncrypted – you can create it with the following SQL:

```
CREATE DATABASE TestAlwaysEncrypted;
```

Creating the Certificate and Column Master Key

First, we'll create the Column Master Key (CMK). We have a few options for a CMK; in this chapter we'll focus on the option of using a certificate stored on the local machine which contains an asymmetric key. You can also use an asymmetric key stored in an external key store such as Azure Key Vault; we look at that option in Chapter 20. When you create the CMK through SSMS, it also creates a CMK object in your database that identifies the location and identity of the actual key.

© Matthew McGiffen 2022
M. McGiffen, *Pro Encryption in SQL Server 2022*, https://doi.org/10.1007/978-1-4842-8664-7_7

If you expand your database in the SSMS Object Explorer, you will find Always Encrypted Keys under the Security folder for the database. Right-click over Column Master Keys and select to create a new one, as shown in Figure 7-1:

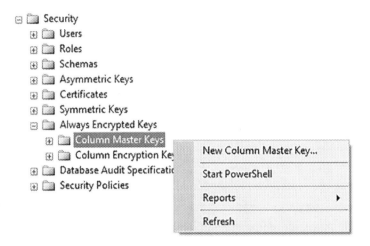

Figure 7-1. *Finding Always Encrypted Keys in SSMS*

Figure 7-2 depicts the GUI that comes up:

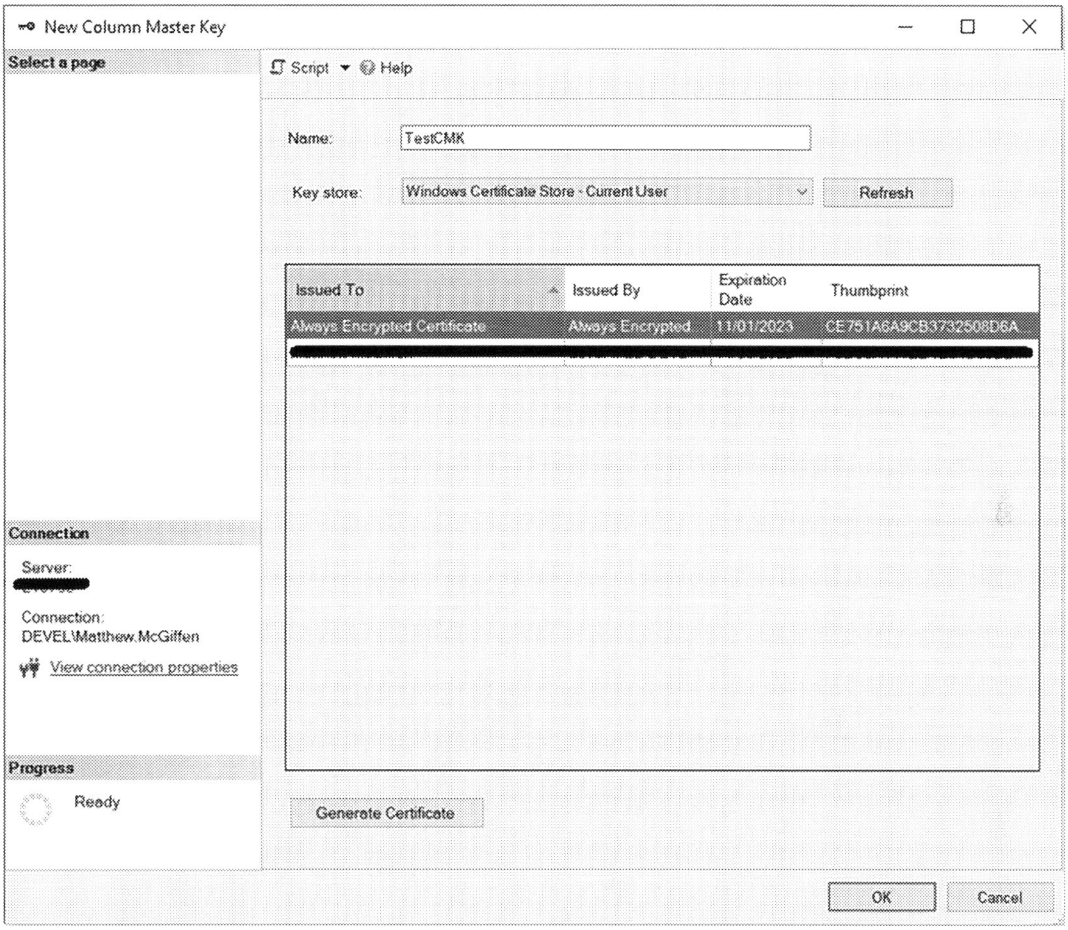

Figure 7-2. *SSMS GUI for creating Column Master Keys and Certificates*

At the top you can see I've given my new CMK the name TestCMK. In the box below we see a list of certificates in the selected key store available for use by Always Encrypted. I created the highlighted one simply by clicking the Generate Certificate button at the bottom. The Key Store for the certificate to be created in defaults to the Current User store. It is worth noting that when you generate a certificate, it is created on the local machine you are running SSMS on – not the SQL Server you are connected to – unless you are running SSMS on the server itself. Your account will need permissions to create certificates in the selected certificate store, or the generate certificate button will be grayed out – in that case you may have to run SSMS as an administrator to resolve the issue.

The decision of whether to create the certificate in the Local Machine or Current User store becomes more relevant once you are deploying the certificate to environments other than your local development environment. In those cases, I prefer to deploy to the Current User store for the account the application runs under – or if deploying to Local Machine, you can set the access for the certificate so only the application user account can access it. This minimizes the set of accounts that can access the certificate.

Click OK and the new CMK will be created. We can then see it listed under the Column Master Keys folder in SSMS, as shown in Figure 7-3:

Figure 7-3. *Your new Column Master Key*

To understand what this key actually is, I'm going to right-click and generate the SQL definition. This also shows you the code if you want to create the SQL Server CMK object through T-SQL:

```
CREATE COLUMN MASTER KEY [TestCMK]
WITH
(
    KEY_STORE_PROVIDER_NAME = N'MSSQL_CERTIFICATE_STORE',
    KEY_PATH = N'CurrentUser/My/CE751A6A9CB3732508D6A7E8368E5B3770CF7328'
);
```

We only have two values, KEY_STORE_PROVIDER_NAME and KEY_PATH. All this is telling us is where to find the certificate we just created; KEY_PATH shows the path in the certificate store including the certificate's thumbprint. If you are following along, your certificate will have its own unique thumbprint. You can see that the Column Master Key object stored in your database is just a pointer to the actual CMK, in this case a certificate stored on client machines.

If you want to create your certificate without using SSMS, you can do so with PowerShell. Here is an example:

```
# Create a column master key in Windows Certificate Store.
$cert = New-SelfSignedCertificate -Subject "AlwaysEncryptedCert"
-CertStoreLocation Cert:CurrentUser\My -KeyExportPolicy Exportable -Type
DocumentEncryptionCert -KeyUsage DataEncipherment -KeySpec KeyExchange
```

In practice, when deploying your applications, you are likely to create the certificate ahead of time and deploy it as part of a deployment package. At a minimum you are also likely to want to use different certificates in your dev/test vs. production environments.

Creating the Column Encryption Key (CEK)

This is the last thing we need before we can set up encryption on our columns. The CEK is a symmetric key that will be used to encrypt our actual data and will be stored in the database encrypted by the CMK. You can find the Column Encryption Keys folder underneath Column Master Keys in SSMS which you saw in Figure 7-3. Again, right-click to create a new key and bring up the GUI shown in Figure 7-4:

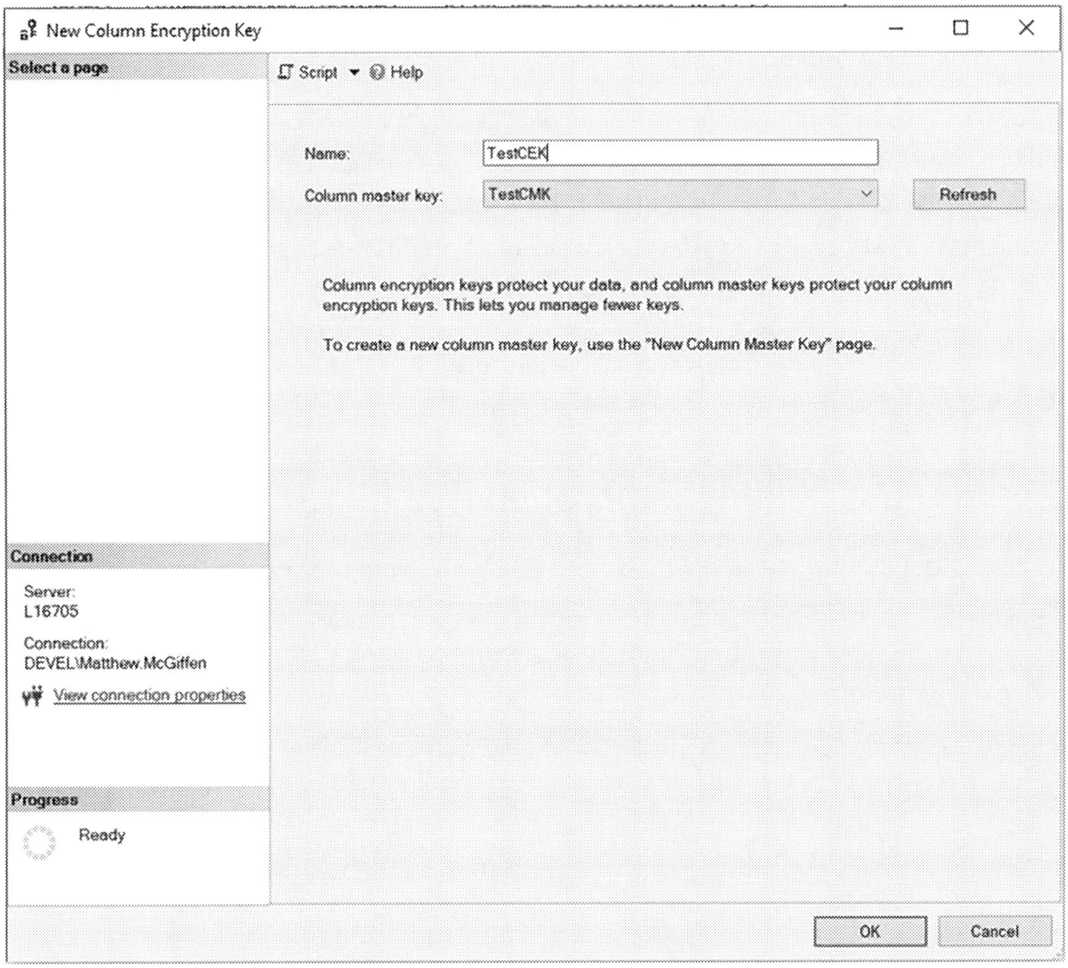

Figure 7-4 shows the New Column Encryption Key dialog:

New Column Encryption Key	— □ ×

Select a page

Script ▼ ⊙ Help

Name: TestCEK

Column master key: TestCMK   ∨   Refresh

Column encryption keys protect your data, and column master keys protect your column encryption keys. This lets you manage fewer keys.

To create a new column master key, use the "New Column Master Key" page.

Connection

Server:
L16705

Connection:
DEVEL\Matthew.McGiffen

👭 View connection properties

Progress

○ Ready

OK   Cancel

Figure 7-4. *Creating a new Column Encryption Key*

You can see I've called mine TestCEK, and in the dropdown, I've selected the CMK that I just created. Click OK and the CEK is created. We can see it in the object browser (Figure 7-5):

⊟ ▥ Always Encrypted Keys
　⊞ ▥ Column Master Keys
　⊟ ▥ Column Encryption Keys
　　🔑 TestCEK

Figure 7-5. *Your new Column Encryption Key*

As with the CMK we'll script the key out through SSMS so you can see what is created and the code involved:

```
CREATE COLUMN ENCRYPTION KEY [TestCEK]
WITH VALUES
(
    COLUMN_MASTER_KEY = [TestCMK],
    ALGORITHM = 'RSA_OAEP',
    ENCRYPTED_VALUE = 0x016E0000016300750072007200650006E00740075007300650
    072002F006D0079002F006300650037003500310061003600610039006300620033000
    3700330032003500300038006400360061003700650038003300360038006500350060
    2003300370037003000063006600370033003200380008B2B50941CCCC53C3EFAE2FC455
    437B95223B879B228D74836F55C50E375186A8E29FEE2CE4AAA9AA95F05EA30F1527C
    B0E6431DD2F925B8D23EDA25C3F1B480736287A7745DD169761778241D9BB4474F780
    2734050C5F8D22A424BFC9B48823F409D3F94808E4FCDB745EB85AC39A96803F5561A
    91BEAFE4094BB34AA74C7CD0F78F95B786F3B5C8793FD9132FED72E52193E59BA3652
    C8CC077F7DC47D49D36E2995A1A0A3727910E22B091F44F36241E13C2D2EAD12F29BB
    6C162928E6136C87A7ED4B63104C6549F00FA5064DE4C7604122C9817836A9C8994CF
    F4054E92DF6E436DCA2E3B897289ECEAB3624FAFA28A99D39B3C6D31AB323ECB51AAE
    F7C2CC604F6B260C048F8DBA4773D7B44D5E6BEE31AD540D3C4A4BCCBB4B192C6CC92
    80138B8D75251572239C5B32F19F9FFD5028CF91D7A0E2F41FD9DE4DAD85BCB4FF0BE
    903868E4036EC495FFB328CA1D1D5BF2F39DF227156E5D619363C079BB87FCEF3D709
    B5C4EAE6EA017473AD2BD26101410D38864791A6A1D94B0F6F801C12A050069210E3C
    E9A412F9D0EE775959A6856C84DB504CCE5CCFCCE5515FCFC2DE60D23140F5941F3D9
    A9E5B7560E452129593C077AACDD2AFD09B885A0198DB13838BFA156B83E7D2855FB8
    B4950F812C14B1AF5078E762D5E4E488C43624CFC711174E9916E076AFEE816FABED6
    E97C299CCE87292F226CF0518EC69F13
);
```

We can see it tells us what CMK this is based on, what Algorithm has been used to encrypt the CEK, and a long binary Encrypted Value. The Encrypted Value is the actual key used to encrypt data, itself encrypted by the CMK. The Encrypted Value seen here is unique to my system. If you create your own CEK, you will have a different value.

The unencrypted value of the CEK never exists on the SQL Server, so both the CMK and CEK are required to interact with encrypted data. This is what makes Always Encrypted so secure – even if you have admin rights on the SQL instance, you don't have access to the unencrypted value of the CEK, so you can't read data unless you have access to the CMK too.

You can deploy a pre-created CEK using the preceding code, but you cannot generate a fresh CEK using T-SQL. Part of the reason for that is that SQL Server cannot access the CMK which is required to encrypt the CEK. You have to use the GUI in SSMS, or if you wish to do it through code, then there are methods available with PowerShell.

Create an Encrypted Column

We're going to look here at how you define a column as encrypted when you create a new table. In a later chapter we will look at encrypting existing data.

Always Encrypted can work with most types of data, but there are some restrictions on which data types you can encrypt – we'll look at that in the section on limitations of Always Encrypted. In general, you can encrypt both numbers and strings, but you are limited in the extra functionality you can have against encrypted columns, such as constraints, and you wouldn't be able to encrypt columns with properties like IDENTITY. A specific restriction that it is good to be aware of is that string-based columns must use a BIN2 collation type. You'll see what I mean by that when we create the table.

With Always Encrypted you can also use one of two types of encryption, randomized or deterministic. The difference is that with randomized encryption, where you encrypt the same value multiple times (where the value exists in multiple rows within your data), the encrypted values will all be different. With deterministic, the same unencrypted value will always end up with the same encrypted value. Randomized encryption is more secure and you should use it where you can, but it does limit your functionality. For instance, you can't have an index on a column with randomized encryption; if you think about it, then that makes sense; if all the underlying values that are the same are stored as different values in the table, then how would it be possible to index them. If you want to index an encrypted column, then it must use deterministic encryption.

Another key restriction is that you cannot query with a WHERE clause against a column with randomized encryption. Let's understand that. Say I have an encrypted text column using randomized encryption and want to find all rows that match a particular value. I have to try doing that by encrypting the value I am searching for and matching that against the encrypted values in the table, but because we are using randomized encryption, my encrypted search value will be different to all the encrypted values in the table even when the unencrypted value might be the same, so no match would be possible. In such scenarios SQL Server will return an error to tell you the operation is not allowed so you don't attempt to execute queries where the result would be incorrect.

Deterministic encryption however is slightly less secure. Imagine that you are encrypting a text column which has a limited number of possible values; it may be possible to use frequency analysis to analyze the number of occurrences of each encrypted value and thereby match/guess what real value each corresponds to.

Let's go ahead and create a table with two encrypted text columns. For the sake of example, we'll use deterministic encryption for one and randomized for the other. The following SQL creates the table:

```
USE TestAlwaysEncrypted;
CREATE TABLE dbo.EncryptedTable(
Id INT IDENTITY(1,1) CONSTRAINT PK_EncryptedTable PRIMARY KEY CLUSTERED,
LastName nvarchar(50) COLLATE Latin1_General_BIN2 ENCRYPTED WITH (
COLUMN_ENCRYPTION_KEY = TestCEK,
ENCRYPTION_TYPE = DETERMINISTIC,
ALGORITHM = 'AEAD_AES_256_CBC_HMAC_SHA_256'
) NULL,
FirstName nvarchar(50) COLLATE Latin1_General_BIN2 ENCRYPTED WITH (
COLUMN_ENCRYPTION_KEY = TestCEK,
ENCRYPTION_TYPE = RANDOMIZED,
ALGORITHM = 'AEAD_AES_256_CBC_HMAC_SHA_256') NULL
);
```

We execute our SQL statement, and the table is created. You can see that what we are doing is specifying the details of encryption for each column we want to encrypt. We specify which CEK to use, which type of encryption (deterministic or randomized), and finally the algorithm used to encrypt the data in the column – though the algorithm specified is the only option at the current time.

Let's just discuss the requirement for a BIN2 collation in more detail as you might be wondering why this is needed. A collation specifies the way data is compared and sorted. One feature of BIN2 is that it is a case-sensitive collation. That means, for instance, that if you search for a string like "Matthew," it won't match with "MATTHEW" or "matthew." If you think about it, then it makes sense that you can't have case-insensitive comparisons on an encrypted column. When you perform a comparison based on encrypted data, what the engine is doing is comparing one encrypted value with another. To enable a case-insensitive comparison there would have to be some deterministic pattern so that you can tell that two different encrypted values differ only by case. That would be more complicated to implement, would weaken the encryption, and isn't supported by the encryption algorithm used by Always Encrypted. The requirement to use a BIN2 collation is driven by what will happen in practice when you compare two encrypted values looking for an exact match and also how such data is sorted. That creates some limitations on things like searching against encrypted columns – we'll talk more about that later.

In terms of setup, that's all you need to do, so you can see Always Encrypted is quite simple to implement.

Summary

Setting up Always Encrypted is straightforward. The key points to understand are:

- You need a certificate and key pair which sit on the client machine or application server; this is the Column Master Key (CMK). Alternatively you can use an asymmetric key in an external key store (see Chapter 20).

- In the database we have a CMK object, but this is just a pointer that tells us where the actual CMK can be found.

- The Column Encryption Key (CEK) is stored in the database but is stored encrypted by the CMK. This key is what is used to encrypt or decrypt data.

- To access data, you need access both to the CEK and the CMK.

- Columns can be encrypted with either deterministic or randomized encryption. Randomized is more secure but very limiting in terms of how you can interact with your data. Deterministic allows for the possibility of attacks by frequency analysis.

- String columns are required to use BIN2 collations which means comparisons are case-sensitive.

In this chapter you've seen how to set up the objects required by Always Encrypted. From there we're ready to start interacting with data – which we'll look at in the next chapter. That's where it starts to get interesting. You'll start to get a real understanding for how Always Encrypted works in practice and how you may be able to use it in your applications.

## CHAPTER 8

Executing Queries Using Always Encrypted

In this chapter we'll look at how you interact with data that is encrypted using Always Encrypted. First, we'll use SQL Server Management Studio (SSMS), and we'll have a look at what happens in the background when you execute a query. We'll also look at stored procedures. Then we'll cover how you can do the same from your application code – using PowerShell for the examples.

One thing to remember is that the encryption activities all occur in the client, be that SSMS or your application. As such the client driver used must support Always Encrypted. If you are using .NET, then you must be on version 4.6.1 or higher. It is also possible to work with Always Encrypted if you are using JDBC, ODBC, or PHP; we'll cover that briefly later on.

For these examples we're going to be using the database we created in the last chapter.

Performing a Basic Insert and Select

In this section we'll look at how you should connect to a database when working with Always Encrypted. We'll then look at the querying patterns you should use when working with encrypted columns.

Connecting to the Database

The first thing we need to do is to make sure we are using a connection to the database that has Always Encrypted enabled. To achieve the same thing when you are connecting from code, then you need to specify "Column Encryption Setting = Enabled" in your connection string. As mentioned earlier you will want to be using a recent version of SSMS – at least version 18.

© Matthew McGiffen 2022
M. McGiffen, *Pro Encryption in SQL Server 2022*, https://doi.org/10.1007/978-1-4842-8664-7_8

From SSMS you connect to the database engine as normal, and then in the Connect to Server dialog, you need to select the Options button. That then displays multiple tabs including one for Always Encrypted which we can see in Figure 8-1:

Figure 8-1. *Enabling Always Encrypted for your connection*

You need to tick the Enable Always Encrypted box and then you can connect as normal. You will also notice the Enclave Attestation URL. We leave that blank for now, but we'll use it when we look at Always Encrypted with Enclaves in later chapters.

Once you are connected, open a new query window. Right-click over the query window and select Query Options. Select the Advanced tab on the left – you should then see the GUI shown in Figure 8-2. Right at the bottom of the available settings is Enable Parameterization for Always Encrypted; make sure this is ticked, and then click OK.

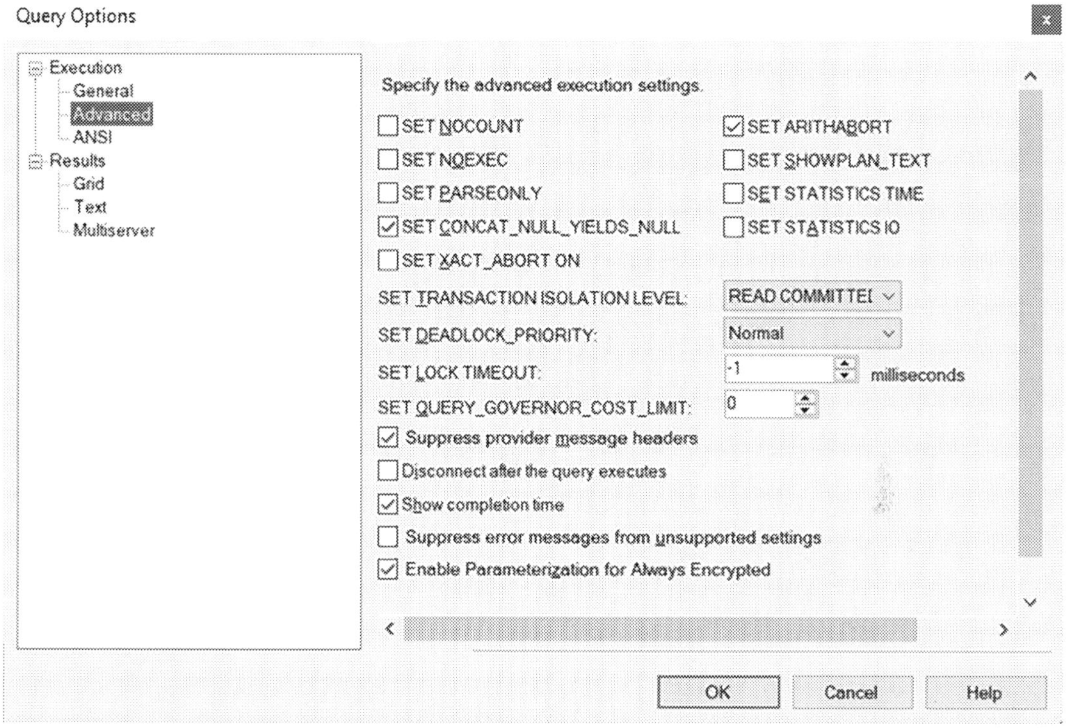

Figure 8-2. *Enabling Parameterization for Always Encrypted*

This setting tells SSMS that when you execute a query; the query should be converted to a parameterized query. Any variables used in the query will be converted to parameters. Those variables that target Always Encrypted columns will end up having their values encrypted before being sent to the database for execution.

If you forget to enable this, then when you attempt to issue a query on an encrypted connection, SSMS usually prompts to ask if you want to enable it.

Inserting Data

We're now ready to try inserting some data. First, we'll attempt something that will fail as it is an instructive example. Make sure your query window is set to the context of the TestAlwaysEncrypted database; then you can attempt to execute the following insert:

```
INSERT INTO dbo.EncryptedTable (LastName, FirstName)
VALUES ('McGiffen', 'Matthew');
```

You will find you get an error similar to this:

```
Msg 206, Level 16, State 2, Line 1
Operand type clash: varchar is incompatible with varchar(8000)
encrypted with (encryption_type = 'DETERMINISTIC',
encryption_algorithm_name = 'AEAD_AES_256_CBC_HMAC_SHA_256',
column_encryption_key_name = 'TestCEK',
column_encryption_key_database_name = 'TestAlwaysEncrypted')
collation_name = 'Latin1_General_CI_AS'
```

What the error message is telling you, in perhaps not very plain language, is that you are attempting to insert an unencrypted value into an encrypted column. The plaintext values must be encrypted before you attempt to insert them. In order to make that happen, we have to use parameters. Try the following instead:

```
DECLARE @LastName nvarchar(50) = 'McGiffen';
DECLARE @FirstName nvarchar(50) = 'Matthew';

INSERT INTO dbo.EncryptedTable (LastName, FirstName)
VALUES (@LastName, @FirstName);
```

Figure 8-3 shows a screenshot of what should happen in your query window. You should see your variable declarations get a wavy blue underline. This denotes that the variable will be treated as a parameter. If you hover your mouse over one of the variables, you will see a pop-up message to that effect. SSMS will also parameterize your query before attempting to execute it. We'll see what that means when we look at what happens in the background when the query gets executed.

Figure 8-3. *Parameterization for Always Encrypted in action*

If you don't see the wavy blue underline, then it is likely you haven't enabled Parameterization for Always Encrypted. That will be confirmed if you execute the query and get the following error:

```
Msg 33277, Level 16, State 6, Line 4
Encryption scheme mismatch for columns/variables '@LastName'. The encryption
scheme for the columns/variables is (encryption_type = 'PLAINTEXT') and the
expression near line '4' expects it to be DETERMINISTIC, or PLAINTEXT.
```

If all is configured correctly, when you execute the query, you will not receive an error and the row will be successfully inserted.

As a quick aside I want to show you something else that will fail as it demonstrates something that is important to understand. Let's try a version of the insert query again with this SQL:

```
DECLARE @LastName nvarchar(100) = 'McGiffen';
DECLARE @FirstName nvarchar(100) = 'Matthew';

INSERT INTO dbo.EncryptedTable (LastName, FirstName)
VALUES (@LastName, @FirstName);
```

The only difference here is that I've been a little bit lazy about the size of my variables. I've set them to nvarchar(100) where the column in the table is nvarchar(50). Normally this wouldn't be a problem as long as I didn't actually supply values longer than the column can hold. In the case of Always Encrypted, however, we get an error similar to the following when we execute this.

```
Msg 206, Level 16, State 2, Line 11
Operand type clash: nvarchar(100) encrypted with (encryption_type =
'DETERMINISTIC', encryption_algorithm_name = 'AEAD_AES_256_CBC_HMAC_SHA_256',
column_encryption_key_name = 'TestCEK', column_encryption_key_database_name =
'TestAlwaysEncrypted') is incompatible with nvarchar(50) encrypted with
(encryption_type = 'DETERMINISTIC', encryption_algorithm_name =
'AEAD_AES_256_CBC_HMAC_SHA_256', column_encryption_key_name = 'TestCEK',
column_encryption_key_database_name = 'TestAlwaysEncrypted')
Msg 8180, Level 16, State 1, Procedure sp_describe_parameter_encryption,
Line 1 [Batch Start Line 6]
```

When working with Always Encrypted and parameters, your parameters must be strongly typed, the type and size used must match what is in the table. Implicit conversions are not allowed. You also cannot insert a previously encrypted value into the table; that will fail with the same sort of error. That prevents someone from attempting to replace an encrypted value with one from another record.

Modifying data with an UPDATE statement works exactly the same way. You must use a parameter for a new value that you want to be stored in the table. One interesting point to note is that if you update multiple rows at once to the same value from a parameter, then the rows will end up with the same encrypted value even when randomized encryption is being used. This is because the parameter only gets encrypted using randomized encryption once.

Reading Data

We can check the outcome of our insert with a simple select query as follows:

```
SELECT *
FROM dbo.EncryptedTable;
```

Figure 8-4 shows the results:

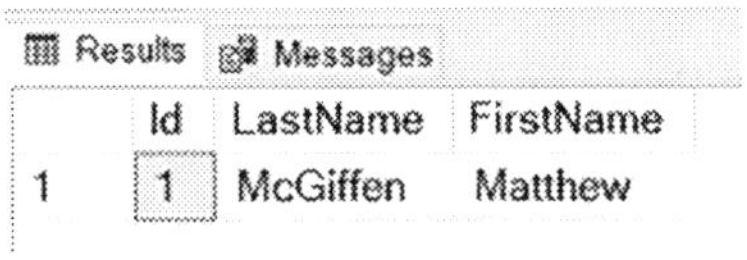

Figure 8-4. *Showing the results of our successful insert*

It's logical at this stage to ask yourself how you know if the data actually got encrypted or not. As our connection has Always Encrypted enabled, the .NET library used by SSMS has automatically decrypted the results before sending them back to the application to be displayed. We can see the actual values stored in the database by opening a new query window and changing the connection. We keep the connection to the same server but go into the options and disable the "Enable Always Encrypted" option. Then we can execute the same select query again. This time we get results like those shown in Figure 8-5:

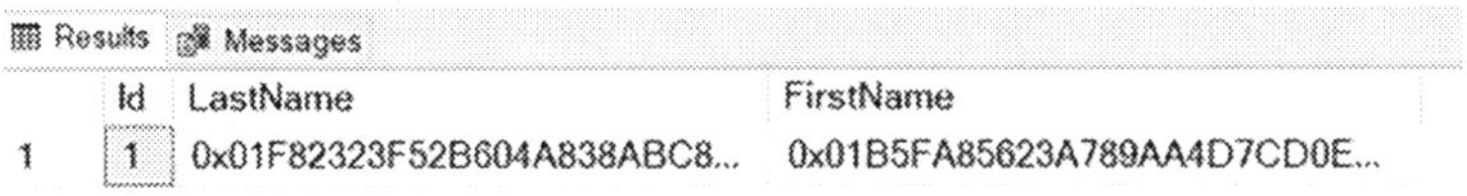

Figure 8-5. *Viewing the actual encrypted values that are stored in the database*

Here we see what is actually stored in the database and can see that our data has been encrypted.

Looking at What Happens in the Background

Let's look at what happens in the background when the query executes. To do this, we're going to run an XEvent Profiler trace and see what actually gets sent to the database.

I debated whether to use Extended Events or the traditional SQL Server Profiler trace for these examples. Without getting into the argument of which is better and why, I have chosen XEvent Profiler which is a simple GUI that uses Extended Events to replicate the functionality of simple Profiler traces. It is the solution that involves the fewest clicks to get going, and so I hope is the easiest for the reader to follow and repeat.

We start an XEvent Profiler trace from SSMS. You generally find it as the bottom item for your server in the Object Explorer. We'll use the TSQL option (Figure 8-6), so right-click on that and select Launch Session.

Figure 8-6. *Starting an XEvent Profiler trace*

What Happens with an Insert Query

Once the session has opened, we rerun our insert query and see what is captured. Here is the SQL again:

```
DECLARE @LastName nvarchar(50) = 'McGiffen';
DECLARE @FirstName nvarchar(50) = 'Matthew';

INSERT INTO dbo.EncryptedTable (LastName, FirstName)
VALUES (@LastName, @FirstName);
```

You can see the results in Figure 8-7:

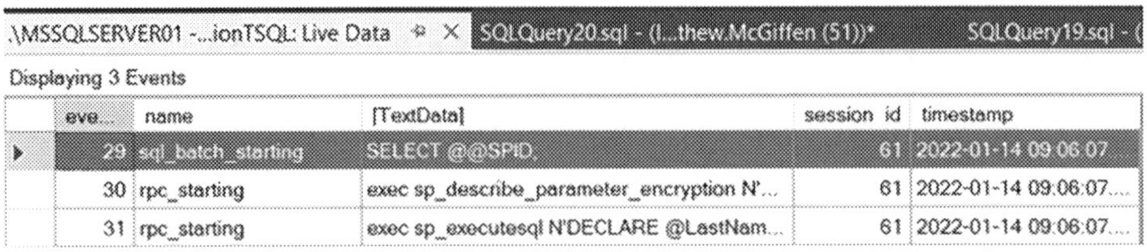

Figure 8-7. *Viewing our XEvent Profiler trace*

We can see there are two queries captured – normally we would just expect to see the one we executed. What we're seeing here is what was described in Chapter 6 when we looked at the steps needed to execute a query over a connection with Always Encrypted enabled. Before executing the query itself, the client must issue a command to retrieve the encryption metadata. It needs to understand if any of the columns targeted by parameters are encrypted, and if so, it needs information about the keys. Let's look at the query in full that is executed:

```
exec sp_describe_parameter_encryption N'DECLARE @LastName AS NVARCHAR (50)
= @pacc87acf4618488b80bc61f6ac68114f;

DECLARE @FirstName AS NVARCHAR (50) = @p4113aa748f2e4ff585556f8eaa618f0d;

INSERT  INTO dbo.EncryptedTable (LastName, FirstName)
VALUES                   (@LastName, @FirstName);

',N'@pacc87acf4618488b80bc61f6ac68114f nvarchar(50),@p4113aa748f2e4ff58555
6f8eaa618f0d nvarchar(50)'
```

Retrieving the encryption metadata is achieved by this call to the *sp_describe_ parameter_encryption* stored procedure. SSMS has parameterized our query and then sent that text over to be parsed by the engine. We can execute the same call to *sp_describe_parameter_encryption* ourselves and see what is returned. We get two result sets. There's a fair amount of information returned, so I'll display them as tables rather than screenshots to make things more readable. The first result set (Table 8-1) gives us information about any Always Encrypted keys we will need to execute our query. In this case there is only one key involved in our query so we just get one row returned, but if there were multiple keys required, we would get a row for each.

Table 8-1. *Showing the metadata for keys required by our query*

Column name	Value
column_encryption_key_ordinal	1
database_id	5
column_encryption_key_id	1
column_encryption_key_version	1
column_encryption_key_metadata_version	0xCBC1DD001CAE0000
column_encryption_key_encrypted_value	0x016E000001630075007200720072006500 6E0074007500730065007...
column_master_key_store_provider_name	MSSQL_CERTIFICATE_STORE
column_master_key_path	CurrentUser/My/ CE751A6A9CB3732508D6A7E8368E5B3770CF7328
column_encryption_key_encryption_ algorithm_name	RSA_OAEP
is_requested_by_enclave	0
column_master_key_signature	NULL

There are a few key columns here:

- *column_encryption_key_ordinal* is an assigned ordinal value used to identify the key and is useful when multiple keys are involved in the query.

- *column_encryption_key_encrypted_value* is the encrypted value of the CEK as stored in the database.

- *column_master_key_store_provider_name* tells the client where the CMK is stored.

- *column_master_key_path* identifies the path to the actual certificate used as the CMK.

Armed with this information, the client driver can obtain the local copy of the CMK and use that to decrypt the encrypted CEK value to obtain the actual encryption key.

The second result set (Table 8-2) gives details of which parameters target encrypted columns:

Table 8-2. *Showing the metadata for parameters used by our query*

Column name	Value	Value
parameter_ordinal	1	2
parameter_name	@pacc87acf4618488b80bc61f 6ac68114f	@p4113aa748f2e4ff585556f8 eaa618f0d
column_encryption_algorithm	2	2
column_encryption_type	1	2
column_encryption_key_ordinal	1	1
column_encryption_ normalization_rule_version	1	1

Here we have two parameters as we are inserting a value into each of the two columns. The results are fairly clear, but let's just go over a few of the values and what they mean:

- *parameter_ordinal* is an ordinal value for the parameter.

- *parameter_name* is the name of the parameter as supplied to the *sp_describe_parameter_encryption* stored procedure.

- *column_encryption_type* describes whether encryption is deterministic or randomized. 1 means randomized and 2 means deterministic. You might also see the value of 0 which means plaintext where a parameter targets an unencrypted column.

- *column_encryption_key_ordinal* denotes which key in the first result set (where there are more than one) should be used.

Armed with all this information and with the CEK now decrypted, the client driver can encrypt the parameters as required and finally issue the query to SQL Server. This is the second query we saw in our XEvent Profiler capture:

```
exec sp_executesql N'DECLARE @LastName AS NVARCHAR (50) = @pacc87acf4618488
b80bc61f6ac68114f;

DECLARE @FirstName AS NVARCHAR (50) = @p4113aa748f2e4ff585556f8eaa618f0d;

INSERT  INTO dbo.EncryptedTable (LastName, FirstName)
VALUES                          (@LastName, @FirstName);
```

```
',N'@pacc87acf4618488b80bc61f6ac68114f nvarchar(50),@p4113aa748f2e4ff58555
6f8eaa618f0d nvarchar(50)',@pacc87acf4618488b80bc61f6ac68114f=0x01F82323F5
2B604A838ABC880ECDEB6CDD26ED47813F507A2EAA78FA1EE10FF47B2ED7C73C1A76580B6C
0753A95DF5C944C5E590C2ED7E0AF59F1B40543170185844A9B8E3B4B0D9C4341B32DE2990E
22C1,@p4113aa748f2e4ff585556f8eaa618f0d=0x012AC8899AACB8F1DDCEF4F6B2EB090F
5E56687FDBB67D237E0E3D6D91C7F96C29F39396C633FB27DD92C7F2FABC18600D154FE1D4
26000CDB401ECD8BFD04AAC3
```

Here the parameterized version of our query has been issued to SQL Server with the plaintext parameters encrypted ready for insertion into the table. The long binary values at the end of the query represent the values "Matthew" and "McGiffen" encrypted using the correct CEK.

Before we move on to other queries, let's pause and think about what this means for us in practice. The key thing to understand is that this call to *sp_describe_parameter_encryption* and the encryption of our parameters within the client driver is core to how Always Encrypted works. Plaintext values that target encrypted columns in the database must be sent via parameters. If your application only interacts through the database via parameterized queries – which is good practice – then you are in a good starting place in terms of implementing Always Encrypted. Otherwise, you are likely to have significant refactoring to do.

Another item worth discussing is the extra call that executing your query entails. It might seem this is going to add performance overhead. In reality the call is very lightweight with CPU consumption of less than a millisecond. On top of that, the results get cached locally so you don't often see repeated calls to get the metadata for the same query. As a consequence of those two points, the performance overhead is generally negligible.

What Happens with a Select Query

Let's repeat the preceding exercise and look at what happens when we execute our select query. We'll start a new XE Profiler session and look at what is captured when we run the following select query:

```
SELECT *
FROM dbo.EncryptedTable;
```

In Figure 8-8, we see the XE Profiler output:

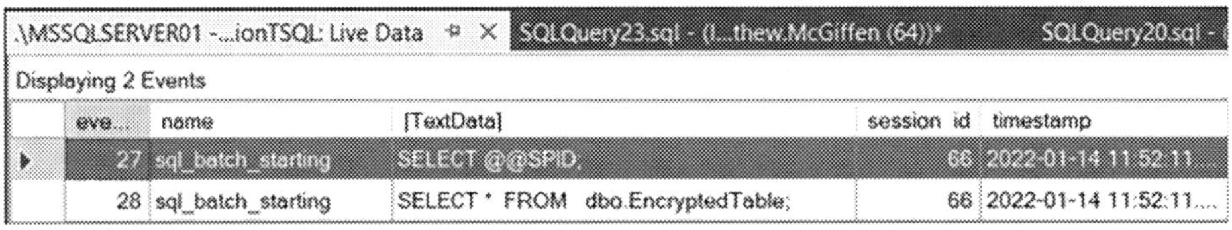

Figure 8-8. *Viewing the XE Profiler capture for a select query*

In this case we're not seeing the extra call to get the metadata which can seem slightly confusing. Surely the client driver needs that information to be able to decrypt the encrypt columns that are returned. The reality is that that metadata does get sent back, but it doesn't need to be asked for. The fact that our connection has encryption enabled means that SQL Server knows it needs to supply that information back to the client, so it does so automatically. In the former case with an insert, we needed the metadata before we could issue the query which is what necessitated the extra call.

For the select query, the results are returned to the client encrypted, along with the metadata. The client driver then decrypts any columns if required to do so before passing the results back to the client application.

Issuing a Query with a Predicate Against an Encrypted Column

So far we've just looked at a very simple select statement that returns all the results in the table. What if we want to search for a particular record? If we want to search based on the value in an unencrypted column – for instance, using the Id column our test table – this works exactly the same as if you didn't have encryption. Decryption of the results happens automatically in the client driver, and functionality of our query is unaffected. What if we want to search for a particular value in an encrypted column – can we do that?

The answer is that it depends; so let's try it. First, let's look at what is obviously not going to work. We'll attempt to execute this SQL:

```
SELECT *
FROM dbo.EncryptedTable
WHERE LastName = 'McGiffen';
```

This fails with an error similar to the following:

```
Msg 206, Level 16, State 2, Line 1
Operand type clash: varchar is incompatible with varchar(8000) encrypted
with (encryption_type = 'DETERMINISTIC', encryption_algorithm_name =
'AEAD_AES_256_CBC_HMAC_SHA_256', column_encryption_key_name = 'TestCEK',
column_encryption_key_database_name = 'TestAlwaysEncrypted') collation_name
= 'Latin1_General_CI_AS'
```

What the error is telling us is that we are trying to compare the value in an encrypted column with a plaintext value which is a nonsense thing to try. Rather than just returning us zero results as there is no match, SQL returns us an error to point out that we are not going about things in the right way. If you've been following so far, it's not going to surprise you that we need to use a parameter – as is done in this SQL:

```
DECLARE @LastName nvarchar(50) = 'McGiffen';

SELECT *
FROM dbo.EncryptedTable
WHERE LastName = @Lastname;
```

This time we get some results, as shown in Figure 8-9:

	Id	LastName	FirstName
1	1	McGiffen	Matthew
2	2	McGiffen	Matthew

Figure 8-9. *Results from a query with a predicate*

The LastName column in our table is encrypted with deterministic encryption. The FirstName column however is encrypted using randomized encryption. Let's see what happens if we try to use the following SQL to query against the FirstName column using the same pattern:

```
DECLARE @FirstName nvarchar(50) = 'Matthew';

SELECT *
FROM dbo.EncryptedTable
WHERE FirstName = @FirstName;
```

In this case we receive an error:

```
Msg 33277, Level 16, State 2, Line 11
Encryption scheme mismatch for columns/variables 'FirstName', '@FirstName'.
The encryption scheme for the columns/variables is (encryption_type =
'RANDOMIZED', encryption_algorithm_name = 'AEAD_AES_256_CBC_HMAC_SHA_256',
column_encryption_key_name = 'TestCEK', column_encryption_key_database_name
= 'TestAlwaysEncrypted') and the expression near line '5' expects it to
be'DETERMINISTIC, or RANDOMIZED, a BIN2 col'ation for string data types,
and an enclave-enabled column encryption key, or PLAINTEXT.
Msg 8180, Level 16, State 1, Procedure sp_describe_parameter_encryption,
Line 1 [Batch Start Line 6]
Statement(s) could not be prepared.
An error occurred while executing batch. Error message is: Internal
error. Metadata for parameter '@pfe3eb6b759d54cdd8c38d6b5e8709633'
in statement or procedure 'DECLARE @FirstName AS NVARCHAR (50) = @
pfe3eb6b759d54cdd8c38d6b5e8709633;

SELECT *
FROM    dbo.EncryptedTable
WHERE   FirstName = @FirstName;

' is missing in resultset returned by sp_describe_parameter_encryption.
```

It's a long error, but the short translation is that we are trying to compare data in a parameter with data in a column that is using randomized encryption, and that is not possible. The error messages you receive when attempting to query Always Encrypted data are not always very clear, so it helps to know the sort of things that are likely to go wrong. Combining that knowledge with the information returned in the error – in this case it states that the encryption for the column is randomized – will help you to quickly understand what the issue is.

Let's look at another query pattern you might attempt. This SQL specifies my surname in capitals:

```
DECLARE @Lastname nvarchar(50) = 'MCGIFFEN';

SELECT *
FROM dbo.EncryptedTable
WHERE LastName = @Lastname;
GO
```

This is very similar to the first query that executed fine; however, in this case we get no results. Remember we saw that encrypted columns must use BIN2 collations which are case-sensitive. As my @LastName parameter doesn't match the case of the values in the LastName column for the records in my table, SQL correctly returns no results. This can be problematic if you want to implement features like searching against encrypted columns where the search term may come from user input and users are used to not having to specify the correct case. There are ways you can work around that; I'll mention one possibility – using a separate search catalog – later on.

Another pattern that will simply not work is the use of LIKE queries. The reason is that "Matthew" may be like "Matt" but the same cannot be said of their respective encrypted values. If we used a form of encryption where that was true, then it would end up being relatively weak and open to attack. If you attempt a LIKE query, you will simply get an error similar to the previous ones.

Indexes and Statistics on Encrypted Columns

Where we want to query with a predicate, it is often useful to have an index on the column being searched. You can only have indexes on columns using deterministic encryption – not randomized. This makes sense as a column with randomized encryption is going to have different values stored even when the underlying plaintext value is the same, so an index would be meaningless. You also can't perform comparisons on such columns so an index wouldn't be useful. An index on a column deterministically encrypted with Always Encrypted will simply be an index of the encrypted values and as such is only useful for equality comparisons, not for sorting or range queries – though neither of these functions are possible against our deterministically encrypted column anyway.

To create an index on a column using deterministic encryption is the same as if the column is not encrypted. Here is an example:

```
CREATE NONCLUSTERED INDEX IX_LastName
ON dbo.EncryptedTable(LastName);
```

While we can't index on our columns using randomized encryption, we can include them in the leaf pages of an index so that their values do not have to be retrieved using a Key Lookup operation. So the following SQL would also work:

```
CREATE NONCLUSTERED INDEX IX_LastName_Include_FirstName
ON dbo.EncryptedTable(LastName) INCLUDE(FirstName);
```

In common with any other index, a statistics object is created that maintains information about the distribution of data in the index. We can view the data held in the statistics object with the following command:

```
DBCC SHOW_STATISTICS('dbo.EncryptedTable','IX_LastName');
```

Figure 8-10 shows the output of this command:

	Name	Updated	Rows	Rows Sampled	Steps	Density	Average key length	String Index	Filter Expression	Unfiltered Rows	Persisted Sample Percent
1	IX_LastName	Aug 19 2022 10:32AM	2	2	1	0	85	NO	NULL	2	0

	All density	Average Length	Columns
1	1	81	LastName
2	0.5	85	LastName, Id

	RANGE_HI_KEY	RANGE_ROWS	EQ_ROWS	DISTINCT_RANGE_ROWS	AVG_RANGE_ROWS
1	0x0115C15450E81B97D39A7020290CCCFC67D8F9CF05BE16	0	2	0	1

Figure 8-10. *Showing the statistics against an index on a deterministically encrypted column*

We only have a couple of rows in our table, but if you're familiar with statistics objects, you'll see this is pretty much the same as we would see where there is no encryption. What is interesting is to look at the last result set. Normally this would show actual data values in the RANGE_HI_KEY column; here we can see that we have an encrypted value. From this, we can understand that the statistics are based on the encrypted values. This underlines the point already made, that our index is an index of the encrypted values of our data. That makes sense as SQL Server is never aware of the unencrypted values, so it wouldn't be possible for it to create or maintain indexes (or statistics) of the plaintext values.

This is different when using Always Encrypted with Enclaves where indexes on columns with randomized encryption are allowed. In that case, those indexes, and associated statistics objects, are actually based on the plaintext values. We talk about how that works in Chapter 16.

Working with Stored Procedures

We've looked at how querying directly against your encrypted tables works, but hopefully your application works using stored procedures rather than direct access to data. This is usually considered a better model from a security point of view, and if you're interested in encryption, then I expect that security in general is a key concern for you.

Let's create some stored procedures to Create, Read, and Update. The only one missing there from the standard CRUD set is Delete, but deletes are unchanged with Always Encrypted as you don't need to be able to encrypt or decrypt data in order to remove it.

Here's my set of stored procedures; you can execute this script to add them to your copy of the database and follow through the examples. First, we have a basic insert, the same as we have performed already. Next is an update based on the Id value. Finally, I have a select which looks for data in the table matching the value supplied for the LastName column:

```
--Working with Stored Procedures
CREATE PROCEDURE dbo.EncryptedTable_Insert
    @LastName nvarchar(50),
    @FirstName nvarchar(50)
```

```
AS
BEGIN
        INSERT INTO dbo.EncryptedTable (LastName, FirstName)
        VALUES (@LastName, @FirstName);
END
GO

CREATE PROCEDURE dbo.EncryptedTable_Update
        @Id int,
        @LastName nvarchar(50),
        @FirstName nvarchar(50)
AS
BEGIN
        UPDATE dbo.EncryptedTable
        SET
                LastName = @LastName,
                FirstName =  @FirstName
        WHERE Id = @Id;
END
GO

CREATE PROCEDURE dbo.EncryptedTable_SelectBy_LastName
        @LastName nvarchar(50)
AS
BEGIN
        SELECT Id, LastName, FirstName
        FROM dbo.EncryptedTable
        WHERE LastName = @LastName;
END
GO
```

First let's try something that's not going to work with the following query:

```
EXEC dbo.EncryptedTable_Insert
        @LastName= 'Smith',
        @FirstName = 'John';
```

This fails with the sort of error we are by now quite familiar with. I won't bother to reproduce it here again. The clear issue is that we are attempting to issue plaintext values against an encrypted column once more. This fails even though we use parameters within the stored procedure. The values must be supplied as parameterized SQL from the client and be encrypted before they hit SQL Server.

Let's try the same operation again; this SQL does things the right way:

```
DECLARE      @LastName nvarchar(50) = 'John';
DECLARE      @FirstName nvarchar(50) = 'Smith';

EXEC dbo.EncryptedTable_Insert
     @LastName= @LastName,
     @FirstName = @FirstName;
```

This time the operation succeeds and if we check the table, we will see an extra row, as shown in Figure 8-11:

Figure 8-11. *Seeing the results of an insert via a stored procedure*

Let's look at executing the other stored procedures. This SQL executes the update procedure:

```
DECLARE @Id int = 1
DECLARE      @NewLastName nvarchar(50) = 'McGiffen';
DECLARE      @NewFirstName nvarchar(50) = 'Matt';

EXEC dbo.EncryptedTable_Update
     @Id = @Id,
     @LastName= @NewLastName,
     @FirstName = @NewFirstName;
```

In this case we're updating one of the rows with my name to give the shortened version "Matt" of my first name. The query executes without error so let's again check the contents of the table (Figure 8-12):

Results | Messages

	Id	LastName	FirstName
1	1	McGiffen	Matt
2	2	McGiffen	Matthew
3	3	John	Smith

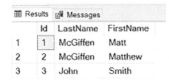

***Figure 8-12.** Seeing the results of an Update via a Stored Procedure*

Finally let's execute our stored procedure that searches for a given last name with the following SQL:

```
DECLARE      @LastName nvarchar(50) = 'McGiffen';

EXEC dbo.EncryptedTable_SelectBy_LastName
     @LastName= @LastName;
```

Here are the results (Figure 8-13):

Results | Messages

	Id	LastName	FirstName
1	1	McGiffen	Matt
2	2	McGiffen	Matthew

***Figure 8-13.** Results searching encrypted data from a stored procedure*

So again we can see that works in a straightforward manner. Stored procedures continue to work with Always Encrypted, as long as when executing them you follow the same parameterized pattern as if you execute queries against the database directly. Of course, there are restrictions on what you can and can't do with encrypted data - we'll get to that in a subsequent chapter.

Querying Always Encrypted Data from Your Application

As we've seen, although Always Encrypted is a SQL Server feature, the encryption is carried out client side. As such it seems worthwhile to look at how you interact with it from code. We're going to use PowerShell for the examples. It's highly unlikely that it would be the programmatic language you use for your applications, but the principles are the same and PowerShell makes it very easy to run such examples in the console - I'm using Windows PowerShell ISE.

Working with Direct Queries

Let's look at our basic insert first with this PowerShell code:

```
$connectionstring = "Data Source=.\MSSQLSERVER01; Integrated Security=SSPI;
Initial Catalog=TestAlwaysEncrypted; Column Encryption Setting=Enabled"
$query = "INSERT INTO dbo.EncryptedTable (LastName, FirstName) VALUES
(@LastName, @FirstName);"
$connection = new-object system.data.SqlClient.SQLConnection
($connectionString)
$connection.Open()

$command = new-object system.data.sqlclient.sqlcommand($query,$connection)

$LastName = new-object System.Data.SqlClient.SqlParameter
$LastName.ParameterName = "@LastName"
$LastName.SqlDbType = "nvarchar"
$LastName.Size = 50
$LastName.Value = "Jones"

$FirstName = new-object System.Data.SqlClient.SqlParameter
$FirstName.ParameterName = "@FirstName"
$FirstName.SqlDbType = "nvarchar"
$FirstName.Size = 50
$FirstName.Value = "Fred"

$command.Parameters.Add($LastName)
$command.Parameters.Add($FirstName)

$command.ExecuteNonQuery()
$connection.Close()
```

If you want to follow this example yourself, you just need to change the Data Source in the connection string to point to your own SQL Server instance. Once you've done that, execute the script; it should complete without error.

The only aspect of this script that is different because we are using Always Encrypted is the "Column Encryption Setting=Enabled" parameter in the connection string. The rest of the script is a standard example of what you might do with or without encryption. In principle this is hopefully the same for your real application code – the only change

117

you need to make is in the code that makes the connection to the database, and that is true as long as your queries don't run up against any of the limitations of Always Encrypted.

Let's try something we know is going to fail just to demonstrate what happens. Remove "Column Encryption Setting=Enabled" from the connection string, and try executing the script again. This time we get an error:

```
Exception calling "ExecuteNonQuery" with "0" argument(s): "Operand
type clash: nvarchar is incompatible with nvarchar(50) encrypted with
(encryption_type = 'DETERMINISTIC',
encryption_algorithm_name = 'AEAD_AES_256_CBC_HMAC_SHA_256', column_
encryption_key_name = 'TestCEK', column_encryption_key_database_name =
'TestAlwaysEncrypted')
Incorrect parameter encryption metadata was received from the client. The
error occurred during the invocation of the batch and therefore the client
can refresh the parameter encryption
metadata by calling sp_describe_parameter_encryption and retry."
```

This sort of error is quite familiar to us by now. As we have turned column encryption off, we are trying to insert an unencrypted value into an encrypted column, and we know that doesn't work.

Let's execute a select from PowerShell to check our row got inserted. We'll use a predicate so we can just get the individual row back:

```
$connectionstring = "Data Source=.\MSSQLSERVER01; Integrated Security=SSPI;
Initial Catalog=TestAlwaysEncrypted; Column Encryption Setting=Enabled"
$query = "SELECT Id, LastName, FirstName FROM dbo.EncryptedTable WHERE
LastName = @LastName;"
$connection = new-object system.data.SqlClient.SQLConnection
($connectionString)
$connection.Open()

$command = new-object system.data.sqlclient.sqlcommand($query,$connection)

$LastName = new-object System.Data.SqlClient.SqlParameter
$LastName.ParameterName = "@LastName"
$LastName.SqlDbType = "nvarchar"
```

```
$LastName.Size = 50
$LastName.Value = "Jones"

$command.Parameters.Add($LastName)

$reader = $command.ExecuteReader()

while($reader.Read())
{
    Write-Host ($reader.GetValue(0), $reader.GetValue(1), $reader.
    GetValue(2))
}
$reader.Close()
$connection.Close()
```

You should get a single row of output similar to the following:

```
4 Jones Fred
```

Working with Stored Procedures

Let's now look at a similar example working with the stored procedures we created and executing them from application code. First let's update the row we just created using our update stored procedure; we'll change Fred's name to Frederick with this PowerShell code:

```
$connectionstring = "Data Source=.\MSSQLSERVER01; Integrated Security=SSPI;
Initial Catalog=TestAlwaysEncrypted; Column Encryption Setting=Enabled"
$query = "dbo.EncryptedTable_Update"
$connection = new-object system.data.SqlClient.SQLConnection
($connectionString)
$connection.Open()

$command = new-object system.data.sqlclient.sqlcommand
$command.CommandType = [System.Data.CommandType]::StoredProcedure
$command.CommandText = $query
$command.Connection = $connection
```

```
$Id = new-object System.Data.SqlClient.SqlParameter
$Id.ParameterName = "@Id"
$Id.SqlDbType = "int"
$Id.Value = 4

$LastName = new-object System.Data.SqlClient.SqlParameter
$LastName.ParameterName = "@LastName"
$LastName.SqlDbType = "nvarchar"
$LastName.Size = 50
$LastName.Value = "Jones"

$FirstName = new-object System.Data.SqlClient.SqlParameter
$FirstName.ParameterName = "@FirstName"
$FirstName.SqlDbType = "nvarchar"
$FirstName.Size = 50
$FirstName.Value = "Frederick"

$command.Parameters.Add($Id)
$command.Parameters.Add($LastName)
$command.Parameters.Add($FirstName)

$command.ExecuteNonQuery()
$connection.Close()
```

Execute the script, and then we'll use our select stored procedure to check that the update was successful with the following PowerShell:

```
$connectionstring = "Data Source=.\MSSQLSERVER01; Integrated Security=SSPI;
Initial Catalog=TestAlwaysEncrypted; Column Encryption Setting=Enabled"
$query = "dbo.EncryptedTable_SelectBy_LastName"
$connection = new-object system.data.SqlClient.SQLConnection
($connectionString)
$connection.Open()

$command = new-object system.data.sqlclient.sqlcommand
$command.CommandType = [System.Data.CommandType]::StoredProcedure
$command.CommandText = $query
$command.Connection = $connection
```

```
$LastName = new-object System.Data.SqlClient.SqlParameter
$LastName.ParameterName = "@LastName"
$LastName.SqlDbType = "nvarchar"
$LastName.Size = 50
$LastName.Value = "Jones"

$command.Parameters.Add($LastName)

$reader = $command.ExecuteReader()

while($reader.Read())
{
    Write-Host ($reader.GetValue(0), $reader.GetValue(1), $reader.
    GetValue(2))
}
$reader.Close()
$connection.Close()
```

As in the previous example you should get a single row of output like this:

```
4 Jones Frederick
```

So, we can see our update ran successfully.

Hopefully this demonstrates how simple it is to work with Always Encrypted from code. All other things being equal, the only change you need to make is to update the connection string to enable Column Encryption.

Summary

The query patterns we've looked at in this chapter have been very simple, but they demonstrate the principles of working with Always Encrypted. These basic building blocks scale up quite happily for even the most complex of queries. The same rules and methods apply in all cases.

In demonstrating how querying works, we've also seen some of the limitations of working with Always Encrypted, and hopefully it has been clear why these limitations exist. We list the full set of limitations later on, but in most cases they logically derive from things we have already seen. There are some key points to remember:

- Encryption activities occur in the client, not on the server side.

- When working from SSMS, you must enable Always Encrypted when connecting to the database. For many activities you also need to enable "Parameterization for Always Encrypted" for your query.

- When working from code, you need to specify "Column Encryption Setting=Enabled" in the connection string.

- Always Encrypted works fine with both direct queries and stored procedures.

- Plaintext values that target encrypted columns must be supplied via parameters. The encryption of parameter values is key to how Always Encrypted works transparently.

- Parameters must be strongly typed; implicit conversions will not work.

- You can only issue predicates in a WHERE clause against encrypted columns using deterministic encryption. This will not work against columns using randomized encryption.

- LIKE comparisons will not work against encrypted columns.

- Encrypted text columns use a BIN2 collation and are case-sensitive.

So far, we've looked at how you work with Always Encrypted when you are creating a new database, deploying tables, and inserting data for the first time. It is likely you'll also want to be able to implement Always Encrypted for existing applications. Key to that will be how you go about encrypting existing data. We look at that in the next chapter.

CHAPTER 9

Encrypting Existing Data with Always Encrypted

So far, we've just looked at the situation where you implement Always Encrypted for a new database. In many cases, however, you're likely to be wanting to implement Always Encrypted for existing applications. Key to that will be being able to encrypt existing data.

As we've seen, one of the fundamentals of Always Encrypted is that SQL Server itself never has access to the unencrypted values of your data, and it doesn't have access to the unencrypted Column Encryption Key. As such it's not possible for SQL Server to encrypt your existing data; all encryption activities must occur on the client side. Therefore, encrypting existing data is not going to be as simple as just issuing an ALTER TABLE command to change an existing column to being encrypted.

That changes if you are using Always Encrypted with Enclaves which was introduced in SQL Server 2019. With enclaves, SQL can perform in-place encryption of your data, so that would be the method you use if you are implementing enclaves; we'll see that in action in Chapter 15.

To encrypt existing data, data is going to need to be transferred back to a client that has access to the keys; then it can be encrypted at the client end before being sent back to the database again. If we talk about encrypting data in a single table, then the usual process will be similar to the following:

1. Create a schema only copy of the table with encryption enabled.

2. Copy the data back to the client.

3. Encrypt the data.

© Matthew McGiffen 2022
M. McGiffen, *Pro Encryption in SQL Server 2022*, https://doi.org/10.1007/978-1-4842-8664-7_9

4. Bulk insert the data back into the copy of the table.

5. Drop the old table and rename the new one.

As part of the process, you may also have to manage any constraints, indexes, etc. on the table. This process might feel like it's going to be quite complicated for you to code and test by hand. Fortunately, SSMS has a wizard that will do all this for you. Or you can write and execute a script in PowerShell – SQL Server Management Objects (SMO) allows you to do this with not much more than a single command. We also look at how you can achieve the same result using the Import and Export Wizard which is based on SSIS.

It's worth mentioning that if you have a lot of data, this can be a long and intensive operation whichever method you choose. Microsoft has mentioned that some customers reported it taking days. It is also best considered as an offline operation. As such you need to think about how you are going to manage it in practice for a production system and benchmark performance in a test system if possible. If you have a number of columns you need to encrypt, then you may want to consider doing them incrementally rather than in a single sweep.

Let's start by looking at the Always Encrypted Wizard.

Encrypting Data Using the Always Encrypted Wizard

Up until now we haven't looked at the Always Encrypted Wizard, which is a tool you can use for all of your Always Encrypted setup. When using a wizard, everything is done for you, so it's not always clear what has been done in the background and how everything works. A key focus of this book is to give you a real understanding of the technologies detailed, so I've focused on doing things in a more manual manner. The wizard is useful in this case though as it provides us with a method of encrypting existing data.

We need to start with a database that has some data we wish to encrypt. I'm going to continue with the same database we've used so far, but we'll create a new table and populate it with some data using the following script:

```
USE TestAlwaysEncrypted;

CREATE TABLE dbo.EncryptingExistingData (
Id INT IDENTITY(1,1) CONSTRAINT PK_EncryptingExistingData PRIMARY KEY
CLUSTERED,
NumericData INT,
```

```
TextData nvarchar(128)
);

INSERT INTO dbo.EncryptingExistingData (NumericData,TextData)
SELECT object_id, name
FROM sys.objects;
```

Now let's look at the wizard. You can access it by right-clicking in the SSMS Object Explorer at the database, table, or even column level, selecting Tasks and Encrypt Columns. That brings up the start page shown in Figure 9-1:

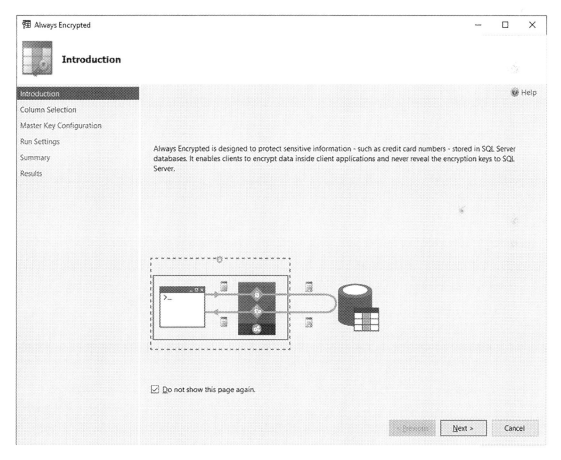

Figure 9-1. *The Always Encrypted Wizard*

We can click **Next**, which will take us straight into being able to select which columns we want to encrypt as well as the keys and type of encryption to use (Figure 9-2):

125

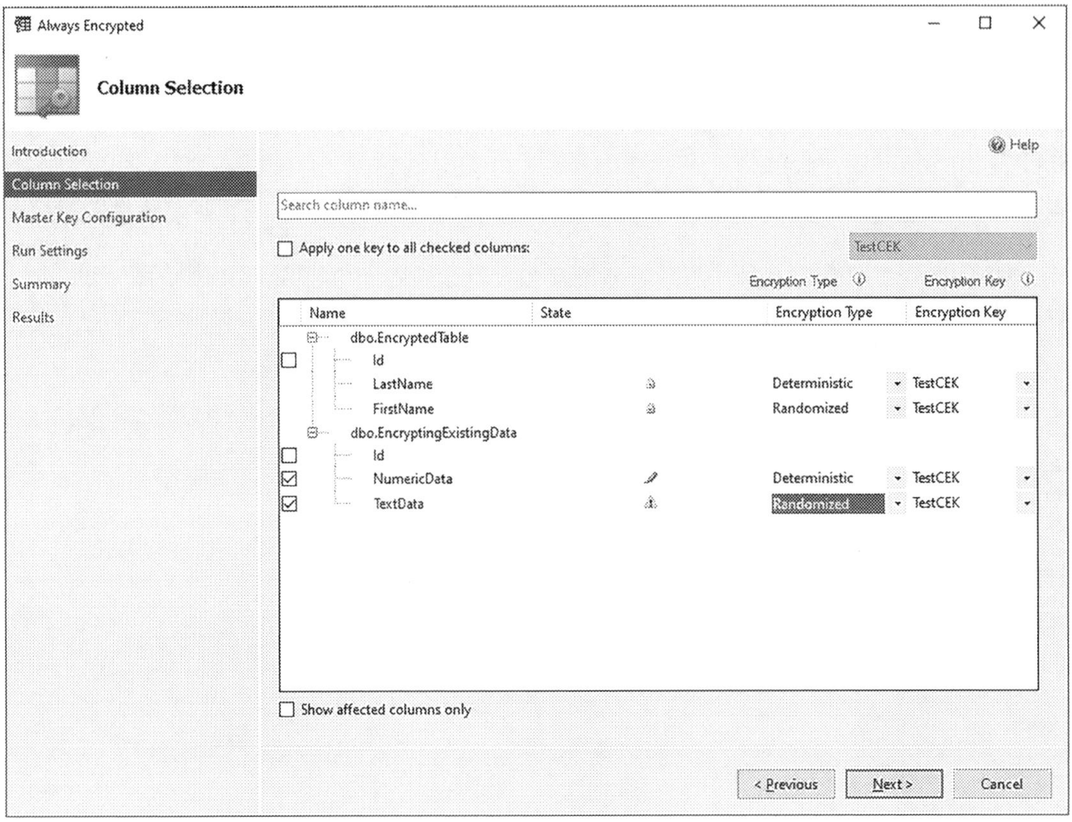

Figure 9-2. Configuring Column Encryption using the wizard

You can see the table we previously encrypted is listed and shows the encryption type and CEK used for each column. We'll use the same CEK for our new table. I've ticked the NumericData and TextData columns to say I want to encrypt them. I've selected Deterministic encryption for NumericData and Randomized for TextData. Then I selected TestCEK from the Encryption Key dropdown.

When you click **Next**, it takes you through to the Master Key Configuration page. In this case the page will just say we have nothing to do as we are using existing keys. Click Next again to proceed to the Run Settings page (Figure 9-3):

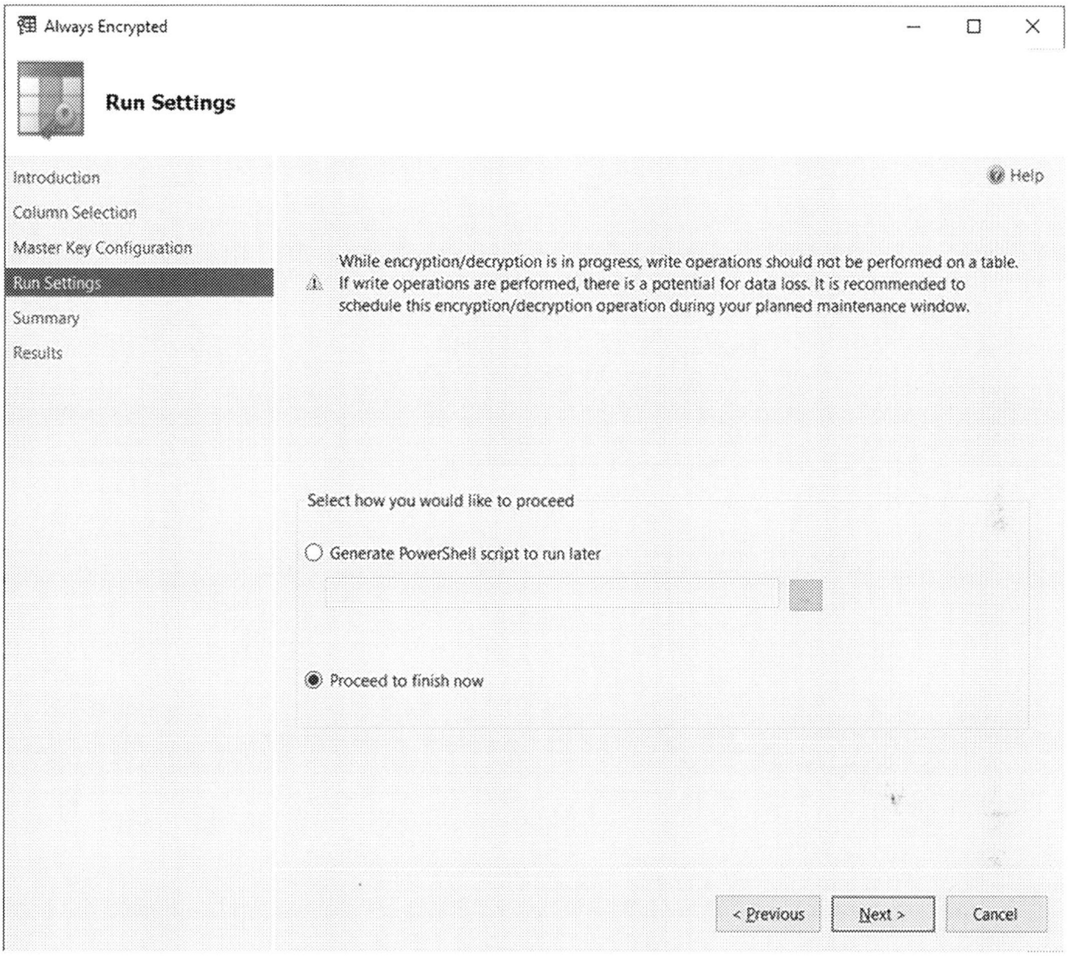

Figure 9-3. *Run Settings for encrypting existing data*

There is nothing you need to set on this page but there are a couple of points worth noting. The first is the warning that states write operations should not be performed against the table while the operation is in progress. I'd add that read operations are also likely to be impacted. As the warning states, you should really do this as part of scheduled outage for your application if working in a production environment.

The other thing I want to note is the option the wizard gives you to generate a PowerShell script for later execution rather than performing the action now. We'll look at that shortly when we see how the same operation can be carried out from code. For now, click Next and then Finish on the next screen to proceed.

We finally get a results screen that – hopefully – tells us the operation was successful. It's quite quick in this case as we don't have a lot of data. It can be slow though for large tables. When complete, click Close and then we'll go and have a look at the table.

First let's script out the new table's definition in SSMS; we see that in the following:

```
CREATE TABLE [dbo].[EncryptingExistingData](
    [Id] [int] IDENTITY(1,1) NOT NULL,
    [NumericData] [int] ENCRYPTED WITH (COLUMN_ENCRYPTION_KEY =
    [TestCEK], ENCRYPTION_TYPE = Deterministic, ALGORITHM =
    'AEAD_AES_256_CBC_HMAC_SHA_256') NULL,
    [TextData] [nvarchar](128) COLLATE Latin1_General_BIN2 ENCRYPTED WITH
    (COLUMN_ENCRYPTION_KEY = [TestCEK], ENCRYPTION_TYPE = Randomized,
    ALGORITHM = 'AEAD_AES_256_CBC_HMAC_SHA_256') NULL,
 CONSTRAINT [PK_EncryptingExistingData] PRIMARY KEY CLUSTERED
(
    [Id] ASC
)WITH (PAD_INDEX = OFF, STATISTICS_NORECOMPUTE = OFF, IGNORE_DUP_KEY = OFF,
ALLOW_ROW_LOCKS = ON, ALLOW_PAGE_LOCKS = ON, OPTIMIZE_FOR_SEQUENTIAL_KEY =
OFF) ON [PRIMARY]
) ON [PRIMARY]
GO
```

We can see the NumericData and TextData columns are now encrypted according to the settings we specified. Let's look at the data next. Open a new query window, and make sure that Column Encryption is disabled for the query (you do this by right-clicking, selecting Connection, Change Connection, and then unticking Enable Always Encrypted in the Always Encrypted tab found in the options). Then we can issue the following select query:

```
USE TestAlwaysEncrypted;
```

```
SELECT *
FROM dbo.EncryptingExistingData;
```

Your results should look something like those shown in Figure 9-4:

	Id	NumericData	TextData
1	1	0x0174D803CB427D16E2EC3F49FFB9F14B74F435742D26B5F9C...	0x01D882A28F6464967447A79B97858BFE572F33E0AE26150509...
2	2	0x0118F11D4C1B5C15806932C52A0F4BA3D7E9087FCDE734D17...	0x011622A152E6C3526D4A2369C161A365E8C862E503EAB96FE...
3	3	0x01235B68AE31A8D6C3AF0973D6654AEEAB92CA2E27D99DAC...	0x01E0059F92B6BEE8C6A60ADBA69723673999FE1982ACA634E...
4	4	0x01050B61164CBDF28E344DEFD734CDE80146E97013124CE7A...	0x01A97A0728A50D1223EFD118C12E864EAA4557110E7DB97D2...
5	5	0x01A0A23030451ACDB866B17228359324CE57DBB75B29E8CBB...	0x0186911477DA81975C3551BD4A81020475630B6FB8C02017C8...
6	6	0x0163B361C8C58E2700D05FA7A18BB1873E85F44ECFC7EE25F...	0x01790A63DDA746DC45FC6AECCEB51C12D8ADE727A3CA09...
7	7	0x01332C7DD346CEE64D44F7EDC8F76DB4B1B4DCC09AEDB9...	0x017BB35C519F1CDFEE33F181C6067AA1CB5E0092727A1B71...
8	8	0x0160A27CF7E86B528FBF2BD5B9446046FC53FB3F956F5029B...	0x01D4F361D593657A253CD482FC8DBCBBF690C91671154BD...
9	9	0x01B7CDAA7296CC9EB99CFA3FB7FCA1578B970400669D2874...	0x014FD3237D30CA8E805845DB5B88272F3819ABBB233CAAFF...
10	10	0x0183368CE12EBDC5788D48B7B90F86F07039085FF2DA22DD...	0x017BB25596661FA582FA2FC75ED016C1245519B9297D983270...

Figure 9-4. *Showing the encrypted data*

We can see our existing data has been successfully encrypted. The wizard (and the PowerShell method we will look at next) also deals with managing dependencies on your table such as foreign keys, so you don't have to worry about that as an additional task.

Encrypting Data Using PowerShell

We can perform the same operation directly using PowerShell. Before we start, we'll remove and recreate the table we just encrypted, so we can again use it as the target for column encryption. You can do that with this script:

```
USE TestAlwaysEncrypted;
DROP TABLE dbo.EncryptingExistingData;
GO

CREATE TABLE dbo.EncryptingExistingData (
Id INT IDENTITY(1,1) CONSTRAINT PK_EncryptingExistingData PRIMARY KEY
CLUSTERED,
NumericData INT,
TextData nvarchar(128)
);

INSERT INTO dbo.EncryptingExistingData (NumericData,TextData)
SELECT object_id, name
FROM sys.objects;
```

Now we run through the wizard again, but when we get to the page that allows us to generate PowerShell for the operation, we select that instead (Figure 9-5):

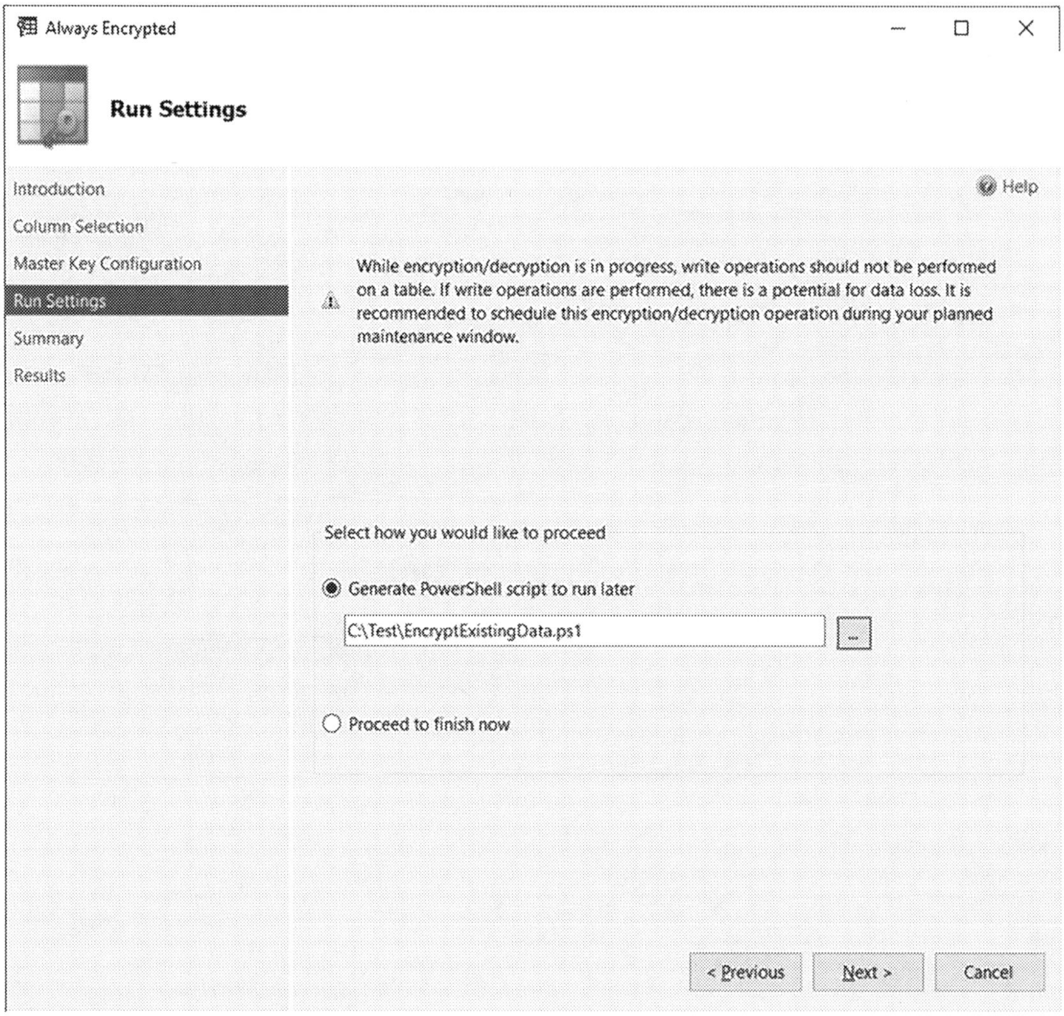

Figure 9-5. *Generating PowerShell to encrypt our existing data*

You need to specify a name and path to save the PowerShell script. Once you've done that, you can click through the wizard to the end. Let's now have a look at the PowerShell file that was created:

```
# Generated by SQL Server Management Studio at 12:54 on 28/01/2022

Import-Module SqlServer
# Set up connection and database SMO objects

$sqlConnectionString = "Data Source=.\MSSQLSERVER01;Initial Catalog=Test
AlwaysEncrypted;Integrated Security=True;MultipleActiveResultSets=False;
Connect Timeout=30;Encrypt=False;TrustServerCertificate=False;Packet
Size=4096;Application Name=`"Microsoft SQL Server Management Studio`""
$smoDatabase = Get-SqlDatabase -ConnectionString $sqlConnectionString

# If your encryption changes involve keys in Azure Key Vault, uncomment one
of the lines below in order to authenticate:
#    * Prompt for a username and password:
#Add-SqlAzureAuthenticationContext -Interactive

#    * Enter a Client ID, Secret, and Tenant ID:
#Add-SqlAzureAuthenticationContext -ClientID '<Client ID>' -Secret
'<Secret>' -Tenant '<Tenant ID>'

# Change encryption schema

$encryptionChanges = @()

# Add changes for table [dbo].[EncryptingExistingData]
$encryptionChanges += New-SqlColumnEncryptionSettings -ColumnName
dbo.EncryptingExistingData.NumericData -EncryptionType
Deterministic -EncryptionKey "TestCEK"
$encryptionChanges += New-SqlColumnEncryptionSettings -ColumnName dbo.
EncryptingExistingData.TextData -EncryptionType Randomized -EncryptionKey
"TestCEK"

Set-SqlColumnEncryption -ColumnEncryptionSettings
$encryptionChanges -InputObject $smoDatabase
```

Before you can execute this, you need to have the SQL Server Management
Objects for PowerShell installed. If you haven't already, then you need to run
PowerShell as an Administrator and then execute a command similar to the
following:

Install-Module -Name SqlServer -RequiredVersion 21.1.18256

You may be prompted to download additional packages to support this installation
and, if you have an existing version installed, will be instructed how to proceed.

This is actually a very simple script and easy to extend if you want to add extra
columns to be encrypted. You just need an array which contains the settings for each
column – in this case, it is our $encryptionchanges object. Let's look at how one of the
items in the array is defined:

```
$encryptionChanges += New-SqlColumnEncryptionSettings -ColumnName
dbo.EncryptingExistingData.NumericData -EncryptionType
Deterministic -EncryptionKey "TestCEK"
```

You can see that we specify the ColumnName with a three part identifier that
includes the schema and table names – dbo.EncryptingExistingData.NumericData. We
also specify the encryption type and the CEK to be used.

Updating the encryption settings for the tables and columns specified, as well as
encrypting existing data, is then carried out by a single simple command:

```
Set-SqlColumnEncryption -ColumnEncryptionSettings
$encryptionChanges -InputObject $smoDatabase
```

You can see that Microsoft has implemented a good level of automation support
for Always Encrypted. The fact that an operation that is quite complex like this can be
carried out with a single command is quite impressive and makes our lives much easier.

Execute the script. You are likely to see a pop-up progress bar saying that data is
being encrypted and a data migration carried out. All going well the script should then
complete successfully.

Let's go back to SSMS and we'll check the contents of our table one more time – again you need to make sure column encryption is disabled for your query and then issue the following select:

```
USE TestAlwaysEncrypted;

SELECT *
FROM dbo.EncryptingExistingData;
```

We should see encrypted results, as in Figure 9-6:

	Id	NumericData	TextData
1	1	0x0174D803CB427D16E2EC3F49FFB9F14B74F435742D26B5F9C...	0x01053499A013111C70550845D175FFA7141E7CEABC9D5D426...
2	2	0x0118F11D4C1B5C15806932C52A0F4BA3D7E9087FCDE734D17...	0x01F349E25B1699740ADFCDC4E489AF883A20188A6AAB15E4...
3	3	0x01235B68AE31A8D6C3AF0973D6654AEEAB92CA2E27D99DAC...	0x010AA75F159CFF602AC91DE7D70A28CBD5C5A869590CECC...
4	4	0x01050B61164CBDF28E344DEFD734CDE80146E97013124CE7A...	0x01C6E77F3C31F412A97DA2DD2A4A59C5D7315A2A6BDE738...
5	5	0x01A0A23030451ACDB866B17228359324CE57DBB75B29E8CBB...	0x013148AF2DC3FF31C09B5FC8AA704C8EF1DA94E920DC18...
6	6	0x0163B361C8C58E2700D05FA7A18BB1873E85F44ECFC7EE25F...	0x016B6E346B87B1C9843AA765334C8AFC0760E68709F1A64DE...
7	7	0x01332C7DD346CEE64D44F7EDC8F76DB4B1B4DCC09AEDB9...	0x01E73F46133848AE3D8F06069159647865CA46ED7467F4E29C...
8	8	0x0160A27CF7E86B528FBF2BD5B9446046FC53FB3F956F5029B...	0x01F6AB921C0EF951E695A8EAF03B1B50C58B2282ACD12A36...
9	9	0x01B7CDAA7296CC9EB99CFA3FB7FCA1578B970400669D2874...	0x01C0EDAA2738FFBADEDBE70ABE8575FE7F38980A8D42B46...
10	10	0x0183368CE12EBDC5788D48B7B90F86F07039085FF2DA22DD...	0x011C4D8B94074ED946880EEBD04D67D520CB03E017639A18...

Figure 9-6. *Showing the results of encryption from PowerShell*

You can see that encrypting existing data using Powershell is a very simple and powerful operation. One point to consider though is where you may have a large amount of data and many columns across multiple tables to encrypt. You could achieve this with a single Set-SqlColumnEncryption call. It may be better though to have multiple calls, for instance, one for each table. That breaks up the work and makes it easier to resume in case of error – particularly network errors. As mentioned in the introduction you may also want to do it in incremental chunks, doing one or more columns at a time during a given outage, rather than a single big hit. Also, as with all code, you should test in another environment before applying to production.

Encrypting Data Using the Import and Export Wizard

The last method we're going to look at for encrypting existing data is using the Import and Export Wizard which is based on SSIS. This is a good approach if you're not comfortable with PowerShell and would prefer to do something in the GUI – but you also want to be able to create a deployable package that can be reused in other environments.

There are two approaches you can take using the wizard. One is to create a schema only copy of your whole database, one that has no data. Then you can configure encryption for the columns you require it on. Finally, you copy all the data from your old database to the new. This has the advantage of being quite a clean approach. You can get the new database correct first, and then once the data copy is complete, you simply need to drop or rename the old database and then rename the new one with the original name. The downside is that you are having to copy all the data, including data that you don't need to encrypt. Where the data targeted for encryption is a small subset of the overall dataset – which is probably the usual case – this is generating a lot of unnecessary work.

We're going to focus here on the second approach which is doing things table by table. For each table in which you have columns you wish to encrypt, we:

1. Create an empty copy of the table with encryption configured as required for the columns.

2. Export data from the old table to the new.

3. Rename/remove the old table.

4. Rename the new table to the original table name. Any named constraints may also need to be renamed as part of this process.

If you have dependencies on or to the affected tables – such as foreign key constraints or indexes – then you will also need to manage the process of removing and re-adding these. We're going to keep it simple though and just look again at our single table scenario.

As before I'm going to drop my table and recreate it, so we have the unencrypted version. The following script does that:

```
USE TestAlwaysEncrypted;
DROP TABLE dbo.EncryptingExistingData;
GO

CREATE TABLE dbo.EncryptingExistingData (
Id INT IDENTITY(1,1) CONSTRAINT PK_EncryptingExistingData PRIMARY KEY
CLUSTERED,
NumericData INT,
TextData nvarchar(128)
);
```

```
INSERT INTO dbo.EncryptingExistingData (NumericData,TextData)
SELECT object_id, name
FROM sys.objects;
```

Next, I'm going to create the new encrypted version of the table with the following SQL:

```
CREATE TABLE dbo.EncryptingExistingData_Encrypted(
     Id int IDENTITY(1,1) NOT NULL CONSTRAINT PK_EncryptingExistingData_
     Encrypted PRIMARY KEY CLUSTERED,
     NumericData int ENCRYPTED WITH (COLUMN_ENCRYPTION_KEY = TestCEK,
     ENCRYPTION_TYPE = Deterministic, ALGORITHM = 'AEAD_AES_256_CBC_HMAC_
     SHA_256') NULL,
     TextData nvarchar(128) COLLATE Latin1_General_BIN2 ENCRYPTED WITH
     (COLUMN_ENCRYPTION_KEY = TestCEK, ENCRYPTION_TYPE = Randomized,
     ALGORITHM = 'AEAD_AES_256_CBC_HMAC_SHA_256') NULL
);
```

Now we're ready to use the wizard. Right-click over your database in the SSMS Object Explorer and select Tasks, Export Data. That brings up the start page for the wizard (Figure 9-7):

Figure 9-7. *The Import and Export Wizard*

We click through the first page and get straight on to configuring our data source. First, we need to select a driver. In theory, you should be able to use any SQL Server client driver for the source, but in practice, I have run into issues with this. As such I recommend you use the .NET Framework Data Provider for SqlServer which will instruct the wizard to use .NET 4.6 which supports Always Encrypted. In the connection settings, we need to specify that Integrated Security should be used, as well as supplying our Data Source and Initial Catalog. All this is shown in Figure 9-8.

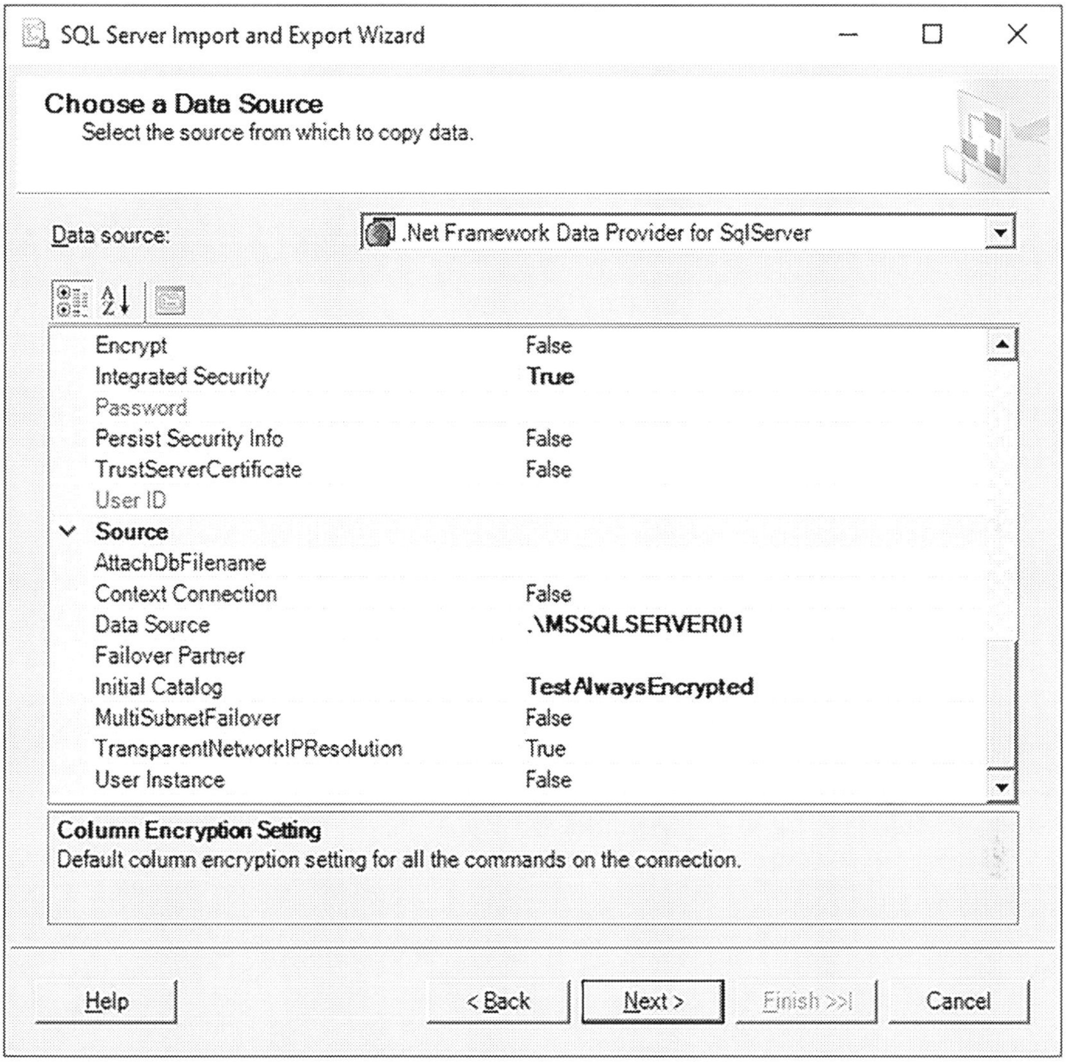

Figure 9-8. *Configuring the Data Source*

We click "Next" and are prompted to choose the destination. We'll use the same driver and connection details. The only difference is that we must ensure that the Column Encryption Setting is Enabled (Figure 9-9):

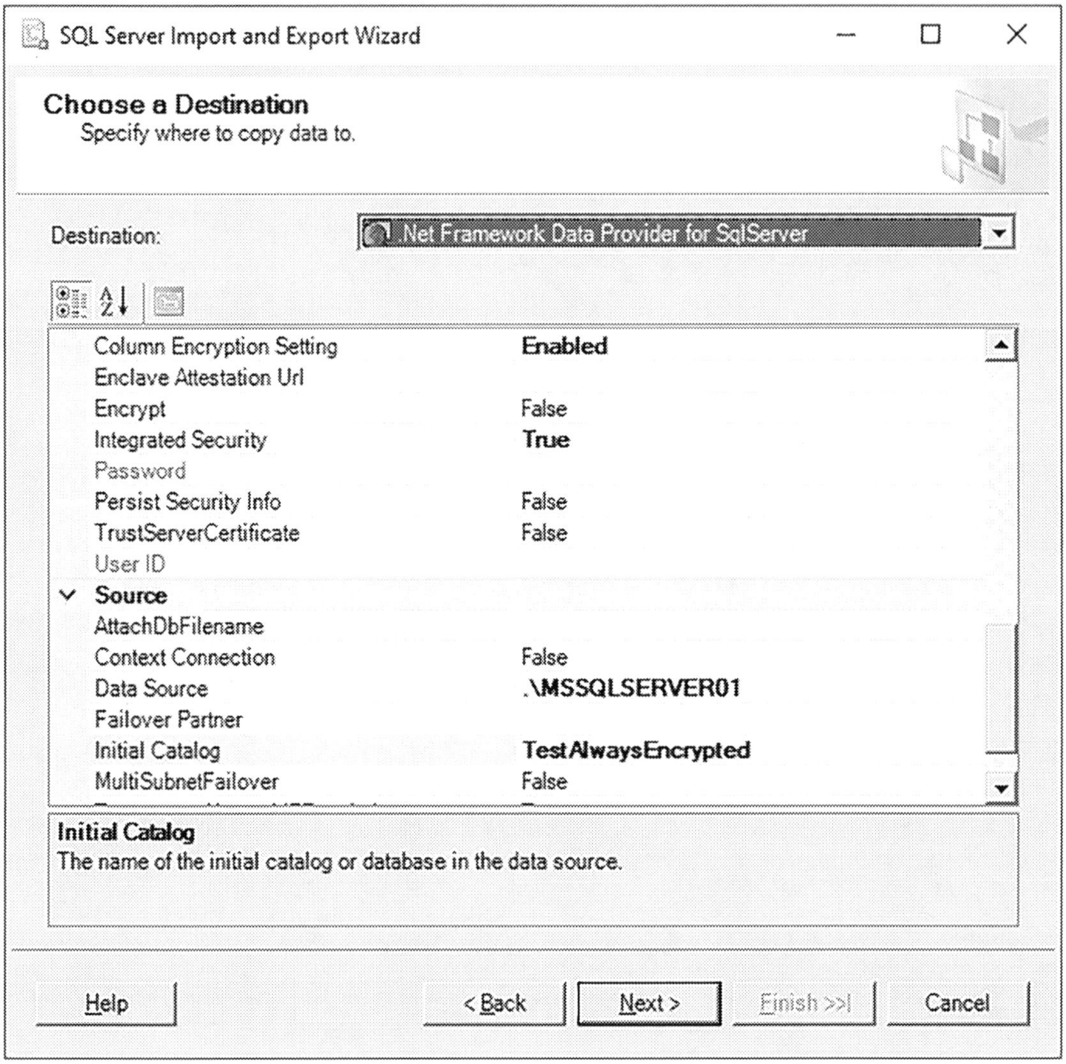

Figure 9-9. *Configuring the Column Encryption Setting for our destination*

We click Next to reach the Specify Table Copy or Query screen (Figure 9-10). We select "Copy data from one or more tables or views," which is the default option, and then click **Next** again.

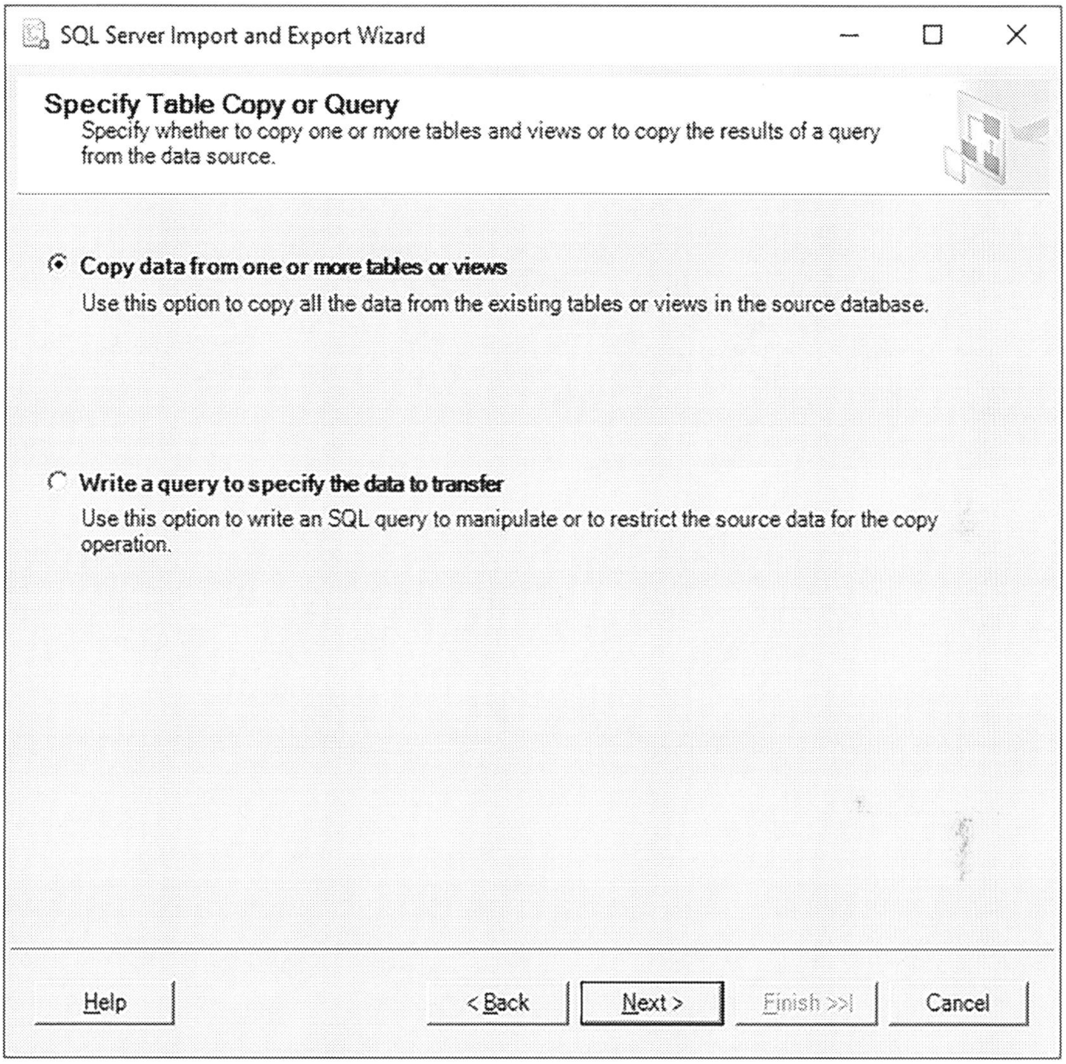

Figure 9-10. *Specifying the type of data transfer*

In the next screen we can select our source and destination tables. I have selected our table holding unencrypted data as the source and selected the copy of it which has encryption enabled as the destination (Figure 9-11):

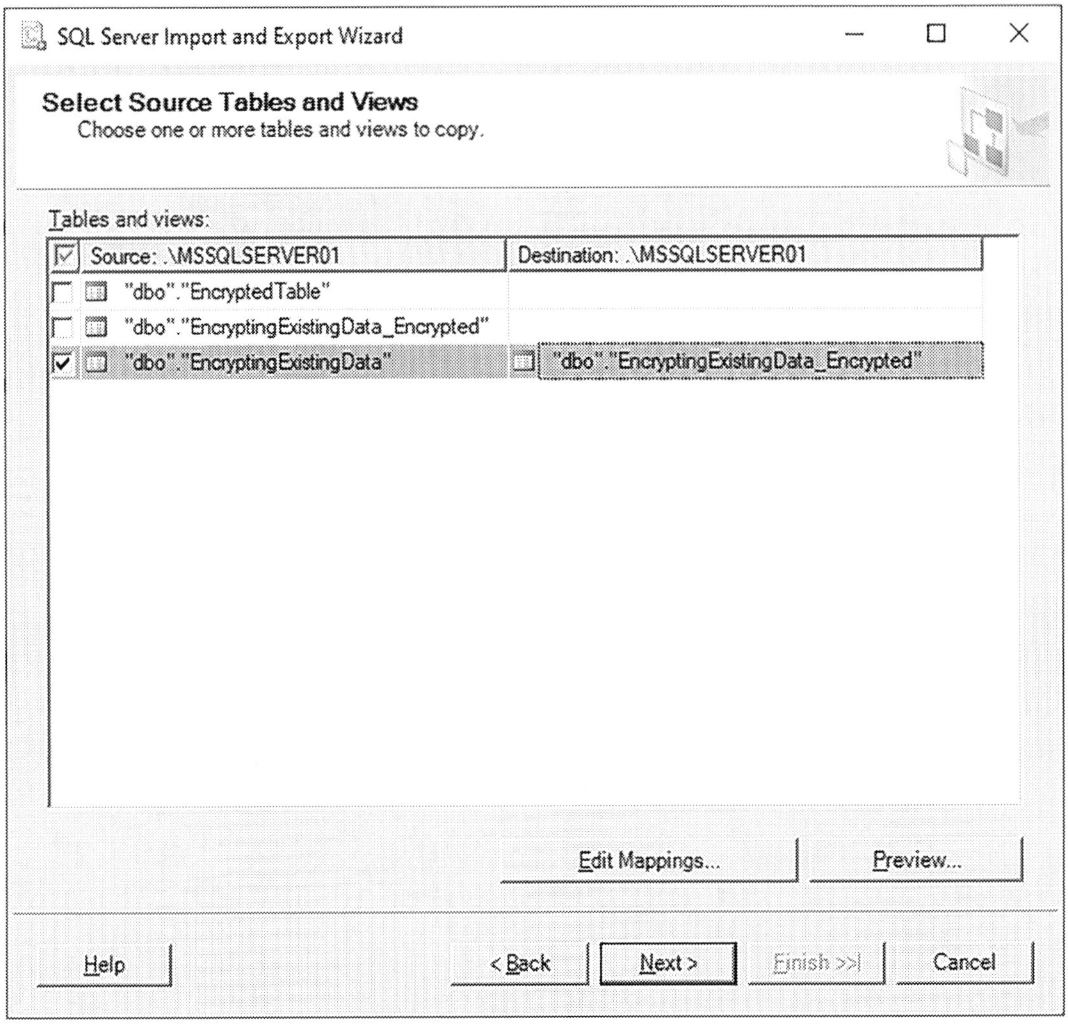

Figure 9-11. *Specifying the table(s) to copy*

We click Next again and are prompted to save or run our package. We will run it immediately, but you can save it so the package can be reused if you wish. You can also reuse the package against other environments as long as you change the connection settings. Let's now just click all the way through to Finish. The final screen shows us progress as our execution proceeds through to completion. This is one of the reasons you may choose to use this method for encrypting your data – rather than the Always Encrypted Wizard or PowerShell – as it provides richer feedback on progress and a more user-friendly experience (Figure 9-12):

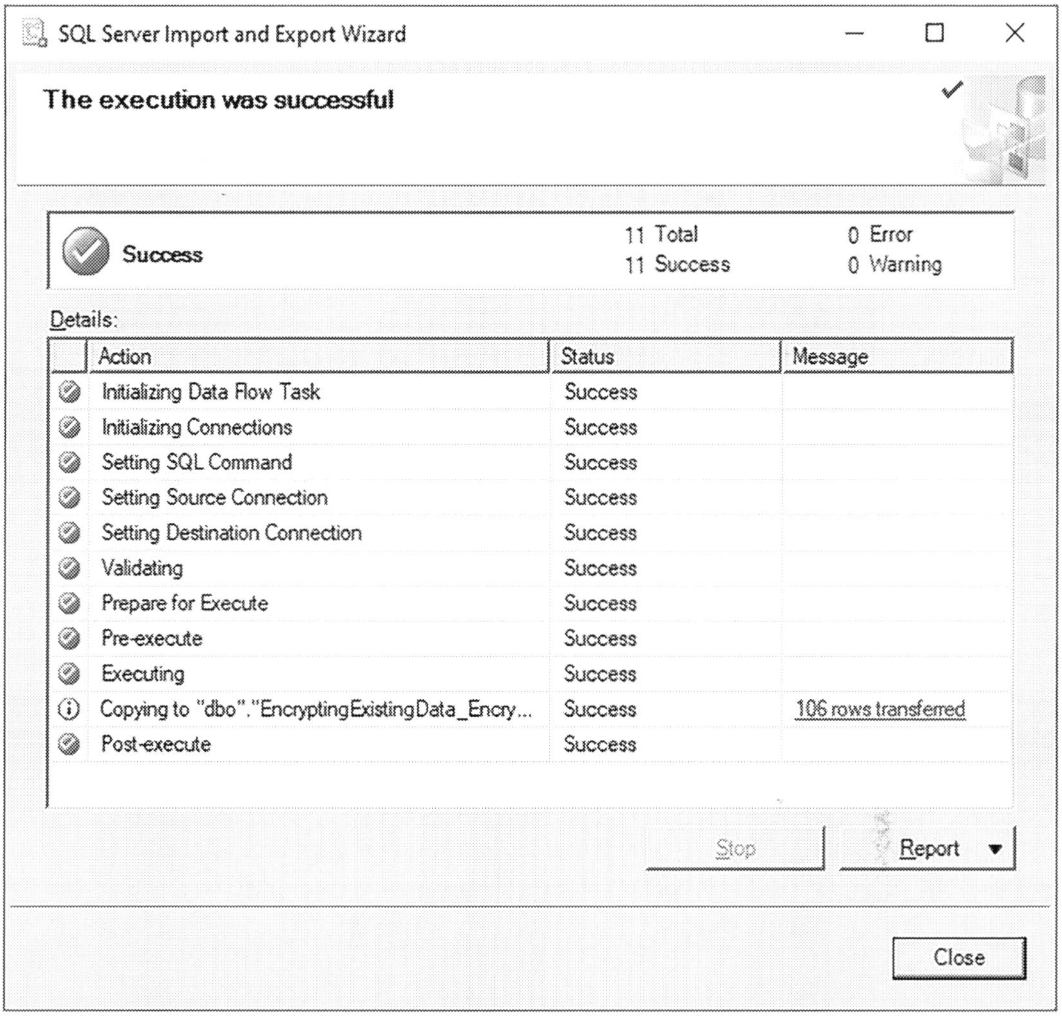

Figure 9-12. *Viewing progress and completion of our data copy*

We can see that the package completed successfully and the number of rows that were copied. As before we can check our new table has data that has been successfully encrypted by issuing a select query against it in a query window with column encryption disabled:

```
USE TestAlwaysEncrypted;

SELECT *
FROM dbo.EncryptingExistingData_Encrypted;
```

We should then see our encrypted records, as in Figure 9-13:

	Id	NumericData	TextData
1	1	0x0174D803CB427D16E2EC3F49FFB9F14B74F435742D26B5F9C...	0x0136A83F8352DB90E220EB9D5E24497AE06E82ADCC335879...
2	2	0x0118F11D4C1B5C15806932C52A0F4BA3D7E9087FCDE734D17...	0x0150E5B6761A8969DEFD6E0D3BEBBC33352EC010EFBBE70...
3	3	0x01235B68AE31A8D6C3AF0973D6654AEEAB92CA2E27D99DAC...	0x01C663536AAD1DF4D71872E681AD608939084C3E9505F7257...
4	4	0x01050B61164CBDF28E344DEFD734CDE80146E97013124CE7A...	0x01F27F199194A904FBACBA711106474C014967951BEDE896E...
5	5	0x01A0A23030451ACDB866B17228359324CE57DBB75B29E8CBB...	0x01C0F87121F5C86A141BA6B1E4DBFEBF0F8973BC0CB7FC4...
6	6	0x0163B361C8C58E2700D05FA7A18BB1873E85F44ECFC7EE25F...	0x01587BB429F33C9F0696418BF16E74843FD5092CC91AB4103...
7	7	0x01332C7DD346CEE64D44F7EDC8F76DB4B1B4DCC09AEDB9...	0x0155D2EE82695265023E84CE5A2B5A8C8149389F187C92493F...
8	8	0x0160A27CF7E86B528FBF2BD5B9446046FC53FB3F956F5029B...	0x01712A26AC742D564B0C4051BFF58B99805EB44D8ECCCA46...
9	9	0x01B7CDAA7296CC9EB99CFA3FB7FCA1578B970400669D2874...	0x01E5F928FD50CE62AE7C1F5498A5A83326108F9223306E7591...
10	10	0x0183368CE12EBDC5788D48B7B90F86F07039085FF2DA22DD...	0x0153CBFC16EC56BC1906492826A4AACF4BDCFFCCE54C8B3...

Figure 9-13. *Seeing our records encrypted by the Import and Export Wizard*

As a final step you now need to rename or remove the old table and replace it with the new table. In this example you will also need to make sure the primary key constraints are renamed. Working with your own applications, you may at this stage need to re-add any foreign keys or other dependencies that referenced the original table.

Summary

As SQL Server can't read encrypted data, or view the plaintext values of CEKs, to encrypt existing data, the data must be copied to a trusted client, encrypted, and then inserted back into the database. This will involve using a copy of the original table that has encryption enabled. That table will then replace the original once the data encryption and transfer is complete.

Encryption of existing data should be carried out as an offline operation during a schedule application outage. You might get away with doing it online but it's not advisable and could lead to data loss.

There are three main methods you might use to encrypt existing data:

- The Always Encrypted Wizard

- PowerShell (or another language that can leverage SQL Server Management Objects)

- The Import and Export Wizard/SSIS

The first two options perform more of the operation transparently for you – including managing foreign key dependencies and indexes; however, the third may be preferable in terms of user experience and being able to monitor progress.

This brings us to the end of this chapter. In the next we will look at the limitations you might face when working with Always Encrypted as well as try to understand why those limitations exist.

## CHAPTER 10

Limitations with Always Encrypted

In the previous chapters we've looked at how Always Encrypted works, how to set it up, and how to work with it in practice.

Along the way we've seen a few restrictions, such as the need to use BIN2 collations for text-based columns or the requirement to use parameter-based queries against encrypted columns. There are a number of other limitations, but on the whole these aren't representative of an incomplete or poorly implemented technology. Rather, they are the natural consequences of the type of protection we are implementing. Anything that increases our safety and security has an impact on the way we can do things.

As you've worked through this section, you've probably already started to realize for yourself some things that just aren't going to be possible based on what Always Encrypted is and how it works.

In this chapter we'll look at the full set of limitations, but we'll also try and understand as much as possible why such things might not be possible or simply not make sense with Always Encrypted. I find it's useful to think in those terms, and then even if you can't remember if something is allowed or not, you can usually have an instinct for what the answer will be. I find people often ask me if a certain scenario would work; understanding the "why" generally leads me in the right direction for an answer.

I've roughly grouped the limitations based on the reasons why they are not allowed. For each group I discuss the logical thinking of why certain types of operations would not work.

SQL Server Only Ever Sees Encrypted Data

SQL Server never sees your unencrypted data. Encryption and decryption occur wholly on the client side. All SQL Server is ever aware of is the binary encrypted value that

145

© Matthew McGiffen 2022
M. McGiffen, *Pro Encryption in SQL Server 2022*, https://doi.org/10.1007/978-1-4842-8664-7_10

represents your data, so that limits the questions it can answer about the data – or the validations it can perform. Imagine trying to have a check constraint on an encrypted integer value that it must be less than 100. SQL doesn't have a clue whether that binary value represents a number less than 100 or not. That is anticipated and so you're not allowed to create the constraint.

Equally, it can't compare the data to a fixed unencrypted value. If you ask it to return all the rows with a value of "1," for instance, that's not going to match any of your encrypted values. SQL Server could of course be obtuse and say none of the rows match the data. What actually happens though – and which is much better – is that you get an error.

The limitations that arise from this would be the same with any other form of client-side encryption. It's clear to see why none of the following can be used with encrypted columns:

- Identity Columns.

- Calculated Columns.

- User defined types – there is no way of validating the value matches the type correctly.

- Partitioning Columns.

- Performing calculations on encrypted columns.

- DATETIME functions like DATEADD or DATEPART.

- Default Constraints.

- Check Constraints.

- Triggers that update encrypted columns or need to evaluate encrypted columns.

- Full Text Search.

- Sparse columns.

- In memory OLTP.

- Change Data Capture (CDC).

- Dynamic Data Masking.

- Table Value Parameters targeting encrypted columns.

Strong Encryption Isn't Predictable

Sticking with the example of integers for the moment, let's say you want to return all values greater than a given value – or in a range. That might be possible if encrypting a series of values would result in an encrypted set of values that fell in the same order when sorted. If you think about that, it would be a pretty weak form of encryption. A lot could be inferred from the encrypted data, and in many cases it would probably be fairly feasible to crack. So, strong encryption doesn't work like that. Any ordering or predictability is going to be lost once encrypted. That means you're not going to be able to do range-type queries.

Then image a text value. Let's say for sake of argument that my name "Matthew" had an encrypted value of "abcdefg." Then let's say that if you encrypted my full name "Matthew McGiffen," the first part of the encrypted string would stay the same so the encrypted version of that would be "abcdefg" + something else. Again, you're making it pretty easy to crack. So, for a strong form encryption, that's not going to be the case. The result of that is that you're not going to be able to do things along the lines of LIKE searches; it's also why a BIN2 collation is in place for our columns.

Again, let's look at a list of things that are therefore not possible:

- LIKE comparisons

- Sorting using ORDER BY

- Range queries

Deterministic vs. Randomized

We've mentioned that you get the choice of two types of encryption, deterministic and randomized. Both are strong in and of themselves; the only difference is that deterministically encrypted values encrypted with the same key always have the same encrypted value for the same unencrypted value, whereas with randomized, they're always different. That means with deterministic, there are some things you can do that you can't with randomized. Like we saw earlier, you can search for a given value in a deterministically encrypted column – as long as that value is specified in a parameter that can be encrypted by the client before sending it over to SQL Server. The encrypted value will match the values in the column that we are looking for.

Think about that with randomized though, client side the value I'm looking for gets encrypted using the randomized algorithm before sending over to SQL. All the values in the column that would match that have different encrypted values – so SQL Server is not going to find any matching data. Like earlier, it could just return no records, but what it actually does is raise a helpful error to remind us that what we are trying is nonsensical.

Equally, allowing an index on a randomized column would be a bit pointless. It would just be a list of records in random order, with no way of looking up a given unencrypted value in the index. Again, it's much better that we get an error if we try to create such an index.

There are a number of things you can use if you are using deterministic encryption that are not possible if you're using randomized:

- Equality comparisons

- Unique constraints

- DISTINCT

- JOIN

- GROUP BY

- Indexes

- Foreign Keys

Data Types

A number of data types are prohibited from being encrypted using Always Encrypted.

The following data types are allowed:

- bit\tinyint\smallint\int\bigint

- char\ncharvarchar\nvarchar

- decimal\money\float\real

- date\time\datetime\datetime2\smalldatetime\datetimeoffset

- binary\varbinary

The following data types are not allowed:

- text\ntext\image

- XML\hierarchyid\geography\geometry

- SQL_VARIANT

- rowversion (timestamp)

- Built-in alias types such as SYSNAME

In most cases it's reasonably clear why these types might not be supported. For instance, text\ntext\image are deprecated, so it doesn't necessarily make sense to do the work to support them. Many of the other types exist to allow specific types of calculations or functions to be executed against them – such as geography. As we can't perform calculations on encrypted columns, it doesn't make a lot of sense to allow such types.

Miscellaneous

There are some prohibitions that don't easily fit into the preceding categories; we'll include them here for completeness:

- FOR XML, FOR JSON PATH.

- StretchDB.

- Temporal Tables – you can create a new table with encryption and then turn it into a temporal table, but you can't use any of the methods we've discussed for encrypting existing data against temporal tables, as the tools do not support them.

Summary

There can seem like a lot of restrictions when you are using Always Encrypted, but in most cases they are logical ones. The main limitations are around how you can interact with encrypted data, and you will need to think about how you work around these sorts of things:

- Searching against encrypted data

- Performing calculations on encrypted data

You need to think carefully about which columns you want to encrypt. Where you can run into problems is where you feel you must encrypt a particular column, but you require functionality against it that is not possible. That's where you'll need to think about reworking application functionality to achieve the required outcome.

We talk more about the wider considerations you might want to be thinking about when implementing Always Encrypted in Chapter 12. In the next chapter, we're going to look at Key Rotation.

## CHAPTER 11

Key Rotation with Always Encrypted

Key rotation is the process of refreshing your encryption keys. It's generally seen as good practice to do this periodically or if you have a serious breach and think they could have been accessed or stolen by an unauthorized individual. When you're planning an implementation of Always Encrypted, you should make sure you understand this process and how your organization is going to manage it over time.

In terms of Always Encrypted there are two potential flavors of key rotation, though one is much more common than the other. We have both a CMK (Column Master Key) and a CEK (Column Encryption Key); in general, it is seen as sufficient to just rotate one of them. If we rotate just the CMK, then the underlying value of the CEK which directly protects our data doesn't need to change. That saves us from having to decrypt and re-encrypt data, and the operation is therefore mostly a matter of updating metadata.

CMK Rotation

The most common approach is just to rotate your CMK. Your certificate which contains the CMK has an expiry date to encourage this good practice. Although you can continue to use the CMK after this date has passed, you really want to be thinking about rotating it before this happens.

© Matthew McGiffen 2022
M. McGiffen, *Pro Encryption in SQL Server 2022*, https://doi.org/10.1007/978-1-4842-8664-7_11

The process is simple, both conceptually and in practice. The stages are:

1. Create a new Always Encrypted certificate containing the new CMK. Store the certificate alongside the existing certificate used as the current CMK.

2. Where you have multiple application or web servers that require the key, the certificate should be deployed on all of them. In the demos in this chapter, we'll proceed straight to rotation after creating the CMK, so don't forget you need to perform this extra step in production environments.

3. Create the new CMK object in your database that specifies the location and identity of the certificate.

4. Add the new CMK to the CEK. In practice that will decrypt the CEK using the existing CMK, re-encrypt it with the new CMK, and store that value alongside the existing encrypted value in the CEK metadata.

5. Remove the values relating to the old CMK from the CEK metadata. A CEK can support up to two sets of values specifying the CMK to use and the relevant encrypted value for the underlying key. This is to allow for this key rotation process while keeping your data online. In practice there may be some performance hit to having two values, so it is best to remove the old one as soon as possible. The performance issue is due to the fact that the client driver doesn't know which of the two CMKs are valid for its own environment, so it may have to attempt to retrieve both.

6. Remove the old CMK metadata from the database.

7. Remove the old certificates from application/web servers.

Note, you should make sure you keep your old certificates somewhere safe as they will be required if you ever need to access data from backups for a period when they were still active.

To reiterate, this process doesn't involve the need to perform any decryption or encryption on your data. The underlying CEK that was used to encrypt that data hasn't changed – just the protection used around the keys. That is why this operation can be done with the database fully online.

There are a few ways you can achieve CMK rotation in practice. We'll start by looking at the methods you can use from SSMS. Then we'll look at how you can achieve the same through code (using PowerShell for the examples); this may be useful to you if you wish to implement key rotation as part of an automated DevOps process.

Rotating the CMK Using the SSMS GUI

There is a GUI within SSMS you can use to do most of the work for you. We'll look at that first, using our existing database we set up in earlier chapters. Before attempting to rotate the CMK, we must create a new CMK. Then we can rotate the CEKs that use the old CMK to use the new one.

Right-click Column Master Keys in the Object Explorer in SSMS, and select the option to create a new one (Figure 11-1):

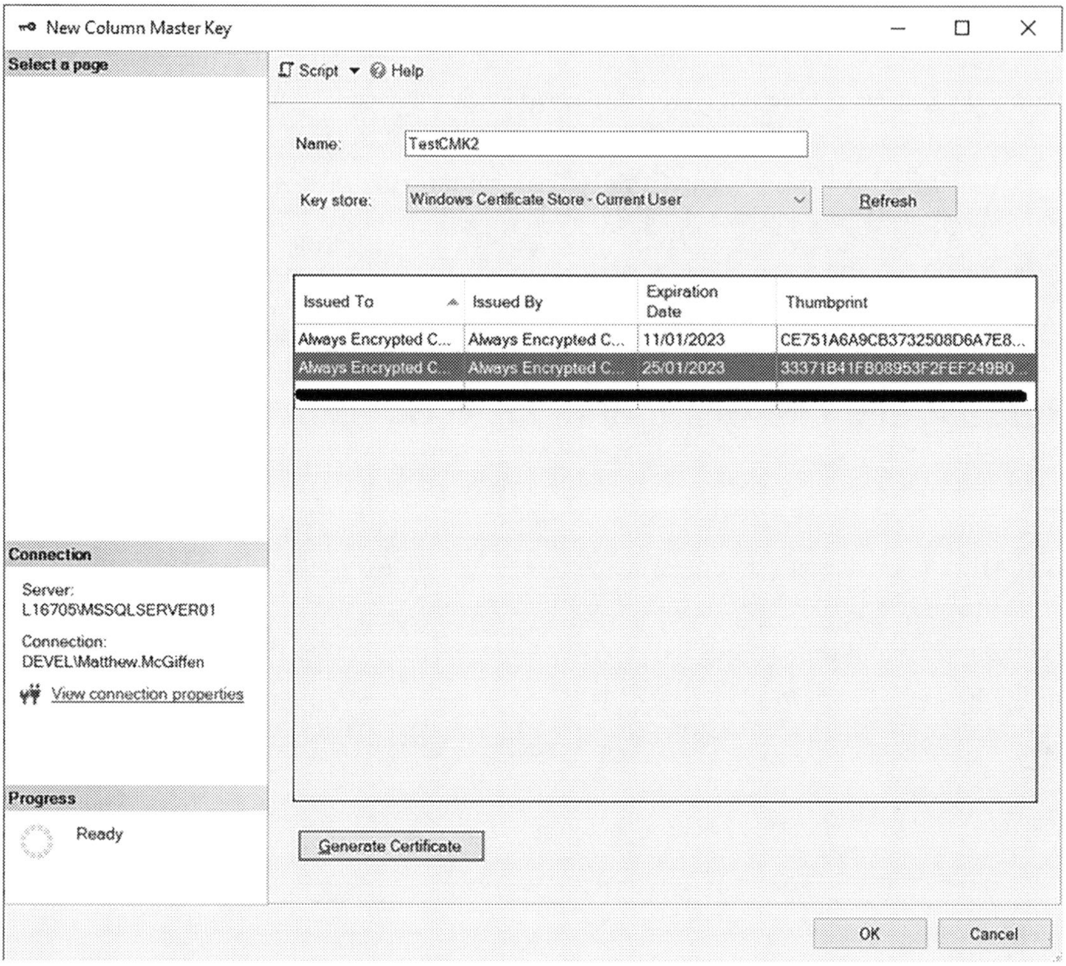

Figure 11-1. *Creating a new CMK for key rotation*

I created a new certificate first (using the Generate Certificate button) as it's the certificate that is the actual CMK. If you find the option to generate a certificate is grayed out, then your account may not have access to the selected key store, in which case running SSMS as an administrator may solve the issue. Then I enter the name I want for my new CMK object in my database, in this case TestCMK2. Finally, I click OK.

I can now see I have two CMK objects in my database (Figure 11-2):

Figure 11-2. *Viewing my new CMK*

We are now ready to start key rotation. Right-click the CMK we want to rotate (the one currently in use) and select Rotate; you then see the GUI shown in Figure 11-3:

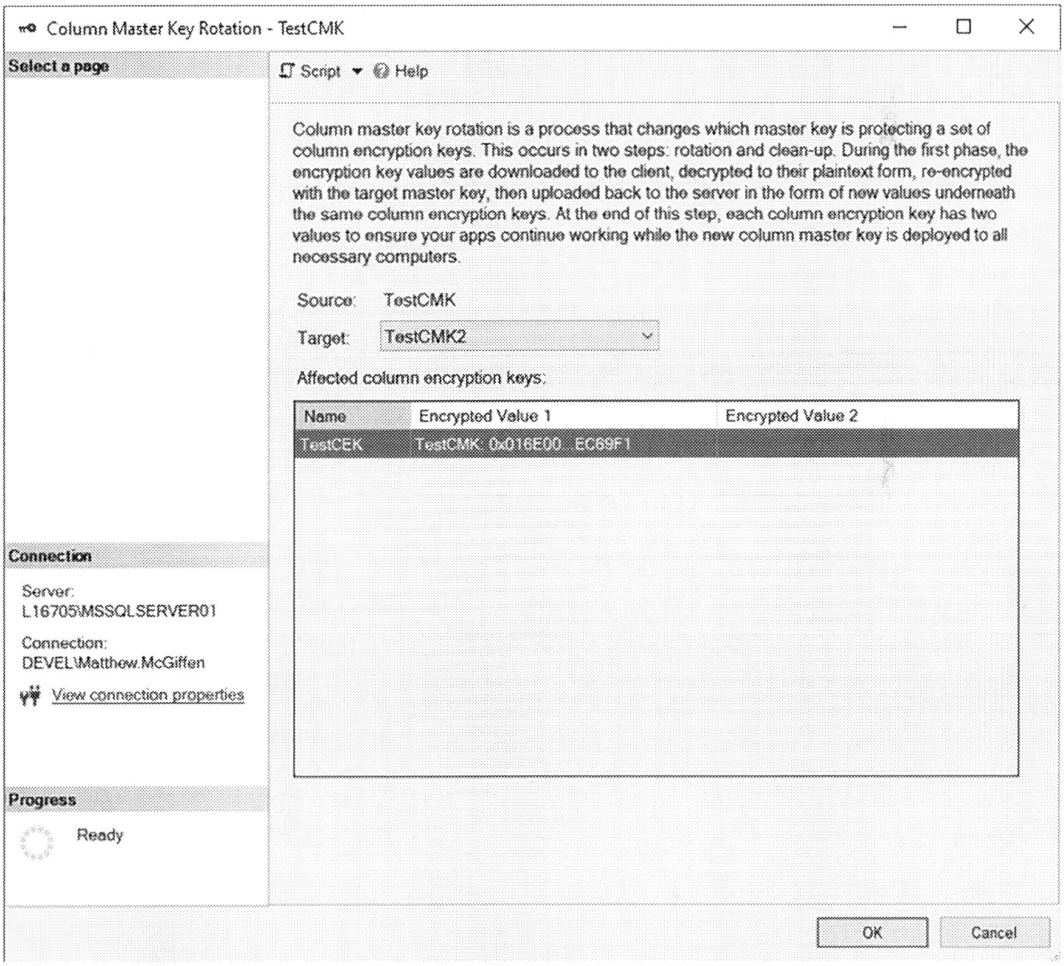

Figure 11-3. *The Column Master Key Rotation Wizard*

In the source field we see the key we have just selected to rotate. I use the Target dropdown to select my new key. In the "Affected column encryption keys" box we can see a list of all Column Encryption Keys that will be affected. In our test database we have just the one, but in practice you could have many CEKs using the same CMK. You can click OK, and the operation is partially completed.

I say partially completed because what happens is that the CEK is now protected by both CMKs. We can see that if we script out the CEK in SSMS. Here is the generated SQL from my machine:

```
CREATE COLUMN ENCRYPTION KEY [TestCEK]
WITH VALUES
(
	COLUMN_MASTER_KEY = [TestCMK],
	ALGORITHM = 'RSA_OAEP',
	ENCRYPTED_VALUE = 0x016E000001630075007200…
),
(
	COLUMN_MASTER_KEY = [TestCMK2],
	ALGORITHM = 'RSA_OAEP',
	ENCRYPTED_VALUE = 0x016E000001630075007200…
)
GO
```

I've truncated the encrypted values so we can see things more clearly. Under the CEK we have two sets of encrypted values: one is the key encrypted by the old CMK and one by the new one. If you're repeating this on your own system, then you will see your own encrypted values.

To complete the process, we need to perform a cleanup operation. Rick-click the old CMK (TestCMK) and select Cleanup (Figure 11-4):

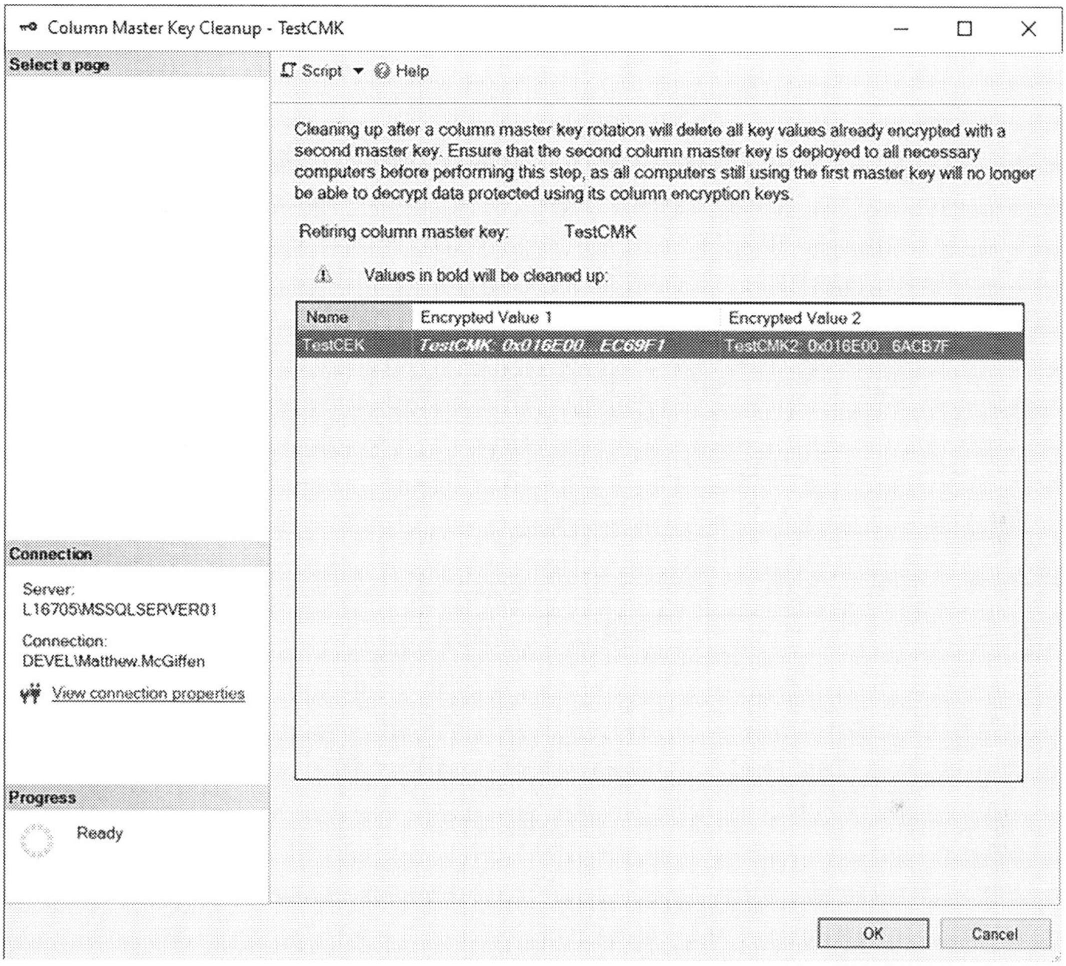

Figure 11-4. Column Master Key Cleanup through the GUI

Once you click OK, the encrypted value stored against your CEK object that was encrypted with the old CMK will be removed. This will only happen if you already have completed the first step of rotating the key. We can confirm this has happened by scripting out the CEK again once we are done. Again, here is the generated definition from my machine:

```
CREATE COLUMN ENCRYPTION KEY [TestCEK]
WITH VALUES
(
    COLUMN_MASTER_KEY = [TestCMK2],
    ALGORITHM = 'RSA_OAEP',
```

157

```
        ENCRYPTED_VALUE = 0x016E0000001630075007200...
)
GO
```

We can see we now have just the one encrypted value. CMK rotation is complete. As a final step you may want to remove the old CMK object from your database which you can do by right-clicking the old key and selecting delete. This operation will fail if you still have CEKs using it. Once you have removed the CMK object, you might also want to go and remove the certificate from your certificate store. You should make sure you keep a copy of it though, in case you ever have to restore an older version of the database that still uses it. The certificate would be required to read the data.

Rotating the CMK Using T-SQL

Usually in practice, for instance, for production deployments, you are not going to want to rotate the CMK as a manual task and will prefer to use a code or script-based solution. One option is to use T-SQL for this. In practice however some of the steps detailed earlier can't be carried out directly from T-SQL, and these include generating the certificate and generating the new values of your CEKS encrypted by the new CEK. As such what you end up doing is following through the process using the GUI in a test or development environment and then generating the required SQL from that process so you can use the SQL for deployments. When you generate the certificate, you will need to make sure it is deployed to all your application servers.

From the example we followed performing rotation through the GUI, we can generate the T-SQL for the CMK object stored in the database:

```
CREATE COLUMN MASTER KEY [TestCMK2]
WITH
(
        KEY_STORE_PROVIDER_NAME = N'MSSQL_CERTIFICATE_STORE',
        KEY_PATH = N'CurrentUser/My/33371B41FB08953F2FEF249B0913B49BE87F7CD3'
);
GO
```

You can see that all we really need to specify is where to find the certificate and the thumbprint uniquely identifying it.

From our CEK we want to extract the T-SQL that defines the value of the key encrypted by our new CMK. Here is mine:

```
(
     COLUMN_MASTER_KEY = [TestCMK2],
     ALGORITHM = 'RSA_OAEP',
     ENCRYPTED_VALUE = 0x016E000001630075007200...
)
```

We can then use this to craft an ALTER ENCRYPION KEY command that adds the new value. If you are running the code for these examples, then you will need to create your own version of the following as your keys will have different values to mine:

```
ALTER COLUMN ENCRYPTION KEY [TestCEK]
ADD VALUE
(
     COLUMN_MASTER_KEY = [TestCMK2],
     ALGORITHM = 'RSA_OAEP',
     ENCRYPTED_VALUE = 0x016E000001630075007200...
);
GO
```

Once that is added, you are then able to remove the value associated with the old CMK with another ALTER ENCRYPION KEY command as follows:

```
ALTER COLUMN ENCRYPTION KEY [TestCEK]
DROP VALUE
(
     COLUMN_MASTER_KEY = [TestCMK]
)
GO
```

You can also generate these scripts directly using the GUI by selecting the required action (rotate or cleanup) and then clicking the script button rather than clicking OK.

Rotating the CMK Using PowerShell

You may wish to perform key rotation from code so that it can be fully automated as part of your deployment pipelines. In these examples, we're going to look at using PowerShell.

You need to have the SQL Server Management Objects for PowerShell installed. If you haven't already, then you need to run PowerShell as an Administrator and then execute a command similar to the following:

Install-Module -Name SqlServer -RequiredVersion 21.1.18256

You may be prompted to download additional packages to support this installation and, if you have an existing version installed, will be instructed how to proceed.

The script we are using is based on a sample supplied by Microsoft which is available online. You can use the script provided with this book, or if you prefer to use the Microsoft one, simply search for "Rotate Always Encrypted Keys Using PowerShell" to get the latest version which you can then modify for your needs. In either case, the key things you need to change are the name of your database server, the database name, and the names for the new and old CMKs. In the following script I've configured these with the values of my test server and database and am starting from where we left off when we did this from SSMS – so I'm going to create a new CMK called TestCMK3 and then rotate to this from my old CMK (TestCMK2). Here is the script:

```
# Create a new CMK (certificate) in the Current User certificate store
$certificate = New-SelfSignedCertificate -Subject "AlwaysEncryptedCert"
-CertStoreLocation Cert:CurrentUser\My -KeyExportPolicy Exportable -Type
DocumentEncryptionCert -KeyUsage KeyEncipherment -KeySpec KeyExchange
-KeyLength 2048

# Import the SqlServer module
Import-Module "SqlServer"

# Connect to the database
$serverName = ".\MSSQLSERVER01"
$databaseName = "TestAlwaysEncrypted"
```

```
$connectionString = "Server = " + $serverName + "; Database = " +
$databaseName + "; Integrated Security = True"
$database = Get-SqlDatabase -ConnectionString $connectionString

# Create a settings object for the new CMK
$newCMKSettings = New-SqlCertificateStoreColumnMasterKeySettings
-CertificateStoreLocation "CurrentUser" -Thumbprint $certificate.Thumbprint

# Create the CMK object in your database
$newCMKName = "TestCMK3"
New-SqlColumnMasterKey -Name $newCMKName -InputObject $database -Column
MasterKeySettings $newCMKSettings

# Initialize rotation - Add protection via the new CMK to your CEKs
$oldCMKName = "TestCMK2"
Invoke-SqlColumnMasterKeyRotation -SourceColumnMasterKeyName
$oldCMKName -TargetColumnMasterKeyName $newCMKName -InputObject $database

# Complete rotation - Remove protection via the old CMK from your CEKs
Complete-SqlColumnMasterKeyRotation -SourceColumnMasterKeyName
$oldCMKName  -InputObject $database

# Remove the old CMK object from your database
Remove-SqlColumnMasterKey -Name $oldCMKName -InputObject $database
```

The script is reasonably self-explanatory, so it should be clear to see what is being done at each step. The steps are very similar to those detailed at the beginning of this chapter:

1. Create a new certificate in the local Certificate Store to use as the new CMK.

2. Connect to the database.

3. Create a new CMK object in the database, in this case TestCMK3 which points at the certificate just created.

4. Initialize Rotation; this adds the value of the key encrypted by our new CMK to each of our affected CEKs.

5. Complete Rotation. This is equivalent to the cleanup operation that removes the encrypted values for the old CMK from our CEKs.

6. Remove the old CMK object from the database.

This script doesn't do anything to the old certificate, so if you wish to delete or move that somewhere, then you must do that as an extra action. Also this script just creates the certificate on the machine it is executed on, so where you have multiple application servers which will all require their own copy of the certificate, you'll need to decide how you wish to manage that.

Rotating the CMK Using PowerShell with Role Separation

As discussed in an earlier chapter, implementing role separation within your organization will give you the greatest security for your encrypted data. Role separation is where no individual is an administrator on both your application and database servers. You can think of this like a lockbox that requires two keys to open, and each key is held by a separate individual. It makes the box much more difficult to open as multiple people need to be involved, but it also makes unauthorized access to the box much more difficult.

Similarly, role separation can create support challenges, but it makes your encrypted data that much more secure. If you fully implement role separation, and there is no automated deployment account that has access to both sets of resources, then key rotation becomes a necessarily more complex process. Microsoft provides PowerShell scripts to help you in this scenario; again these can be found by searching online for "Rotate Always Encrypted Keys Using PowerShell." If you have this need, then it is best you refer to the Microsoft documentation and scripts, but I'll explain the process briefly.

Let's say we have a DBA role and a Security Administrator role.

Part 1: DBA

This step involves retrieving the metadata for the existing keys, so these can be passed to the Security Administrator.

1. Connect to the database using PowerShell.

2. Export the metadata for the existing CMK to file. This will detail where the certificate used currently as the CMK can be found.

3. Export the metadata for the CEKs that use the CMK that is to be rotated. In each case this will include the current encrypted value of the CEK.

4. Pass the created files to the Security Administrator to perform the next step.

Part 2: Security Administrator

This step involves generating the certificate to be used as the new CMK and then generating the new encrypted values for each CEK.

1. Create a new certificate in the key store, generally in the same location as the one currently used as the CMK. As seen earlier, this can be done in PowerShell.

2. In PowerShell, the files received from the DBA can be imported into CMK and CEK settings objects. Then a PowerShell command can generate new encrypted values for each CEK using the new CMK.

3. The details of the new CMK are exported to file.

4. The new encrypted values for each CEK are also exported to file.

5. The files created are shared back with the DBA.

Part 3: DBA

This step involves importing the files passed back from the security administrator in order to generate the new CMK object in the database, as well as adding the new encrypted values to each CEK.

1. In PowerShell, we import the CMK and CEK files received from the Security administrator into variables.

2. Connect to the database.

3. Create a new CMK object using the values loaded in Step 1.

4. Add the new encrypted CEK values loaded in Step 1 to each CEK.

5. Clean up by removing the old encrypted values from each CEK.

6.   Remove the old CMK object.

As you can see the process is a little more complex, but still perfectly achievable. All the scripts are provided by Microsoft to make your life easier.

Rotating the CEK

In extreme cases, or if policy demands, you may feel the need to rotate the CEK. If this occurs, then effectively what you are doing is decrypting the existing data using the old CEK and then encrypting it fresh with a new one. As encryption and decryption must occur client side, the encrypted data must also be transferred across the network.

If you have a large amount of data, this is going to take a proportionately large amount of time, and availability is going to be impacted during that time. In an ideal world, you simply don't need to do this, but if you do, then it's a straightforward task. You can't perform this action via SSMS, but we'll look here at how you can achieve it using PowerShell. Again, we provide a sample script here, or you can find the Microsoft one online. Whichever you use, you will then need to customize it for your own use.

If you are using Always Encrypted with Enclaves, then you have the option to perform CEK rotation via T-SQL, and the operation is carried out within the enclave on the SQL Server box. We look at that in Chapter 15.

CEK rotation via PowerShell is in fact very similar to something we looked at in Chapter 9 and uses the same command from the SQL Server Management Objects.

The Set-SqlColumnEncryption command can be used, not just for initial encryption of a column but also to migrate from one set of encryption settings to another. In the script we'll also create the new CEK and remove the old one.

Following is the script we will use which I've based closely on the Microsoft version. For your own usage, you need to configure your connection details. You also need to specify the names of your keys, the names of your CMK, and your existing CEK, as well as the name you want to use for your new CEK. I'm starting from the point after we rotated the CMK using PowerShell, so my CMK is called TestCMK3. If you are starting from a different point, you may need to change this to your current value.

```
# Import the SqlServer module.
```

```
Import-Module "SqlServer"

# Connect to the database.
$serverName = ".\MSSQLSERVER01"
$databaseName = "TestAlwaysEncrypted"
$connectionString = "Server = " + $serverName + "; Database = " +
$databaseName + "; Integrated Security = True"
$database = Get-SqlDatabase -ConnectionString $connectionString

# Generate a new CEK encrypted by the existing CMK
$CMKName = "TestCMK3"
$newCEKName = "TestCEK2"
New-SqlColumnEncryptionKey -Name $newCEKName -InputObject $database
-ColumnMasterKey $CMKName

# Find all columns encrypted with the old column encryption key, then
create a SqlColumnEncryptionSetting object for each column.
$columnEncryptionSettingsArray = @()
$oldCEKName = "TestCEK"
$tables = $database.Tables
for($i=0; $i -lt $tables.Count; $i++){
    $columns = $tables[$i].Columns
    for($j=0; $j -lt $columns.Count; $j++) {
        if($columns[$j].isEncrypted -and $columns[$j].ColumnEncryption
        KeyName -eq $oldCEKName) {
            $columnName = $tables[$i].Schema + "." + $tables[$i].Name + "."
            + $columns[$j].Name
            $columnEncryptionSettingsArray += New-SqlColumnEncryption
            Settings -ColumnName $columnName -EncryptionType $columns[$j].
            EncryptionType -EncryptionKey $newCEKName
        }
    }
}

# Re-encrypt all columns using thew old CEK to use the new one
```

```
Set-SqlColumnEncryption -ColumnEncryptionSettings
$columnEncryptionSettingsArray -InputObject $database -UseOnlineApproach
-MaxDowntimeInSeconds 120 -LogFileDirectory .

# Remove the old CEK from the database
Remove-SqlColumnEncryptionKey -Name $oldCEKName -InputObject $database
```

First, we connect to the database, and then we create the new CEK.

The next section is the clever bit – credit to Microsoft for this approach. It iterates through all the tables and columns in your database and identifies any that use the current CEK you've specified. For each of these, it adds a new SqlColumnEncryptionSettings object to an array.

Then it does the work, like when we encrypted data in the first place, except this will perform the extra step of decrypting it with the existing CEK first. Still, the whole operation is achieved by a single call using Set-SqlColumnEncryption.

This is working exactly the same way as when we looked at the same command before. It creates an empty copy of your table with the new encryption settings. Then it can decrypt the existing data and bulk-insert it into the new table. Finally, it drops the old table, renames the new one, and aligns any necessary constraints.

You can see in the command here the operation is specified as online. As before though I'd be hesitant in recommending you do this with the expectation that your application would not be impacted while it is running. You should expect issues with availability and the potential for data loss. Personally, I would do this during a scheduled outage.

The final step in the PowerShell script is simply to remove the old CEK from the database.

Once that's completed, we can check back with the DB. You can see we only have the new CEK (Figure 11-5):

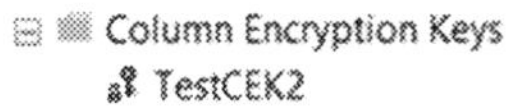

Column Encryption Keys
TestCEK2

Figure 11-5. *Viewing the new Column Encryption Key*

If I view the definition for my table as shown here, I can see the columns are now specified as being encrypted using the new CEK:

```
CREATE TABLE [dbo].[EncryptedTable](
    [Id] [int] IDENTITY(1,1) NOT NULL,
    [LastName] [nvarchar](50) COLLATE Latin1_General_BIN2 ENCRYPTED WITH
    (COLUMN_ENCRYPTION_KEY = [TestCEK2], ENCRYPTION_TYPE = Deterministic,
    ALGORITHM = 'AEAD_AES_256_CBC_HMAC_SHA_256') NULL,
    [FirstName] [nvarchar](50) COLLATE Latin1_General_BIN2 ENCRYPTED WITH
    (COLUMN_ENCRYPTION_KEY = [TestCEK2], ENCRYPTION_TYPE = Randomized,
    ALGORITHM = 'AEAD_AES_256_CBC_HMAC_SHA_256') NULL,
 CONSTRAINT [PK_EncryptedTable] PRIMARY KEY CLUSTERED
(
    [Id] ASC
)WITH (PAD_INDEX = OFF, STATISTICS_NORECOMPUTE = OFF, IGNORE_DUP_KEY = OFF,
ALLOW_ROW_LOCKS = ON, ALLOW_PAGE_LOCKS = ON, OPTIMIZE_FOR_SEQUENTIAL_KEY =
OFF) ON [PRIMARY]
) ON [PRIMARY]
GO
```

As mentioned earlier, hopefully you never have to do this, and for all scenarios you encounter, it is sufficient to simply rotate the CMK. As you can see though, if you need to rotate the CEK, then it is also quite straightforward.

Summary

Key rotation is the process of periodically refreshing keys used by encryption in order to maintain the best level of security.

In general, you would prefer just to rotate your CMKs as this is a metadata-only operation that doesn't require your data to be re-encrypted with new keys and doesn't require application downtime. We've looked at a number of different methods you can use for CMK rotation:

- Through the GUI in SSMS

- Using T-SQL, though some tasks such as certificate creation must be managed outside of SQL Server

- Using PowerShell

- Using PowerShell where you have role separation so more than one individual must be involved

CEK rotation can also be achieved, but it does require data to be decrypted and re-encrypted with new keys. This generally means application downtime and if you have a large amount of encrypted data could be a significant operation.

Key rotation is reasonably straightforward, but there is some level of complexity involved. When performing it from code, you can use the scripts provided here as a starting point, or you may choose to download the latest ones from Microsoft.

Key rotation is an important part of the lifecycle for Always Encrypted – as well as for other forms of encryption. When you are planning to implement Always Encrypted, it is good to consider what your strategy will be for key rotation as this may impact the way you decide to design your implementation and deployment.

In the next chapter we'll close off this exploration of the basic version of Always Encrypted by looking at some other things we may want to think about when implementing column encryption.

CHAPTER 12

Considerations When Implementing Always Encrypted

This is the last chapter on the basic version of Always Encrypted before we move on to look at the version with enclaves. I want to wrap up by looking at some additional items you may want to consider when planning to implement Always Encrypted.

In my opinion Always Encrypted is a great technology, but it's not like TDE where you can pretty much flick a switch and expect everything to work just as it did before. At a minimum level you will need to modify connection strings for applications that access the database, and you may also need to make application changes to work around the natural limitations of column encryption. There may be more change required when you have external systems that need to interact with the database if they want to interact with encrypted data in a way that's not supported. You also need to think about how you release change to the database and how you manage keys over time.

Choosing What Data to Encrypt

This is something you'll want to think about at the outset but also something you'll come back to as you get further into planning your implementation. With column encryption it's not about encrypting every piece of data in the database – but rather, targeting data that is personally identifiable information or sensitive in any way.

The limitations of working with Always Encrypted that we talked about in Chapter 10 are likely to influence your decision. It might be logical to think that we want to encrypt the names of customers – but if you want to perform case-insensitive searches against those columns, then you are going to run into problems. There are ways around that,

© Matthew McGiffen 2022
M. McGiffen, *Pro Encryption in SQL Server 2022*, https://doi.org/10.1007/978-1-4842-8664-7_12

but they require more development effort. That doesn't mean you shouldn't do it, but it may be that you start with targeting other columns first – such as credit card information, email addresses, and columns where a customer may have given you sensitive information about themselves such as medical details.

I have seen projects not get off the ground where an all or nothing attitude is taken. If it is too difficult to encrypt everything that could be deemed personal, then nothing gets done. I'd encourage you to think about encrypting what you can. Any protection is better than none. The old saying "perfect is the enemy of good" can be very much appropriate here.

Just a quick note on how you might go about encrypting columns where you need to support case-insensitive searching, one option is to encrypt the data in place but to maintain a separate search catalog. If it's only case-insensitive searching you need to support, then you can still encrypt the catalog as long as you use deterministic encryption, but just ensure the values are all stored in uppercase (or lowercase works just as well) and that search terms are capitalized before you issue them as a predicate. LIKE queries are harder to support, but it's still achievable.

This sort of approach may feel like a lot of extra work, maintaining copies of the same data, but search catalogs can also be a way of achieving lightning fast searching so you may get more out of implementing such a technique than just being able to encrypt your data.

Source Control and Release Management

In modern software development we often talk about DevOps. DevOps is a term that can have different meanings to different people, but generally we're talking about the approach to source control of your application code and some form of managed or automated release process. Hopefully you have some level of both in place for your database schemas and code. Whatever your process, you'll want to assess if it is impacted by implementing column encryption and what changes you may need to make to accommodate that.

You should also have a story in place for how you are going to deal with key rotation – which we covered earlier – when that needs to happen.

You should be clear about the limitations of Always Encrypted, in particular that you can't just encrypt columns in place, but otherwise, the process of releasing most changes you may make to your application should be unaffected.

When it comes to database and server configuration, there is a lot of variance as to whether people have that in their source control with their application code or whether it is managed separately by system administrators. With TDE, for example, I often see that being managed as a configuration outside of the application code, with the settings and keys managed by administrators, developers don't need to be aware of them. It's not uncommon that TDE would only be enabled in a production environment and not on development and test instances. I'm not saying that is a good or bad thing.

With Always Encrypted, however, we are defining encryption within our table and column definitions, and its implementation causes limitations on the way we can work with data. Therefore, it is critical that we have Always Encrypted fully set up for our database in all environments, be they on a developer's local machine or shared development and test instances. In each case we will need the relevant keys and certificates in order to be able to interact with data. However, and this is very important, you are not going to want to use the same keys that you will use in your production environments. These are the keys that allow access to your – or your client's – sensitive data. They should not be freely available on everyone's machine. Therefore, you need an approach for how you are going to manage having separate keys in different environments. You also may not want to have your production keys in source control at all but stored securely elsewhere.

There are two main approaches for releasing change to databases. One is migration based; for each release you write scripts that enact the changes you need to make. As long as you have control over how the scripts are written and understand the ways in which you need to work with Always Encrypted, then using this approach shouldn't have any major issues.

The other approach uses schema comparisons. A good example of this is where you use SQL Server Data Tools (SSDT) with Visual Studio. You work with a database project which defines the latest development state of your database. If you use a development environment such as SSDT, you commonly release changes through a tool that analyzes the differences between your source control and your target database and applies whatever changes are required to make your target match your source. The latest versions of SSDT have full support for Always Encrypted.

In order to compile an SSDT database project with column encryption, the CEK and CMK objects must exist in your database project. As discussed, it makes sense that these are just test versions of the keys. When you deploy to production, your CMK and CEK objects in the target database are not going to match what's in the source, and you don't want your automated schema-based comparison to overwrite them with the test version. As such you need to be able to deal with this. With Visual Studio and SSDT this is straightforward, and I'll show you that. For other tools you'll need to identify the appropriate way of doing the same.

Let's look at my project in Visual Studio (Figure 12-1). This project matches the TestAlwaysEncrypted database that we have been working with, at the state we left it in at the end of the last chapter. We can see my CEK and CMK objects are defined within the project.

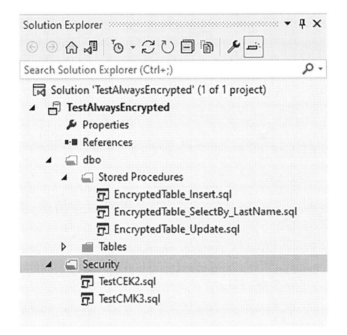

Figure 12-1. *Viewing our database project in Visual Studio*

To deploy the project, I can right-click it and select Publish; we see the GUI that appears in Figure 12-2. I select the destination and make any other changes I need. In an automated deployment, you would script this action:

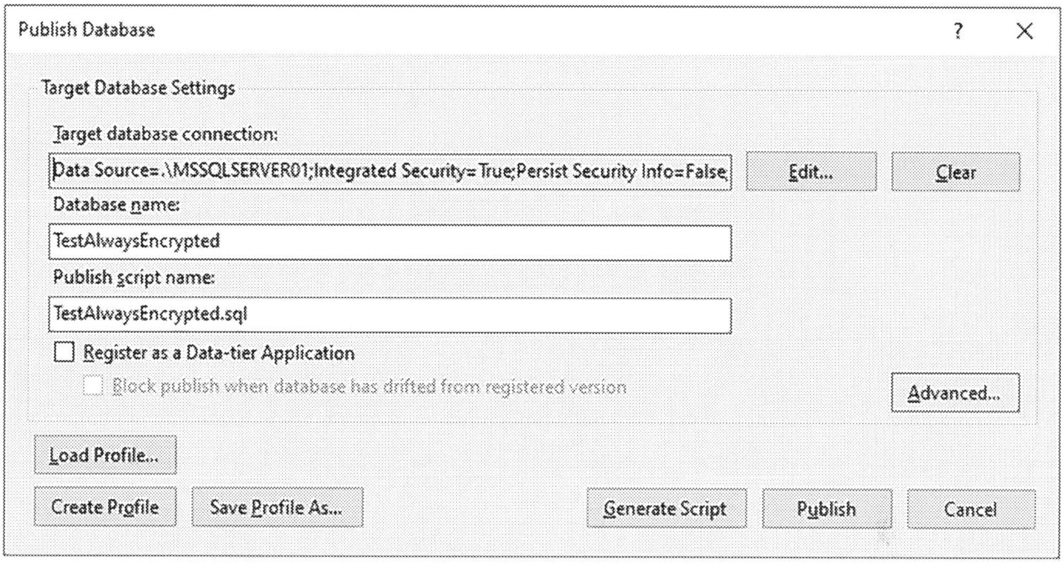

Figure 12-2. *Deploying a database project using SSDT*

To ignore the keys and certificates you can go to the Advanced Publish Settings (Figure 12-3). Select the Ignore tab, and in the excluded object types, you should select to exclude CMKs and CEKs:

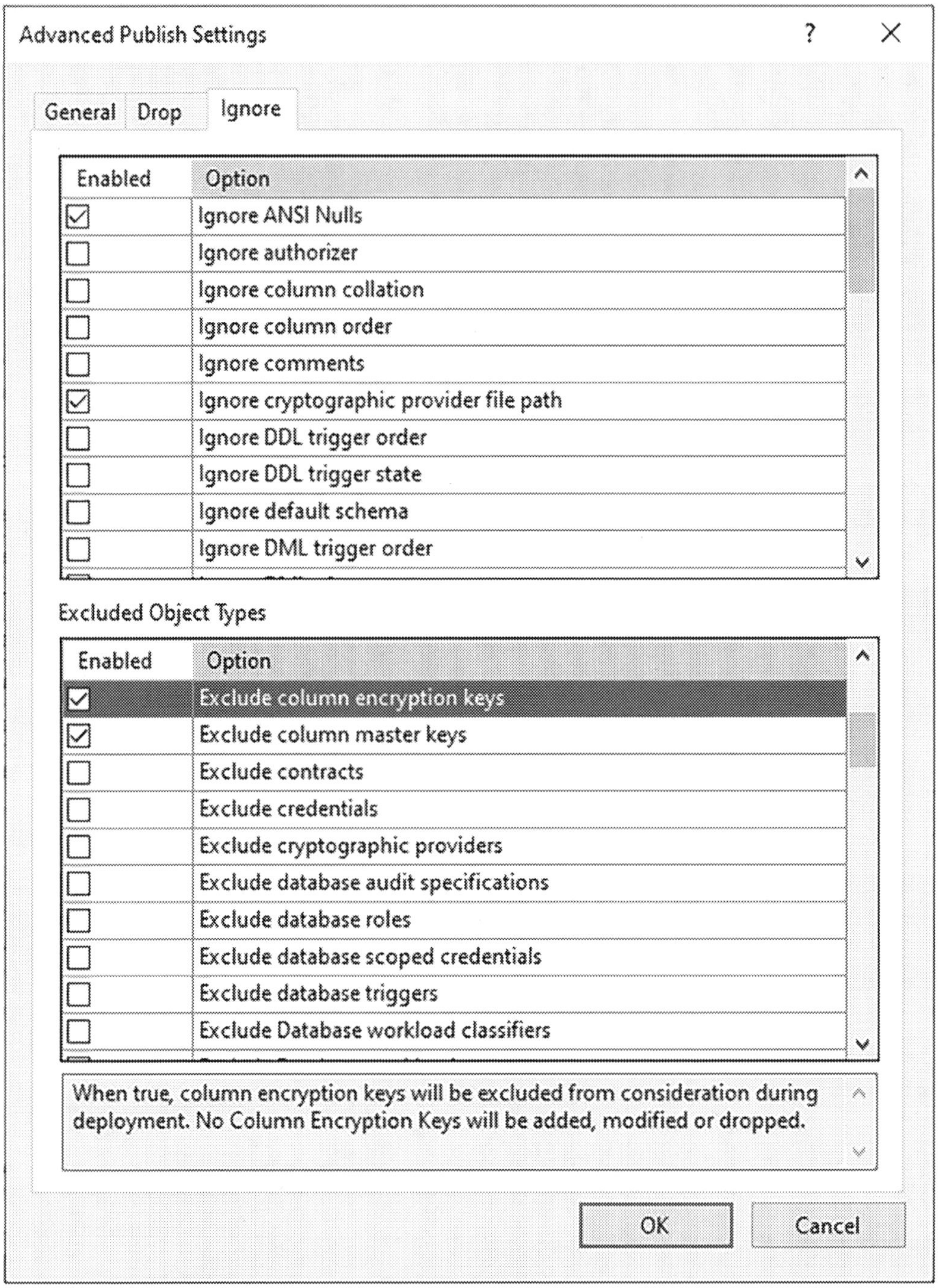

Figure 12-3. *Advanced publish settings for my Visual Studio project*

Once you've made those settings, you can publish your project without fear of the existing keys being overwritten. There are equivalent settings for each of these you can use from the command line, and you can find them in the documentation for SQLPackage.exe. You won't want to do this for your initial deployment as you are creating the database for the first time and the keys must exist in order for the tables to be deployed with encryption enabled. It is useful however to be able to do this for subsequent production deployments – or to other environments that use different keys to those held in source.

ETL

We routinely use ETL – extract, transform, and load – processes, or variants of that, to move data from our SQL databases to other destinations, usually for data warehousing and reporting purposes. You may be considering how implementing Always Encrypted is going to impact that.

The first question to be asking yourselves is whether you need those processes to interact with the encrypted data. Remember we are usually only encrypting personally identifiable and sensitive information. This might include names, email addresses, important identifiers such as national security numbers, and things like credit card information.

If your ETL is concerned with reporting and data warehousing, then should you be loading that information? Do the relevant data protection laws allow you to process that information, and do you have the right consents? Do you actually need that data in order to generate your aggregated reports?

Let's assume that you do need to perform some ETL on your encrypted data. Is it going to be encrypted in the same manner where it is copied to, and if not, is it just as likely to be exposed as if you hadn't encrypted it in the first place?

That said, you may need to do it and to understand what changes will be required to your ETL processes in order for them to continue working after Always Encrypted has been implemented.

Remember, Always Encrypted is designed to be transparent; all encryption and decryption is carried out within the client library used for connecting to SQL Server. So far, we've only really mentioned .NET, but other client drivers support Always Encrypted including ODBC and JDBC.

If your ETL process uses a client driver that supports Always Encrypted, then you shouldn't have any problems as long as you're not trying to do things that are not allowed – for instance, using a query as a data source that requires a predicate against a column encrypted with randomized encryption. The key is that you must specify that the Column Encryption Setting is enabled for your connections that target encrypted data, and the ETL client must have access to the certificate used as the CMK.

In Chapter 9 we looked at how you can use the Import and Export Wizard to encrypt existing data. That was effectively an ETL process, moving data from one table to another and using SQL Server Integration Services (SSIS) to perform the actual task.

Performance

Let's talk about the performance impact of Always Encrypted. Following is the diagram (Figure 12-4) we looked at earlier that shows all the stages of executing a query with column encryption.

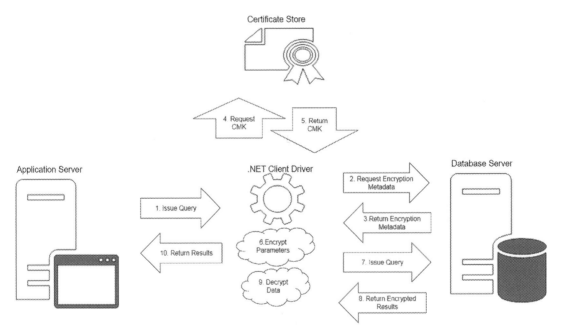

Figure 12-4. *Stages of executing a query with Always Encrypted*

We can see on the right, against the database server, that the only additional work we are doing – compared to issuing a regular query – is in asking for and retrieving the encryption metadata. This gets cached on the client side, so after you've executed a particular query once, the metadata for that query doesn't need to be requested again until the cache needs to be refreshed. That means that the impact on the database side is next to nothing – the occasional call to a very lightweight functionality.

It's worth noting that you might not see this if you try to assess performance using SSMS. SSMS doesn't take advantage of the caching, so each query executed on a connection with encryption enabled will request the encryption metadata – this can make it look like there is a fixed extra overhead on every query you issue.

All the real extra work exists on the client side, in the process of encrypting parameters being sent to the database as well as decrypting results that come back. For the parameters, encrypting a couple of values is going to be the work of microseconds.

Similarly, decrypting values in the result set is going to be minimal work unless the result set is large. We have to be talking about large amounts of data being retrieved and decrypted before we're going to notice significant overhead. One good thing though is that on the client side it is relatively cheap and easy to scale up or out – as opposed to the database side where we can only (in most cases) have a single instance serving our requests and the cost of licensing the software is comparatively high.

Overall then, the performance impact of Always Encrypted on our database server is not something we need to worry about.

Client Drivers

While all the examples I've shown in this book have used .NET to connect to the database, as I've mentioned a few times, other drivers are supported. So you're not necessarily blocked from using Always Encrypted if your application doesn't use .NET.

The key requirements are that you are using a supported driver and that when you connect to the database, you specify that the Column Encryption Setting is enabled.

The full list of supported client drivers is shown in Table 12-1:

Table 12-1. *Client drivers that support Always Encrypted*

Client driver	Minimum required version
.NET Framework Data Provider for SQL Server	4.6.1
JDBC driver	6.0
ODBC Driver for SQL Server	13.1
Microsoft Drivers for PHP for SQL Server	5.2
Microsoft .NET Data Provider for SQL Server	. NET Framework 4.6 or .NET Core 2.1

You can find more details about working with each of the drivers, other than .NET which we've looked at, in the Microsoft documentation.

Summary

In this chapter we've looked at a number of things you might want to think about before you jump in feet first with Always Encrypted. Key points are:

- When choosing what data to encrypt, don't let perfect be the enemy of good.

- Where Always Encrypted limits what you can do with data, like searching, you may just need to think of new ways you can achieve the same functionality.

- You need to consider whether the tools you use for source control and release management support Always Encrypted.

- ETL still works as long as your ETL tool uses client drivers that support Always Encrypted. Think though about whether it is appropriate to be moving your encrypted data around and using it for other purposes outside the application.

- Always Encrypted has little impact on database performance. Where there is a hit, such as decrypting large result sets, the extra effort occurs on the client side.

- Besides .NET, there are a number of other client drivers that support Always Encrypted – such as JDBC. As long as your application uses one of these, then you should be fine.

In the next chapter we'll start to look at the version of Always Encrypted that uses enclaves to support greater functionality – but at the cost of additional setup and maintenance.

PART IV

Column Encryption using Always Encrypted with Enclaves

## CHAPTER 13

Introducing Always Encrypted with Enclaves

In SQL Server 2019 the potential to use enclaves was added to Always Encrypted. An enclave is a secure partition of memory, in this case on the SQL Server machine, that appears as a black box to anything outside of the enclave. There is no way to view the data or code inside the enclave from outside of it, which makes it a trusted and secure environment in which to perform cryptographic operations. Code that runs in the enclave must also be signed and cannot be modified.

In looking at Always Encrypted so far, we've seen that many of the key limitations occur because all the cryptographic activity occurs on the client side and SQL Server never has access to the plaintext keys or data. By using a secure enclave on the SQL box, we can allow SQL to perform some functions and access plaintext values while ensuring that the data and keys still can't be viewed by someone who has high privilege access over the SQL box. Even by running a debugger you cannot view the contents of memory inside an enclave.

Microsoft has used this to allow certain functions that before wouldn't have been possible. Those functions fall into two categories:

- Rich querying

- In-place encryption and decryption of data

Rich querying is mainly about allowing a wider range of comparison operators. Remember previously we could only perform equality comparisons and then only if our data used deterministic encryption. With enclaves, Microsoft has added support for a wider range of comparison operators such as greater than and less than as well as allowing for range queries such as BETWEEN, IN, and LIKE. These are however only supported on columns using randomized encryption. Importantly, we can now also have indexes on columns using randomized encryption. This is very important;

183

M. McGiffen, *Pro Encryption in SQL Server 2022*, https://doi.org/10.1007/978-1-4842-8664-7_13

otherwise, our queries performing comparisons against those columns could perform very badly. The hope is that this reduces the amount of application rework people need to make in order to be able to implement Always Encrypted.

The in-place encryption and decryption of data allows for initial encryption of columns which can now be achieved with a simple ALTER TABLE command. It also can be used for CEK (Column Encryption Key) rotation. In both cases all the processing required can be done on the SQL box without the data needing to be passed back and forth across the network which makes it much faster and less prone to issues.

The allowed functions are intended to be a starting point and represent the feedback Microsoft received from customers about the functions most required and which the limitations around with the basic version of Always Encrypted caused the most problems in planning to implement it. It is planned for the set of functions and capabilities available within the enclave to be added to over time.

Attestation

An important concept required to support the enclave, and ensure it is secure, is the idea of attestation. Attestation is the process of verifying that the enclave is legitimate and has not been tampered with in any way – either from a software or hardware point of view – to ensure that a sophisticated hacker cannot use the enhanced functionality allowed with an enclave in order to access our data.

For Attestation we use an attestation service installed on separate server; in the case of Always Encrypted, we use Microsoft Host Guardian Service (HGS). HGS supports two different attestation modes:

Host Key – this simply verifies the identity of the server hosting SQL by using an asymmetric key pair. The private key is stored on the SQL box and the public key is shared with HGS. Only the key is verified in terms of attesting that the SQL Server is trusted.

TPM – TPM stands for Trusted Platform Module which is a chip installed on the motherboard of most modern computers. The TPM contains a unique Endorsement Key that can be used to verify the identity of the computer. TPMs also store information about the boot processes of the computer as hashed measurements. These measurements can be used during attestation to verify the security configuration of the computer hasn't been tampered with. HGS requires that the TPM version must be 2.0.

TPM attestation is the more secure form and is what Microsoft recommend for production usage when working with Always Encrypted with Enclaves. It provides a level of protection where it can be verified that even the hardware hasn't been tampered with in order to try and crack the enclave. It is however harder to set up than host key attestation. Microsoft recommends that host key mode be mainly used for test and development servers. If you do choose to use host key attestation in production, you should make sure that the private key for the SQL box is well protected and also accept that you could be vulnerable to sophisticated hardware and software attacks; you may however decide that it provides enough protection for your purposes.

Setting up attestation is where you face additional challenges in implementing Always Encrypted with Enclaves, and we'll look at that in detail in subsequent chapters. You may find that it's not something you want to do due to the extra complications and ongoing management and support; that's partly why we covered Always Encrypted without enclaves as a separate item. Once you've gone through setting up enclaves in a test environment, you will hopefully be able to judge whether it's something you'd want to use – or whether you'd rather stick with the basic version. For now, let's take an overview of how it all works. The other consideration is that you may want to use Always Encrypted but not be ready to move to SQL Server 2019 or later; in the real world, it's not uncommon for people to be running a number of versions behind the latest.

Executing Queries That Use the Enclave

When we issue a query that requires one of the new types of functionality that is supported, the enclave will require the CEK to be sent over securely from the client. Before that happens, the client must verify that the enclave is valid and trusted. Assuming that verification – the attestation – is successful, then the CEK can be supplied, and the query sent for execution. Let's look at the attestation process first, and then we'll look at how the key is supplied and the query executed.

The Attestation Process

Figure 13-1 shows the attestation process that is triggered when we issue a query that requires the use of the enclave. It's important to understand that attestation is something that is required when SQL Server requests access to a CEK in order to be able to execute a query in the enclave. Once the CEK is received, it is then cached within the enclave, so it does not need to be asked for again for other queries that need the same CEK – as such, the attestation process doesn't need to be re-instigated that often.

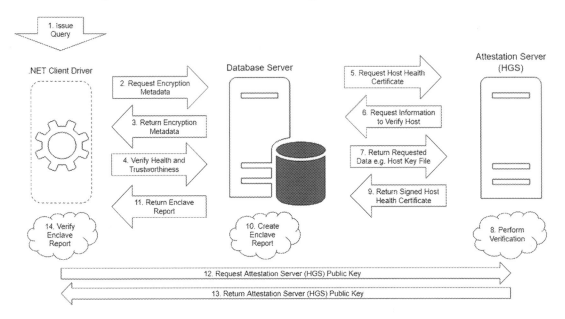

Figure 13-1. *The attestation process in action*

1. **Issue Query**

   The query is issued in the normal manner; as we've already seen with Always Encrypted, if we want to be able to target encrypted columns, then the connection must specify that column encryption is enabled.

2. **Request Encryption Metadata**

   Just as we saw with the basic version of Always Encrypted, for any query issued where column encryption is enabled, the client must request the encryption metadata from SQL Server before it actually attempts to execute the query.

3. **Return Encryption Metadata**

   As before, the encryption metadata is returned to the client. Now though we have an additional option. Let's say it is a LIKE query we are executing. SQL Server will identify that query must be executed within the enclave and that to do so it will require the relevant CEK. The request for the CEK is included as part of the metadata.

4. **Verify Health and Trustworthiness**

   The client sees that SQL is requesting the CEK and that is what kicks off the actual attestation process. The client wants to verify the health and trustworthiness of the SQL Server and particularly the enclave, before it is willing to send over the key. It passes this request to the SQL Server. Effectively this is asking SQL to prove it is who and what it says it is.

5. **Request Host Health Certificate**

   SQL Server contacts the Attestation server to gain a health certificate it can pass back to the client. In this case the Attestation server is using the Host Guardian Service (HGS) which is a Windows service that can be used for attestation.

6. **Request Information to Verify Host**

   In Host Key mode the attestation service just needs to verify the public key from the SQL Server. In TPM mode, the SQL box will already have its configuration registered with the attestation service as part of the setup process. In this step the attestation service requests artifacts to be supplied that will prove the configuration is still secure and hasn't been tampered with.

7. **Return Requested Data**

   The requested items are returned to the attestation service.

8. **Perform Verification**

   The attestation service verifies the configuration.

9. **Return Signed Host Health Certificate**

   Assuming all is as it should be, the attestation service creates a Host Health Certificate and signs it using the service's private key.

10. **Create Enclave Report**

    SQL Server creates an enclave report that includes the signed Host Health Certificate.

11. **Return Enclave Report**

    The enclave report is passed back to the client.

12. **Request Attestation Server (HGS) Public Key**

In order to verify the signature on the Host Health Certificate, the client machine contacts the attestation service directly to obtain the public key.

13. **Return Attestation Server (HGS) Public Key**

The public key is returned to the client.

14. **Verify Enclave Report**

The client can now use the public key to verify that the Host Health Certificate is authentic.

After all that, the SQL Server's health and trustworthiness have been verified, and the client knows it can safely pass the CEK to the enclave. We show that process next as we look at the steps in the query execution.

The Query Execution Process

In many ways the query execution process is unchanged when working with Always Encrypted with Enclaves enabled. We do have some additional steps though as we need to pass over the CEK – and we want to make sure that is passed over securely and can't be accessed in transit or outside of the enclave. Figure 13-2 shows this process:

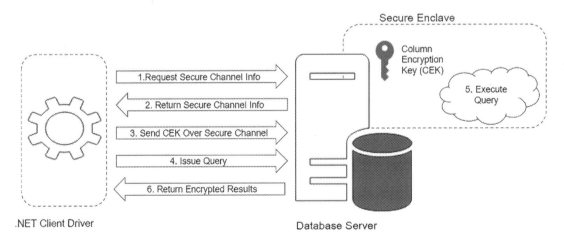

Figure 13-2. *The query execution process with enclaves enabled*

1. **Request Secure Channel Info**

   The CEK needs to be sent directly to the enclave in a manner that
   ensures it is secure. In order to do this the client needs a secure
   channel with the enclave over which they can communicate. The
   channel uses the enhanced TDS protocol, and a shared secret is
   negotiated using the Diffie Hellman protocol.

2. **Return Secure Channel Info**

   The enclave returns the information required for the client to
   communicate securely with it.

3. **Send CEK Over Secure Channel**

   The CEK received in the encryption metadata is decrypted with
   the CMK and then is re-encrypted with the session key for the
   secure channel before being sent to the enclave. The enclave is
   able to decrypt the CEK as it too has access to the session key.

4. **Issue Query**

   Now that the CEK exists in the enclave, the query can be sent to
   SQL Server for execution. Note that the query is also signed.

5. **Execute Query**

   Armed with the CEK, the enclave is now able to execute the query.

6. **Return Encrypted Results**

   We're now back into the workflow from the basic version of
   Always Encrypted. Results are returned including any encrypted
   columns that are selected – still in their encrypted form. Where
   required, the metadata is supplied to allow the client to decrypt
   the encrypted columns.

Once that's all complete, the unencrypted results can be returned back to the
application just like before, and our query execution is complete.

Summary

In this chapter we've taken an overview of Always Encrypted with Secure Enclaves, which is available to you if you are using SQL Server 2019 or higher. Hopefully I've given you a clear understanding of what it offers and how it works.

The key extra functions available with the use of enclaves are:

- Rich queries – these include range and like queries as well as indexes on columns with randomized encryption.

- In-place encryption and decryption of data on the SQL box.

Key points to note about enclaves are:

- The enclave is a secure partition of memory on the SQL Server. Only signed code can execute within it, and the contents cannot be viewed from outside.

- An attestation service is used to verify that the enclave is, and remains, trustworthy and hasn't been tampered with. We use Windows Host Guardian Service (HGS) as our attestation service.

In the next chapter we'll look at how you set up Always Encrypted with Secure Enclaves, including how you set up the attestation server.

CHAPTER 14

Setting Up Always Encrypted with Enclaves

In this chapter we're going to look at how you set up your environment to be able to work with the version of Always Encrypted that uses enclaves. My key aim here is to give you a demo I'm confident you can repeat and that you can set up in a self-service manner. By that I mean you don't need to talk to domain admins to get approval for setting up the attestation service, and you don't need to get extra kit – virtual or physical – in order to be able to evaluate Always Encrypted with Enclaves. To that end we're going to use Hyper-V virtual machines for SQL Server and the attestation server.

We'll start by looking at how you can set it up using host key attestation. This is where the security of the enclave is only verified using the private key belonging to the server hosting your SQL Server instance. The more secure version of attestation is TPM mode; we'll look at that in Chapter 17.

I talked previously about how attestation can check that the server configuration – and therefore the enclave it hosts – is secure and has not been tampered with. When you use host key attestation, this does not happen. The public key of the SQL box is registered as trusted with the attestation service, and all the service does is verify the key. Microsoft only recommend this form of attestation for development and test environments as it will not protect against sophisticated software or hardware hacks. You might though also want to consider it where you just want to set up enclaves to allow for the initial encryption of data in place and then remove the use of the enclave once that is done. Equally, it's possible that you may decide that the level of security provided is "good enough" for you to use where your SQL instance or environment may not support setting up the more secure forms of attestation.

We're going to use Microsoft Host Guardian Service (HGS) as the attestation service. For that we require a separate server, and when setting up the service, a new Active Directory domain will be created. To make that possible for you to do easily without

© Matthew McGiffen 2022
M. McGiffen, *Pro Encryption in SQL Server 2022*, https://doi.org/10.1007/978-1-4842-8664-7_14

access to extra kit, as well as participation from your domain admins, we're going to do it all inside Hyper-V virtual machines. I'll go into as much detail as is practical, including a brief tutorial on how to set up and work with VMs in Hyper-V, but you may need to figure out a few things for yourself if you've never used Hyper-V before.

You'll be able to follow this demo using a single development machine as long as you have enough disk space free for the VMs (50 GB is plenty) and enough memory (8 GB is good, but you can get away with a bit less). In terms of CPU power, 8 CPU cores or more is ideal.

Setting Up Your VMs

First, you'll need to install Hyper-V if you don't already have it enabled on the machine you are using. You can add it using the "Turn Windows Features on or off" control panel applet. Once that's installed you can open Hyper-V Manager and get ready to create your VMs.

You'll also need media to install Windows Server on both VMs and SQL Server on one of them. I'm using Windows Server 2019 Evaluation edition and SQL Server 2019 Developer edition. You can download both from Microsoft; in each case, you will want the ISO image for the installer so you can attach it to your VM as a virtual DVD drive.

In Hyper-V Manager, go to the Action menu, and select New and then Virtual Machine. That brings up the wizard (Figure 14-1):

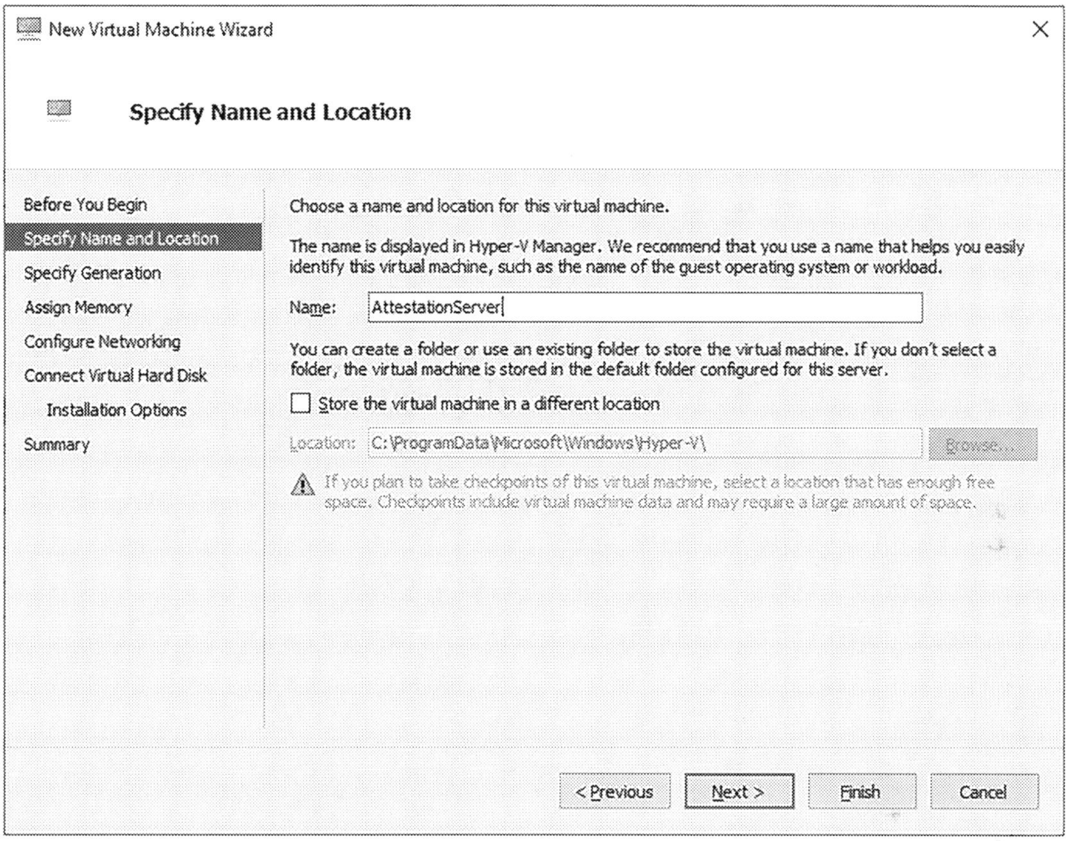

Figure 14-1. *The Hyper-V New Virtual Machine Wizard*

We'll create the VM for HGS first. I've called it AttestationServer; give yours a name and click Next.

In the next screen (Figure 14-2) we have the option to specify which generation of VM should be created:

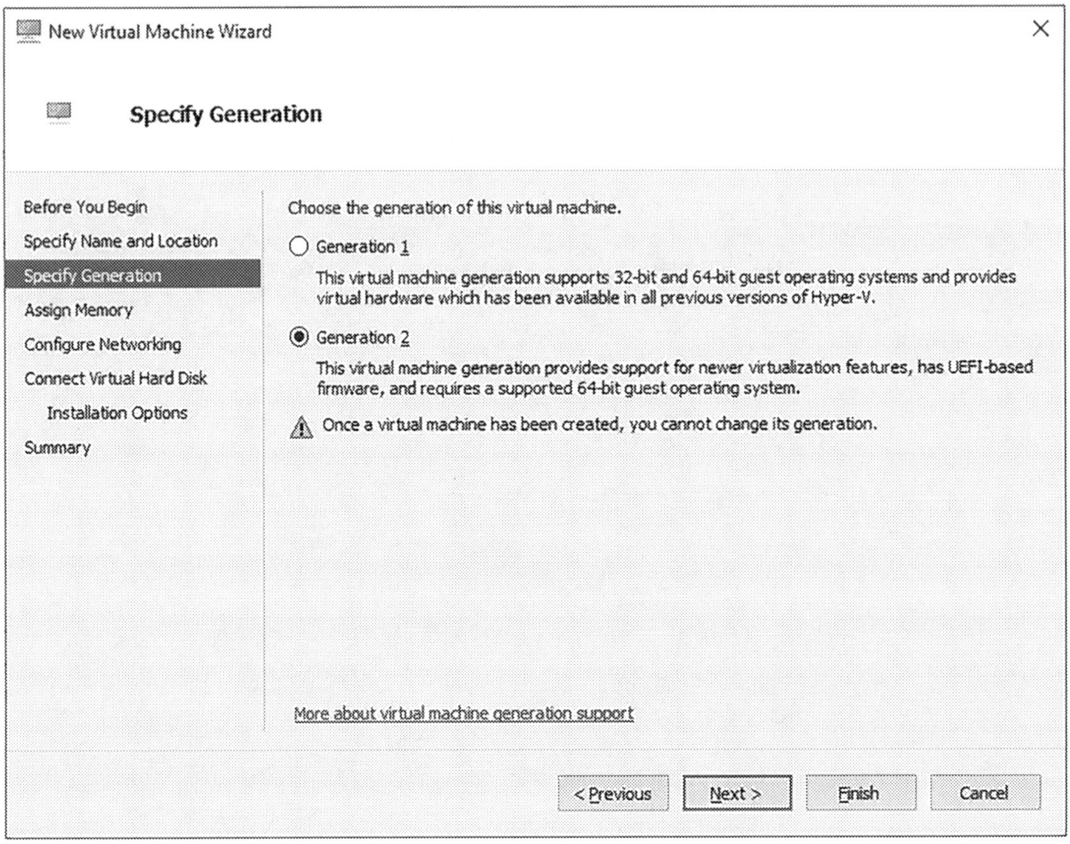

Figure 14-2. *Specifying the generation for your VM*

For this demo it doesn't matter too much which one we pick, but let's go with Generation 2. This is what would be required for our SQL Server for the more secure form of attestation. Click Next to move on to assigning memory for your VM (Figure 14-3).

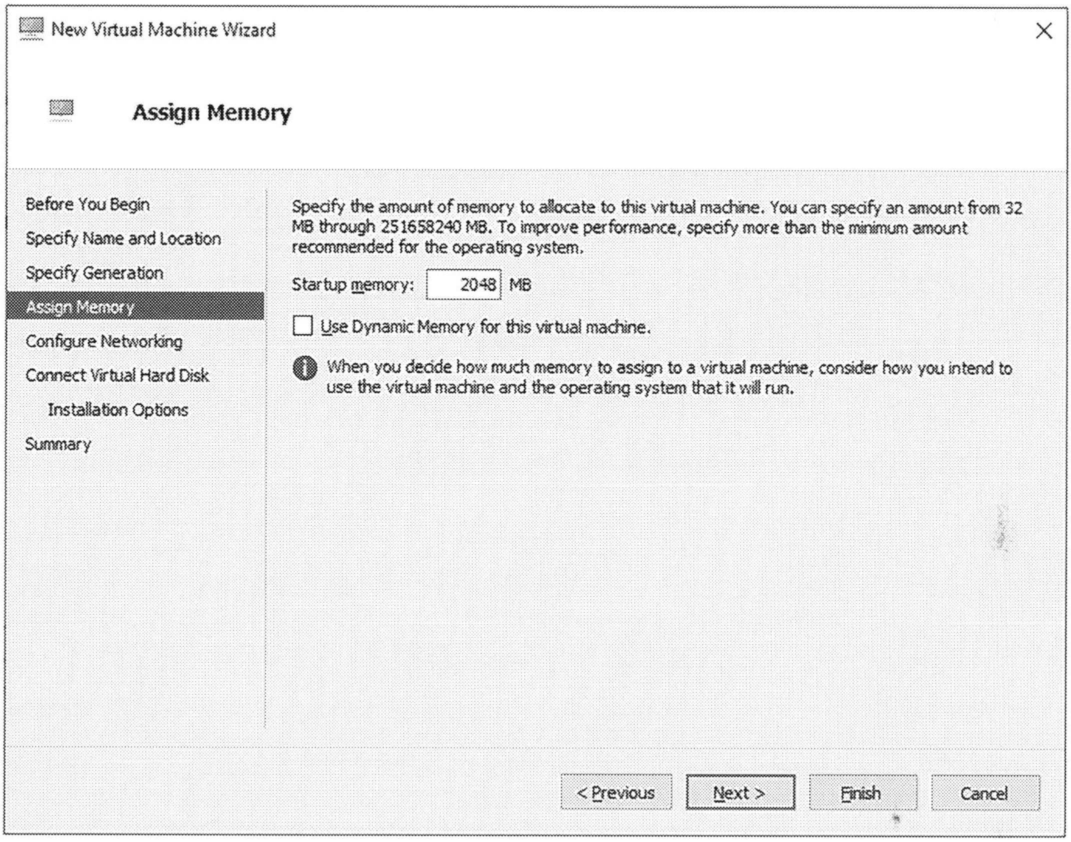

Figure 14-3. Assigning memory to your VM

Give the machine 2048 MB of memory (2 GB). I've found if you use much less, then it will not support the services required. We untick the box to use Dynamic Memory; again that is not too important for this demo, but if you want to create a SQL Server to use with more secure attestation, you cannot use dynamic memory.

Click Next twice to skip through the screen for configuring networking. We'll set that up separately once we have both our VMs. You come to the screen (Figure 14-4) to set up the virtual hard disk (VHD).

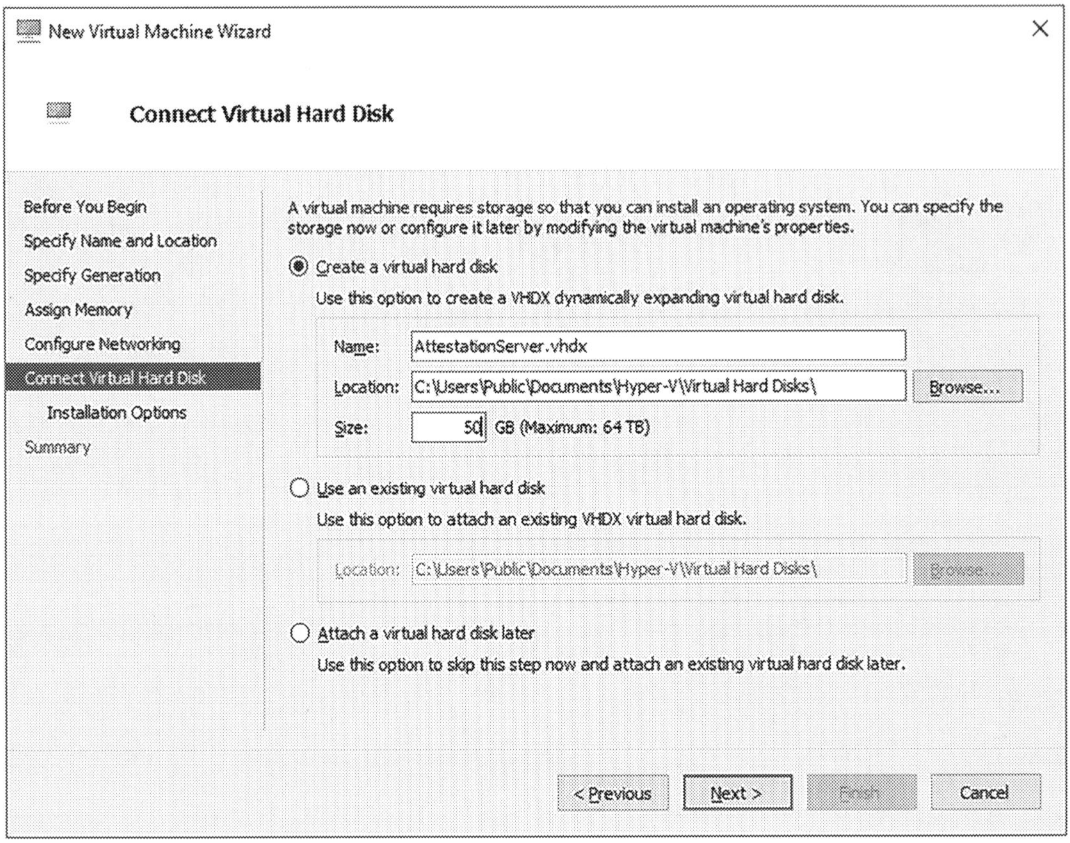

Figure 14-4. *Adding a virtual hard disk to your VM*

I've given my VM 50 GB of disk space though you can get away with less. Click Next for the installation options (Figure 14-5).

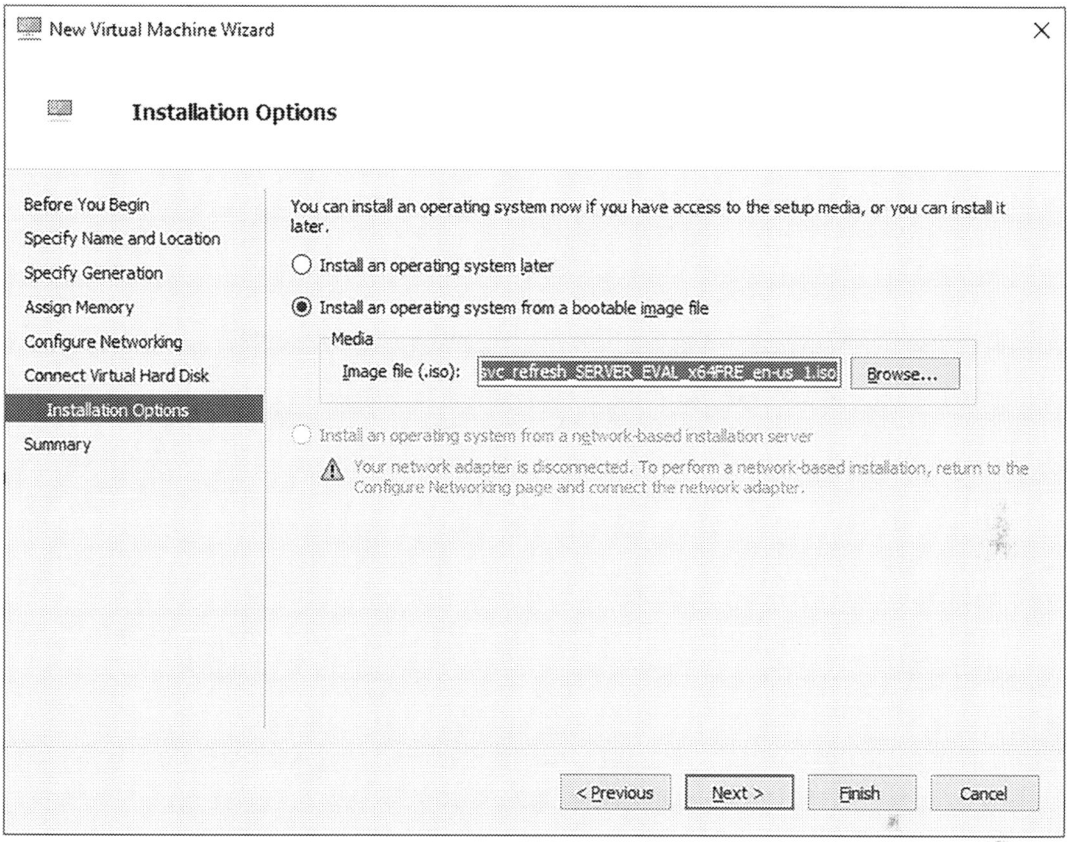

Figure 14-5. *Operating system installation instructions for your VM*

Here I've set the VM to have the OS installed from the ISO image I downloaded for the Windows Server 2019 Evaluation edition. That's the last step, so you can click through to Finish and your VM will be created. We can see our new VM now appears in Hyper-V Manager (Figure 14-6).

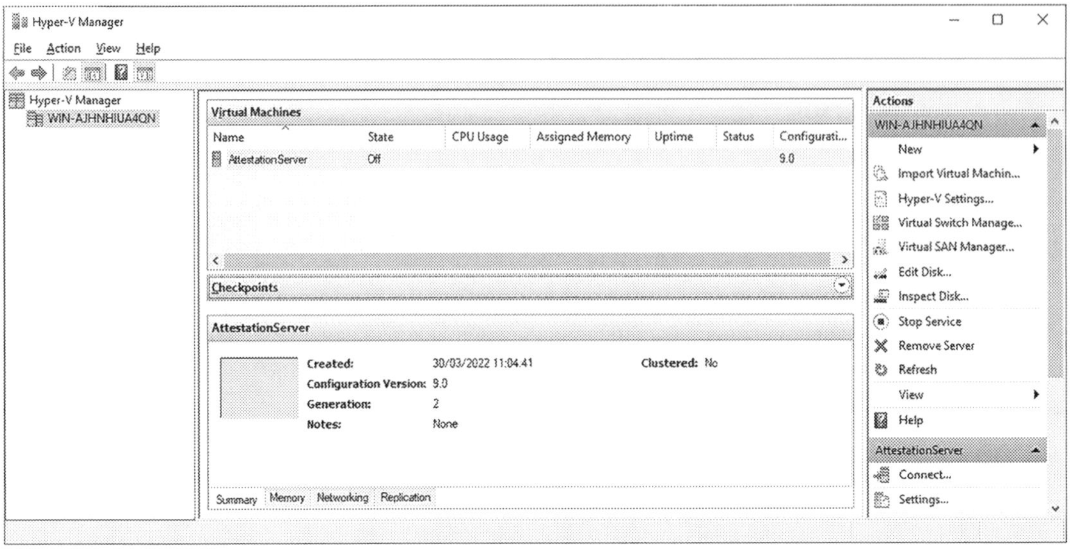

Figure 14-6. *Our new VM in Hyper-V Manager*

One thing the wizard doesn't give you the option to do is to configure the number of vCPUs for the VM, and it will be defaulted to one. You may get away with that for the attestation server, but I configured mine with two. You can access the settings for that by right-clicking the VM in Hyper-V Manager and selecting Settings. Then select Processor in the left-hand pane and specify the number of vCPUs on the right (Figure 14-7).

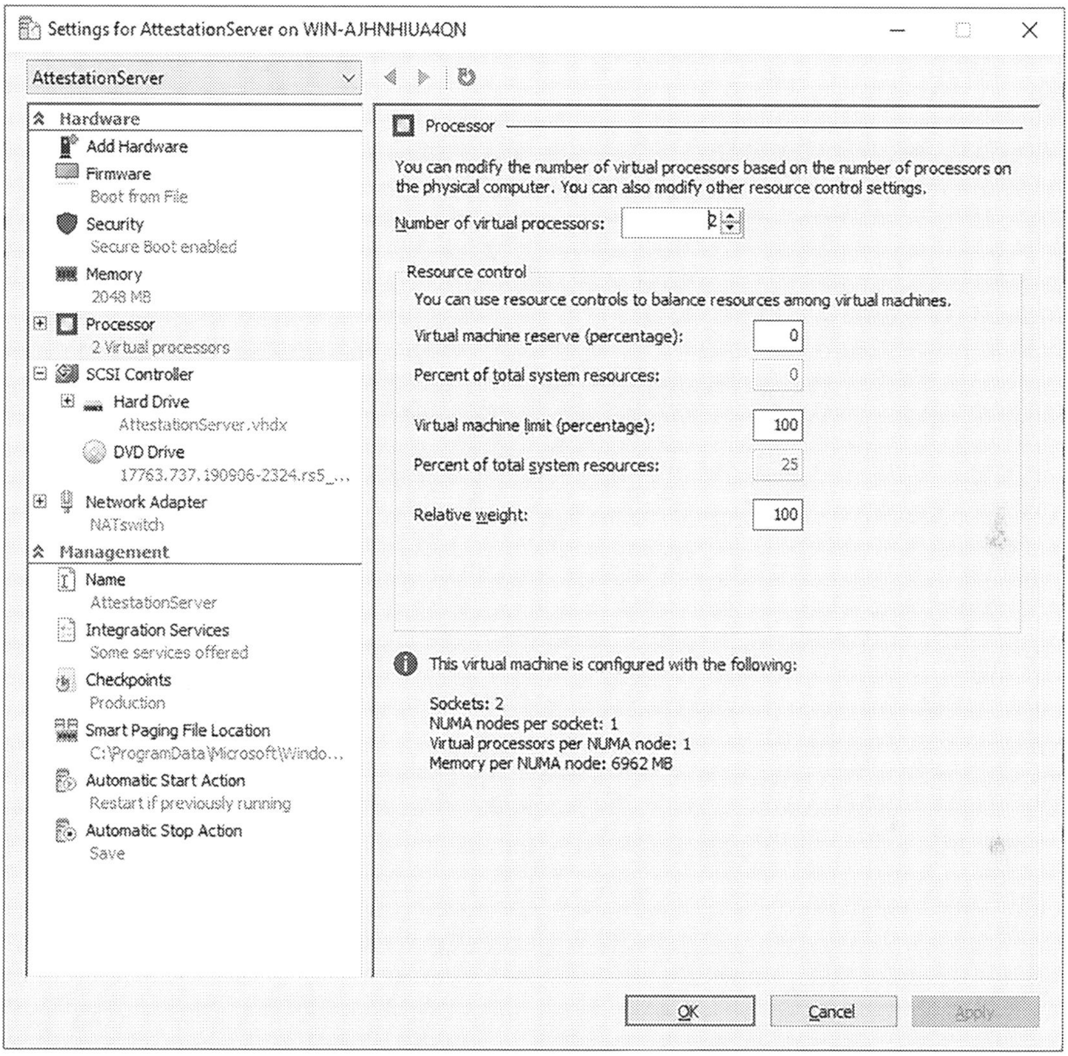

Figure 14-7. *Configuring the number of vCPUs for your VM*

Now we can install the OS. Right-click the VM and select Start, and then right-click again and select Connect. A terminal opens up into the VM. I find I usually get a boot failure initially and have to reboot to get it to pick up the bootable virtual DVD drive. You do this with the Action menu and selecting Ctrl+Alt+Delete, or you can use the button on the toolbar that does the same. When it restarts, you need to press any key to get it to boot into the server installation. The server installation is very simple, so I'll leave you to progress through that on your own. The only important thing to specify is that when prompted to specify the version of Windows Server you want to install, you want to select Windows Server 2019 Datacenter Evaluation (Desktop Experience).

Once that's complete, repeat all these steps to set up a VM to run SQL Server. I've called mine AlwaysEncryptedSQLServer. In the case of SQL Server I configured mine with four vCPUs; if you are tight on capacity, you may get away with two but make sure you specify more that the default of one.

When you're done, you now have two new VMs in Hyper-V manager.

Setting Up Networking

For the sake of the demo and to allow you to have a setup you can test on your single machine, we're going to set up a virtual NAT (Network Address Translation) network between your physical machine and the new VMs we have created. This is supported in Hyper-V for Windows 10 onward.

You can run into issues if you already have a NAT network defined. This may be the case if you're already using Hyper-V and have networking set up. In that case you may want to skip the steps of setting up a new NAT network and use what you already have in place.

The first step is to create a new NAT network on your host machine. Open PowerShell as an administrator. Then run the following command to create an internal switch:

```
New-VMSwitch -SwitchName NATswitch -SwitchType Internal
```

Then run the following command to retrieve the ifIndex for the new adapter; it will show up in the list of Interfaces as vEthernet (NATswitch):

```
Get-NetAdapter
```

Next, we configure a static IP address for that adapter with this command:

```
New-NetIPAddress -IPAddress 192.168.0.1 -PrefixLength 24 -InterfaceIndex
<ifIndex from last command>
```

Finally, we configure NAT with this command:

```
New-NetNat -Name NATnetwork -InternalIPInterfaceAddressPrefix
192.168.0.0/24
```

Now we can go and set up the networking on each VM. We'll do the attestation server first then repeat for the SQL Server box.

First of all, you need to attach your virtual switch to the VM in Hyper-V Manager. Go to the settings for the VM, then select Network adapter on the left, and then select NATswitch from the Virtual Switch dropdown on the right (Figure 14-8).

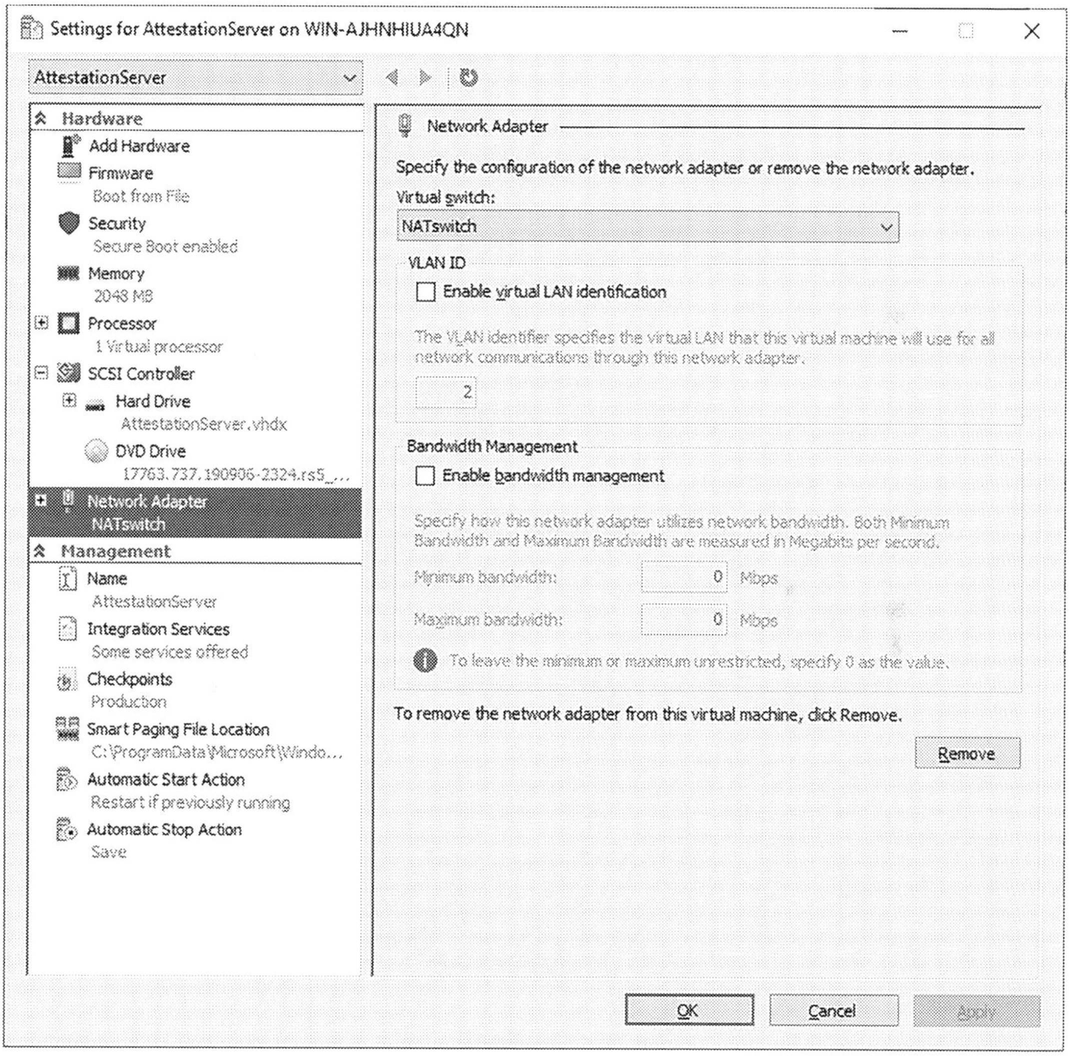

Figure 14-8. *Attaching the virtual switch to your VM*

Next, connect into the attestation server VM using Hyper-V. The easiest way to open the network settings is to go Start, Run, and type in ncpa.cpl. That brings up the Ethernet Properties dialog. From there go to the Properties for Internet Protocol Version 4 (TCP\IP). Then we'll enter the settings shown in Figure 14-9.

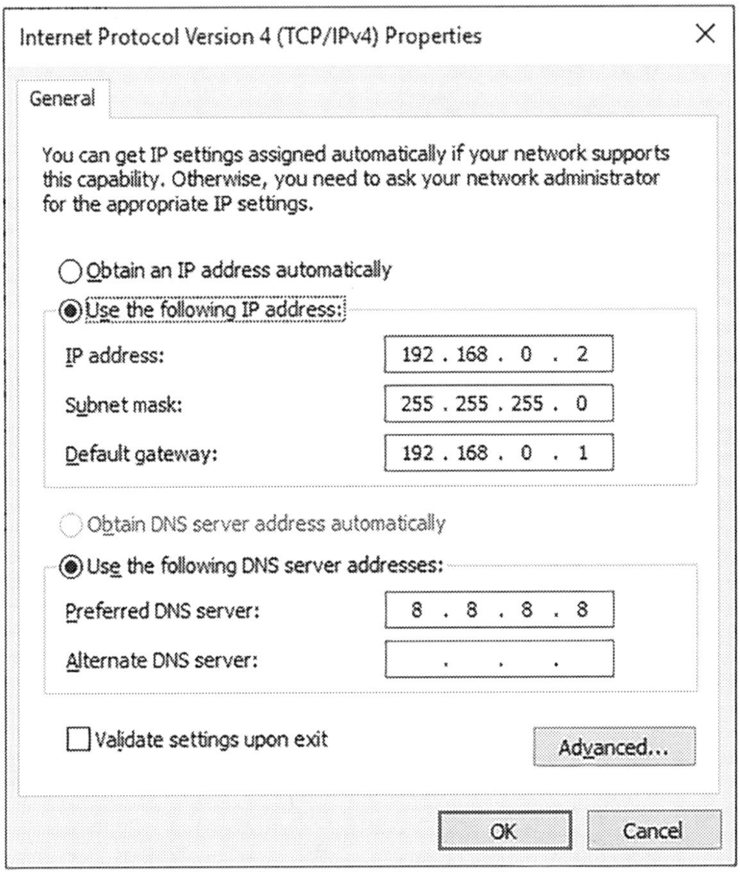

Figure 14-9. *Configuring the IP address for your attestation server VM*

You can now repeat these steps on your AlwaysEncryptedSQLServer VM. In this case give it the IP address 192.168.0.3.

Once the network is set up, it is worth making sure that you can ping both VMs from your host machine and that you can ping both the host and the other VM from each VM. This will confirm that everything is set up correctly. Networking can be the trickiest thing to get right when working with VMs. If you have an issue, you'll need to resolve it before moving on with the demo as the machines need to be able to talk to each other. One thing to check is in your sharing settings for the network and whether the machines are discoverable.

Install and Configure Host Guardian Service (HGS)

HGS is straightforward to set up. The easiest method is to do so within a PowerShell console running with elevated privileges. Connect to your AttestationServer VM, open a PowerShell console selecting to run as an administrator, and then execute the following command:

```
Install-WindowsFeature -Name HostGuardianServiceRole
-IncludeManagementTools -Restart
```

The VM will need to reboot to complete the installation. After that is complete, once again in an elevated privilege PowerShell session, run:

```
$adminPassword = ConvertTo-SecureString -AsPlainText '<password>' -Force
Install-HgsServer -HgsDomainName 'bastion.local' -SafeModeAdministrator
Password $adminPassword -Restart
```

You'll need to specify the password for the preceding command. This command will install the HGS server, and as part of that, a new domain – bastion.local – will be created and the AttestationServer VM will be joined to that domain. You can join the AttestationServer to an existing domain, but the recommendation from Microsoft is that it should sit in its own domain with access from a restricted group of administrators to preserve the maximum security. In this demo it's no pain for us to use a new domain so we will do that.

There will be another reboot after which you can initialize HGS with the following command:

```
Initialize-HgsAttestation -HgsServiceName 'hgs' -TrustHostKey
```

Install SQL Server and Configure as a Guarded Host

On the AlwaysEncryptedSQLServer VM, install SQL Server. You can attach your ISO image for the installation to the VM as a virtual DVD drive and then install from that. An installation with most of the defaults is fine, though you'll want to configure mixed authentication and give a password for the sa user. If you're reading this book, then I'm going to assume you are already comfortable installing SQL Server.

Once installed you will need to configure Windows Firewall to allow SQL Server traffic as it is blocked by default in the Windows Server installation (generally you will be warned about this during the SQL Server installation). You need to make sure you have an inbound rule that will allow traffic coming in on port 1433.

Now is a good time to check that you can connect to SQL Server on your VM from SSMS on your host machine. Connect with the IP address 192.168.03 as the Server Name, and use SQL Server Authentication with the sa account and the password you defined during setup. If you have any issues connecting, then you'll want to resolve those before continuing.

Once SQL Server is installed and you can connect to it, you are ready to configure it as a guarded host. The first step is to enable the Host Guardian feature on the SQL Server VM, which you can do from PowerShell running with Administrative privileges with the following command:

```
Enable-WindowsOptionalFeature -Online -FeatureName HostGuardian -All
```

The feature will require a reboot to complete the installation. Then we need to generate a Host Key which we will export to file as follows:

```
Set-HgsClientHostKey
Get-HgsClientHostKey -Path $HOME\Desktop\hostkey.cer
```

Now we need to copy that Host Key file to our AttestationServer VM. Copy it to the desktop on the AttestationServer VM, and then on that box we can run the following command to register the Host Key for our SQL VM with HGS.

```
Add-HgsAttestationHostKey -Name 192.168.0.3 -Path $HOME\Desktop\hostkey.cer
```

Next, we need to tell the SQL Server where the attestation server lives by issuing the following PowerShell command on the SQL box:

```
Set-HgsClientConfiguration -AttestationServerUrl http://192.168.0.2/
Attestation -KeyProtectionServerUrl http://192.168.0.2/KeyProtection/
```

It's important to check the output from this command to see if the action has been successful. There are a number of pieces of information passed back, and you should check that the AttestationStatus is "Passed."

Finally, we need to configure SQL Server to use enclaves. We can do this from SSMS on our host machine by running the following SQL command:

```
EXEC sys.sp_configure 'column encryption enclave type', 1;
RECONFIGURE;
```

We need to restart SQL Server for that change to take effect. Once that's complete, we can connect again from SSMS and check that the setting has been changed with the following command:

```
SELECT [name], [value], [value_in_use] FROM sys.configurations
WHERE [name] = 'column encryption enclave type';
```

You should see that the value of the setting is now 1.

And with that our setup is complete; hopefully it's not been too painful for you. This is the simpler version of attestation however – host key attestation – where we are setting up a trust based purely on the SQL Server Host Key. We'll look at the more secure form of attestation later on. Setting that up will require a number more steps, and there are more ways it can go wrong.

Summary

In this chapter we've looked at setting up a lab environment using Hyper-V for working with Always Encrypted with Secure Enclaves using host key attestation.

Once you have HGS and SQL Server installed, the main steps are:

- Enable the Host Guardian Service on your SQL Server.

- Generate a host key for your SQL Server.

- Register the host key with HGS.

- Set the location for attestation on the SQL Server.

- Configure SQL Server to use enclaves, and then restart the SQL Server service.

In the next chapter we'll look at how you can use the additional capabilities offered by Always Encrypted with Secure Enclaves to encrypt your existing data.

## CHAPTER 15

In-Place Encryption with Always Encrypted Enclaves

In the last chapter we set up our environment to be able to use the functionality offered by Always Encrypted where encryption activities can be executed within a secure enclave on the database server. In this chapter we're going to look at the in-place encryption functionality this offers us. Microsoft says this was one of the feature additions most requested for Always Encrypted.

Remember, in order to encrypt existing data with the previous version of Always Encrypted, the data must be passed back to a trusted client to be encrypted before being passed back to the database. This added extra overhead as well as being potentially more prone to errors – such as network issues – than if the data could be encrypted in-place. This is particularly true due to the intensive workload that can be required to encrypt a large existing dataset. Some of Microsoft's customers reported that encryption activities could sometimes take days.

We're going to look at in-place encryption and decryption of data but also rotation of Column Encryption Keys. As discussed in Chapter 11, if you need to rotate a CEK, then this requires data to be decrypted and re-encrypted with the new key and would therefore suffer the same limitations. Now that we can perform encryption activities in-place on the SQL Server, that functionality can also be used to achieve CEK rotation with less overhead.

© Matthew McGiffen 2022
M. McGiffen, *Pro Encryption in SQL Server 2022*, https://doi.org/10.1007/978-1-4842-8664-7_15

Setting Up Our Test Database and Keys

First, let's create a database and the encryption keys we require. We'll call the database TestAlwaysEncryptedEnclaves.

Run SSMS on your box hosting your VMs and connect to our database server on 192.168.0.3. Then we can execute the following SQL to create the database:

```
CREATE DATABASE TestAlwaysEncryptedEnclaves;
```

As with the basic version of Always Encrypted, we will need to create a Column Master Key (CMK) and a Column Encryption Key (CEK). We covered creating these objects in detail in Chapter 7, so I will just go over it quickly now; if you need more detail, refer back to that chapter.

To create the CMK, expand the database in the SSMS Object Explorer, and go to the Security folder and then Always Encrypted Keys. Right-click Column Master Keys and select to create a new key. If you don't have one already then you'll also need to create a new certificate to be used as the CMK using the Generate Certificate button, and we'll call our new CMK TestCMK, as shown in Figure 15-1.

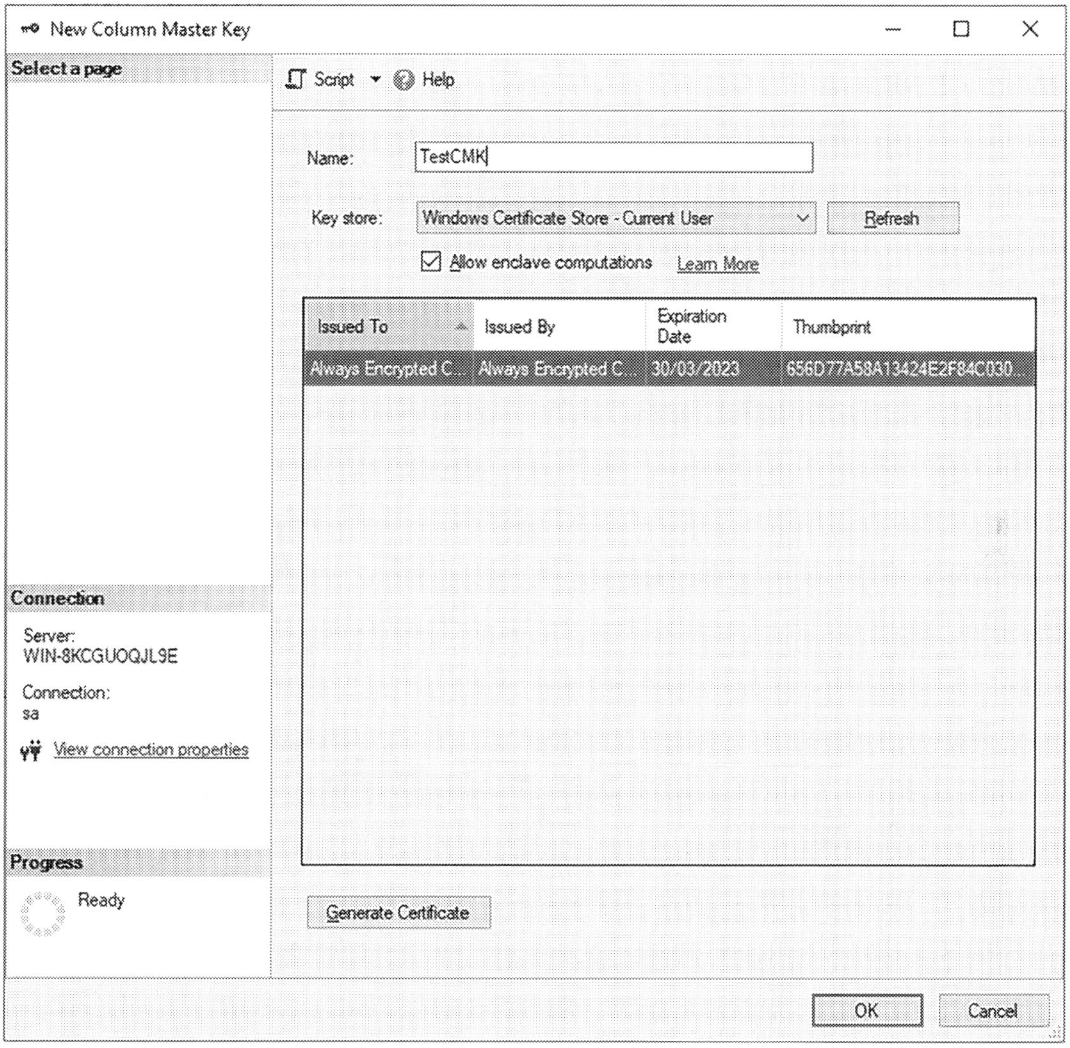

Figure 15-1. *Creating a new CMK*

An important difference here from when we did this in Chapter 7 is that we must make sure the "Allow enclave computations" checkbox is ticked. You can see from this that when we create a CMK, we make it clear what our intention is. This means that when we create a CMK for use with the basic version of Always Encrypted, an attacker can't leverage enclaves as a method of trying to access our data. Equally if we wish to migrate to using enclaves from the basic version of Always Encrypted, we will need to rotate the CMK from one that does not allow enclave computations to one that does.

Once we click okay, we can see the difference in the key definition if we script it out in SSMS. Here is the definition for my CMK:

```
CREATE COLUMN MASTER KEY [TestCMK]
WITH
(
    KEY_STORE_PROVIDER_NAME = N'MSSQL_CERTIFICATE_STORE',
    KEY_PATH = N'CurrentUser/My/656D77A58A13424E2F84C0300968A
    7E9095FA544',
    ENCLAVE_COMPUTATIONS (SIGNATURE =
    0x1D9CDD485F3FCA67E99D5AF2E18ACDB6...
)
GO
```

You can see that in addition to the KEY_STORE_PROVIDER_NAME and KEY_PATH settings that we had before, we also have an ENCLAVE_COMPUTATIONS setting and a signature. The signature is generated by digitally signing the KEY_PATH with the CMK itself. That ensures that the setting cannot be tampered with by an unauthorized user. The signature can be verified by the client driver when accessing the CMK.

Next, we create our CEK which in this case is just the same operation we have performed before. Right-click Column Encryption Keys, and select to create new one. Give it the name TestCEK and select the CMK we just created. We can now see both our objects in the SSMS Object Explorer, as shown in Figure 15-2.

Figure 15-2. Viewing our CMK and CEK in SSMS

In-Place Encryption and Decryption of Data

In order to look at in-place encryption we'll need a table and some data to encrypt. We'll start with a single row before moving on to look at how the encryption performs against a larger dataset. You can create the table and data with this SQL:

```
USE TestAlwaysEncryptedEnclaves;

CREATE TABLE dbo.SomeData(Id INT IDENTITY(1,1), SomeText VARCHAR(255));

INSERT INTO dbo.SomeData (SomeText)
VALUES ('XXXXXXXXXXXXXXXXXXXXXXXXXXXXXXXXXXXXXXXXXXXXXXXXXXXXXXXXXXXXXXXXXXX
XXXXXXXXXXXXXX');
```

Now we're ready to try encrypting some data. First, we need to make sure our connection to the database has Always Encrypted and attestation enabled. Close the current connection and then re-connect. Select Options on the Connect to Server dialog, and go to the Always Encrypted tab shown in Figure 15-3.

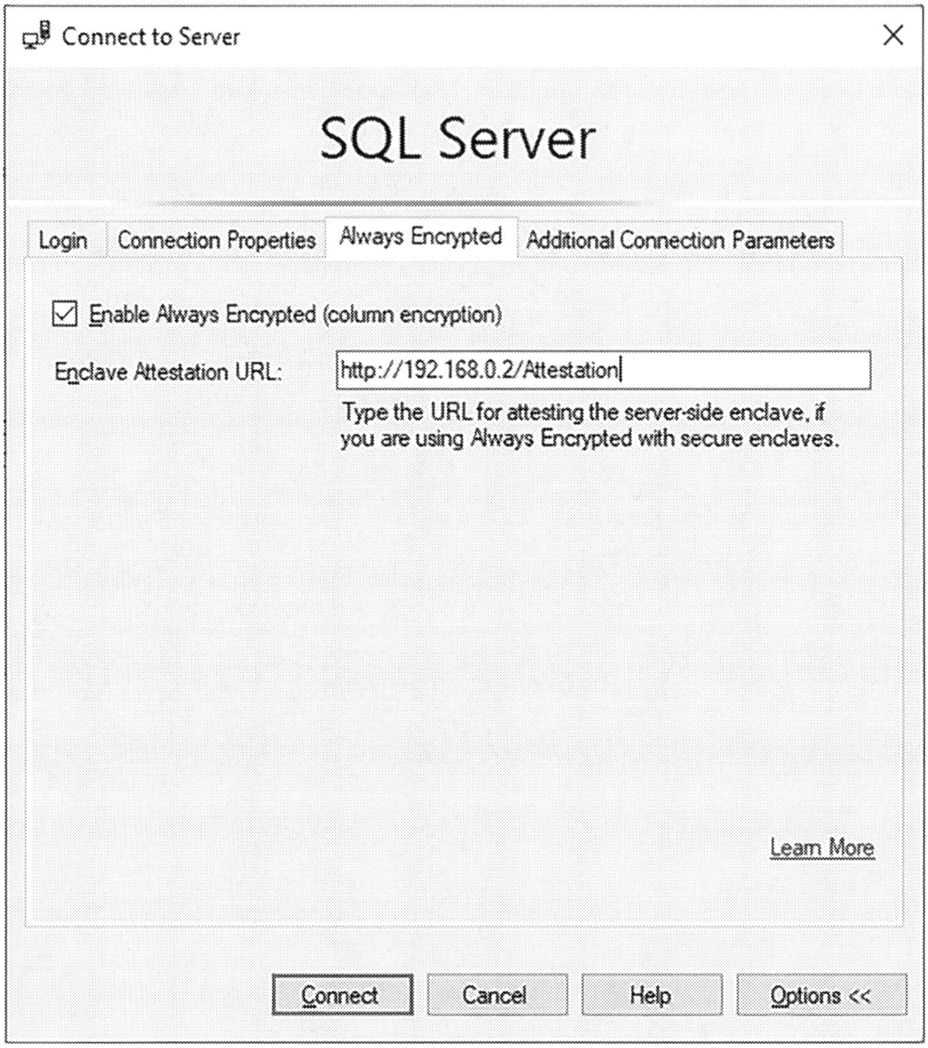

Figure 15-3. *Specifying the Attestation URL for our connection*

Besides specifying to enable Always Encrypted, we now must also specify our Enclave Attestation URL from the attestation server we created in the last chapter – http://192.168.0.2/Attestation. Once you've done that, click connect.

Now in a new query window, we can attempt to change the encryption settings for our table with this straightforward ALTER TABLE command:

```
USE TestAlwaysEncryptedEnclaves;

ALTER TABLE dbo.SomeData
```

```
ALTER COLUMN SomeText varchar(255) COLLATE Latin1_General_BIN2
ENCRYPTED WITH (COLUMN_ENCRYPTION_KEY = [TestCEK], ENCRYPTION_TYPE =
Randomized, ALGORITHM = 'AEAD_AES_256_CBC_HMAC_SHA_256') NOT NULL
WITH
(ONLINE = ON);
```

That should complete almost instantly as we only have one row of data. We can
check it was successful by scripting out the table definition in SSMS. Here is the new
table definition:

```
CREATE TABLE [dbo].[SomeData](
     [Id] [int] IDENTITY(1,1) NOT NULL,
     [SomeText] [varchar](255) COLLATE Latin1_General_BIN2 ENCRYPTED WITH
     (COLUMN_ENCRYPTION_KEY = [TestCEK], ENCRYPTION_TYPE = Randomized,
     ALGORITHM = 'AEAD_AES_256_CBC_HMAC_SHA_256') NOT NULL
) ON [PRIMARY]
```

To check that the data is encrypted, we need to open a new query window and
change our connection to one with Always Encrypted disabled. Then we can view the
encrypted data with a simple select query as follows:

```
USE TestAlwaysEncryptedEnclaves;

SELECT * FROM dbo.SomeData;
```

We see in the output that our data is now encrypted (Figure 15-4).

Figure 15-4. *Viewing our encrypted data*

To decrypt the data, if you should need to do so, is a similarly straightforward
command. You just specify to change the column to one without encryption specified as
shown here:

```
ALTER TABLE dbo.SomeData
ALTER COLUMN SomeText varchar(255) COLLATE Latin1_General_BIN2;
```

Both these operations occur within the enclave on the SQL Server VM. In order to achieve that, the client has had to supply the CEK to the enclave. As discussed earlier, there are a few steps undertaken to achieve this. First, the attestation process is followed to verify that the enclave is secure and trusted. Then a secure channel is negotiated between the client and the enclave over which the CEK can be passed encrypted. The process of supplying the CEK to the enclave is sometimes referred to as hydrating the enclave with the CEK. The CEK remains cached in the enclave, so it can be used by subsequent queries that require it, and we don't have to go through the full attestation process each time.

Performance of In-Place Encryption

We've seen that encrypting one row is, as we would expect, pretty quick. When we plan to implement this against our existing applications, however, we will want an idea of how long it might take to encrypt a column. Let's load our table up with about a gigabyte of data using the following command. Then we can try to get an idea of how encryption performs (you'll need to make sure you've run the previous command to remove encryption from the table first):

```
INSERT INTO dbo.SomeData (SomeText)
SELECT TOP 1000000
('XXXXXXXXXXXXXXXXXXXXXXXXXXXXXXXXXXXXXXXXXXXXXXXXXXXXXXXXXXXXXXXXXXXXXXX
XXXXXXX')
FROM sys.objects a
CROSS JOIN sys.objects b
CROSS JOIN sys.objects c
CROSS JOIN sys.objects d;
GO 10
```

Once that's loaded, we can execute the command to encrypt the table again:

```
ALTER TABLE dbo.SomeData
ALTER COLUMN SomeText varchar(255) COLLATE Latin1_General_BIN2
ENCRYPTED WITH (COLUMN_ENCRYPTION_KEY = [TestCEK], ENCRYPTION_TYPE =
Randomized, ALGORITHM = 'AEAD_AES_256_CBC_HMAC_SHA_256') NOT NULL
WITH
(ONLINE = ON);
```

On my VM, this takes about 230 seconds – just under 4 minutes. Bear in mind though that this VM is relatively under-provisioned compared to a production server. Still, you can see that this is not going to be a quick operation if you have a large amount of data to encrypt. Remember that we are encrypting individual columns here, not the whole database, so even if your databases are terabytes in size, hopefully you are only encrypting a small part of that. If, however, the bulk of your data size is taken up by blobs and documents that need to be encrypted, then that could be a significant undertaking. If I wanted to encrypt a terabyte of data on this VM, it would take nearly 3 days. Even if your kit was ten times as fast, it would take 6 or 7 hours to encrypt a terabyte. If you have a large volume of data to encrypt, then it will be critical that you benchmark performance on your server so you can plan accordingly. While the operation can be specified as online, you should also expect performance impact to queries while the encryption activities are occurring.

Even though you're less likely to need to do it, let's have a quick look at how decryption of the same dataset performs. Here is the SQL again to remove the encryption against our column:

```
ALTER TABLE dbo.SomeData
ALTER COLUMN SomeText varchar(255) COLLATE Latin1_General_BIN2;
```

This took just over 150 seconds on my VM – or 2.5 minutes. In general, I've found that decryption takes about a third less time to complete than encryption.

It's worth noting, as a final point on performance, that both these operations will be significantly quicker and less prone to error, than if you are not using enclaves, where the data must be copied across the network to a trusted client to be encrypted before being then passed back to the database server.

CEK Rotation

The ability to perform in-place encryption activities can also be used if you need to perform CEK rotation. As mentioned previously, it's not desirable to have to do this as it will require data to be decrypted with the existing CEK and re-encrypted with the new one which is going to be an intensive activity. If you do need to do it, however, it is good to be able to use a method that doesn't also require the extra overhead of transmitting the data back and forth across the network. Let's look at CEK rotation in practice.

We'll use the table and data we created in the previous section. Before we start we want to make sure it is currently in an encrypted state; if the last action you followed was to decrypt the data, then simply encrypt it again with this SQL:

```
ALTER TABLE dbo.SomeData
ALTER COLUMN SomeText varchar(255) COLLATE Latin1_General_BIN2
ENCRYPTED WITH (COLUMN_ENCRYPTION_KEY = [TestCEK], ENCRYPTION_TYPE =
Randomized, ALGORITHM = 'AEAD_AES_256_CBC_HMAC_SHA_256') NOT NULL
WITH
(ONLINE = ON);
```

CEK rotation can be performed through an equivalent ALTER TABLE command. We simply specify to change the encryption of the column to use a new CEK. To demonstrate that, first create a new CEK based on the same CMK and call it TestCEK2. It's worth noting that to be able to do the rotation in-place, both the new and the old CEKs must be based on CMKs that allow enclave computation.

Then we can simply execute the following command:

```
ALTER TABLE dbo.SomeData
ALTER COLUMN SomeText varchar(255) COLLATE Latin1_General_BIN2
ENCRYPTED WITH (COLUMN_ENCRYPTION_KEY = [TestCEK2], ENCRYPTION_TYPE =
Randomized, ALGORITHM = 'AEAD_AES_256_CBC_HMAC_SHA_256') NOT NULL
WITH
(ONLINE = ON);
```

In terms of performance, I have found that rotating the key takes a similar amount of time to the initial encryption of the same dataset. So, it looks like there isn't a significant overhead added by the fact that the data must be decrypted with the old key before being re-encrypted with the new one.

Once you've rotated all the columns that use a given CEK, you can then remove the old one from the database.

It's worth noting that if you have an index on a column you wish to rotate the key for (we'll look at indexes in the next chapter), then you'll be blocked from rotating the key and will receive the following error message:

```
ALTER TABLE ALTER COLUMN [ColumnName] failed because one or more objects
access this column
```

This is similar to where you try to change the data type to an incompatible one on a column which you have an index defined. To perform the CEK rotation, you must first drop the index, then rotate the CEK, and then add the index again afterward.

Summary

We've seen in this chapter that when we can use enclaves, the encryption of existing data is a straightforward task and can be carried out in-place on the SQL Server itself. Some key points are as follows:

- In-place encryption with enclaves reduces overhead and risk of error compared against the basic version of Always Encrypted as data does not need to be transferred back and forth across the network.

- Encryption of existing data can now be carried out through a simple ALTER TABLE command.

- Even though performance is improved, it can still take a significant amount of time to encrypt a large dataset.

- In-place encryption can also be used to achieve CEK rotation, which can now also be carried out with just a simple ALTER TABLE command.

In the next chapter we're going to look at the enhanced querying capabilities that Always Encrypted with Enclaves offers us.

## CHAPTER 16

Rich Querying with Always Encrypted Enclaves

In this chapter, we're going to look at the extra querying capabilities available when you're using Always Encrypted with secure enclaves. Alongside that we'll also look at indexes on columns encrypted with randomized encryption, functionality that wasn't available before for very logical reasons we've already discussed.

The new functionality is often referred to a rich querying. Remember that with the basic version of Always Encrypted the only comparisons that could be carried out with encrypted columns were with those using deterministic encryption and were achieved by matching ciphertext values. That allowed for equality comparisons, which would also allow for IN statements as well as GROUP BY and DISTINCT. You could also have indexes on deterministically encrypted columns to allow such queries to perform well.

With enclaves, encrypted data can be decrypted and read inside the enclave. This allows for a larger set of comparisons to be possible. The new functionality is all targeted against columns with randomized encryption, so the functionality for deterministically encrypted columns remains the same. You might ask why it's not available for deterministic columns. The answer is that you only choose to use deterministic – a slightly less secure form of encryption – in order to allow the required functionality. If that functionality is available for randomized encryption, then there is no need to use deterministic.

219

© Matthew McGiffen 2022
M. McGiffen, *Pro Encryption in SQL Server 2022*, https://doi.org/10.1007/978-1-4842-8664-7_16

It's worth noting that if you want to execute queries that would be supported by the basic version of Always Encrypted, you can continue to do so over connections that enable Always Encrypted but do not enable enclave computations – so have not specified an Attestation URL.

The full set of operations now available on columns with randomized encryption – where the keys allow for enclave computation – depends on which version of SQL Server you are using. With SQL 2019 we had:

- Comparison operators – such as equality, less than greater than, etc.

- BETWEEN.

- IN.

- LIKE.

- DISTINCT.

- Joins – though only nested loop joins are supported. We'll look at that more later in this chapter.

- Indexing.

Microsoft stated that this was just an initial set of functionality and extra operations may be supported over time based on customer demand. We see that in SQL Server 2022 where the following functions have been added:

- ORDER BY

- GROUP BY

- Full support for Joins

It's worth noting that the functionality we see available in SQL Server 2022 is also what you will see if you are using Azure SQL database.

Let's go ahead and look at this in practice.

Setting Up Your Database and Data

First, we connect to SQL Server from SSMS on our host machine. We're going to use the lab environment we created in Chapter 14 and connect to our SQL Server via the IP address 192.168.03 again; we'll also specify to enable Always Encrypted and supply the Attestation URL http://192.168.0.2/Attestation.

I'm going to continue using the same database I created in the last chapter, but if you don't have it or need to create it again, then do so now with this SQL:

```
CREATE DATABASE TestAlwaysEncryptedEnclaves;
```

I'm going to create a new table for looking at rich queries, populate it with data, and then encrypt the columns in place. Even when working with enclaves, it's still challenging to insert more than one row of data at a time once the table is encrypted, so for the demos it's easier to do it this way round. You can create the table and data with this script:

```
USE TestAlwaysEncryptedEnclaves;

CREATE TABLE dbo.Person(Id INT IDENTITY(1,1) PRIMARY KEY, LastName
nvarchar(50), FirstName nvarchar(50), Age INT NULL);

INSERT INTO dbo.Person (LastName,FirstName)
SELECT LastName.Name, FirstName.Name
FROM
(VALUES ('Smith'),('Jones'),('Taylor'),('Brown'),('Williams'),('Wilson'),
('Johnson'),('Davies'),('Patel'),('Robinson')) AS LastName(Name)
CROSS JOIN
(VALUES ('David'),('John'),('Michael'),('Paul'),('Andrew'),('Susan'),
('Margaret'),('Sarah'),('Patricia'),('Mary')) AS FirstName(Name);

UPDATE dbo.Person SET Age = (Id*Id) % 100
```

```
ALTER TABLE dbo.Person
ALTER COLUMN LastName nvarchar(50) COLLATE Latin1_General_BIN2
ENCRYPTED WITH (COLUMN_ENCRYPTION_KEY = [TestCEK], ENCRYPTION_TYPE =
Randomized, ALGORITHM = 'AEAD_AES_256_CBC_HMAC_SHA_256') NOT NULL
WITH
(ONLINE = ON);

ALTER TABLE dbo.Person
ALTER COLUMN FirstName nvarchar(50) COLLATE Latin1_General_BIN2
ENCRYPTED WITH (COLUMN_ENCRYPTION_KEY = [TestCEK], ENCRYPTION_TYPE =
Randomized, ALGORITHM = 'AEAD_AES_256_CBC_HMAC_SHA_256') NOT NULL
WITH
(ONLINE = ON);

ALTER TABLE dbo.Person
ALTER COLUMN Age INT
ENCRYPTED WITH (COLUMN_ENCRYPTION_KEY = [TestCEK], ENCRYPTION_TYPE =
Randomized, ALGORITHM = 'AEAD_AES_256_CBC_HMAC_SHA_256') NOT NULL
WITH
(ONLINE = ON);
```

Later we'll add some other tables so we can look at join behavior, but this will do for now.

Rich Querying

Let's look at some examples of the extra functionality we have now when querying our columns with randomized encryption. First let's look at an equality comparison as we couldn't perform that against our randomized columns without enclaves. This SQL searches for records with a last name of Williams:

```
DECLARE @LastName nvarchar(50) = 'Williams';
SELECT LastName,FirstName
FROM dbo.Person
WHERE LastName = @LastName;
```

We can execute this and get the result set shown in Figure 16-1.

	LastName	FirstName
1	Williams	Andrew
2	Williams	David
3	Williams	John
4	Williams	Margaret
5	Williams	Mary
6	Williams	Michael
7	Williams	Patricia
8	Williams	Paul
9	Williams	Sarah
10	Williams	Susan

Figure 16-1. Equality comparison against a column with randomized encryption

I'm going to run that again and capture what gets executed in the background using XEvent Profiler (we looked at how to create an XEvent Profiler session in Chapter 8).

In the XEvent capture I see the call to sp_describe_parameter_encryption that is familiar to us from looking at this with the basic version of Always Encrypted. Here is the call made in this case:

```
exec sp_describe_parameter_encryption N'DECLARE @LastName AS NVARCHAR
(50) = @pf7d20ad250ca47268bf0b34ae2fc4673;    SELECT LastName,
FirstName  FROM   dbo.Person  WHERE  LastName = @LastName;    ',N'@
pf7d20ad250ca47268bf0b34ae2fc4673 nvarchar(50)'
```

I'm going to execute that so we can see what is different when we are executing a query that requires the use of the enclave. We get two result sets back as before. In this case it's just the first I want to show you. Table 16-1 shows the results in table format.

Table 16-1. *Encryption metadata for an enclave enabled query*

Column name	Value
column_encryption_key_ordinal	1
database_id	6
column_encryption_key_id	1
column_encryption_key_version	1
column_encryption_key_metadata_version	0x77FDF2006AAE0000
column_encryption_key_encrypted_value	0x016E0000016300750072007200065006E 007400750073006500...
column_master_key_store_provider_name	MSSQL_CERTIFICATE_STORE
column_master_key_path	CurrentUser/My/656D77A58A13424E2F84C 0300968A7E9095FA544
column_encryption_key_encryption_ algorithm_name	RSA_OAEP
is_requested_by_enclave	1
column_master_key_signature	0x1D9CDD485F3FCA67E99D5AF2E18ACDB 60D17F5C911DC7...

Most of the output in Table 16-1 is what we have seen before, but there is one key difference and that is the *is_requested_by_enclave* column. The value of 1 specified here tells the client that in order to execute the query, the enclave will need the CEK specified. The client driver instigates the attestation process and then (assuming that is successful) negotiates the secure channel with the enclave over which the CEK is passed before the query is executed. All this happens invisibly in the background, and we just see the results of the query – or an error if something goes wrong.

Key to note here is that I still need to use parameters for values that target encrypted columns – even though the column gets viewed in plaintext form inside the enclave, so you could say it seems feasible that we could use literal values. That's not the case though and that limitation also applies to other actions that you might think could be carried out inside the enclave such as calculations on encrypted columns – such operations are still not possible. Also, operations such as inserting the plaintext values from an encrypted table into another table are not possible.

Another thing to note is that we are still restricted to using a BIN2 collation so comparisons will be case-sensitive.

The main new querying functionality offered with enclaves is of course range queries, so let's look at a couple of those. Let's start with a LIKE query targeting the LastName column. Here is the SQL:

```
DECLARE @LastName nvarchar(50) = 'Sm%';

SELECT LastName,FirstName
FROM dbo.Person
WHERE LastName LIKE @LastName;
```

If you're following along with this demo, you'll see that works fine and the results in Figure 16-2 are returned.

	LastName	FirstName
1	Smith	Andrew
2	Smith	David
3	Smith	John
4	Smith	Margaret
5	Smith	Mary
6	Smith	Michael
7	Smith	Patricia
8	Smith	Paul
9	Smith	Sarah
10	Smith	Susan

Figure 16-2. *Results from a LIKE query*

Next let's look at a range query targeting the Age column with the following SQL:

```
DECLARE @LowAge INT = 21;
DECLARE @HighAge INT = 24;

SELECT LastName,FirstName, Age
FROM dbo.Person
WHERE Age BETWEEN @LowAge AND @HighAge;
```

Again, we are able to run this without issue and get the results shown in Figure 16-3.

	LastName	FirstName	Age
1	Jones	David	21
2	Jones	Sarah	24
3	Brown	John	24
4	Brown	Patricia	21
5	Johnson	David	21
6	Johnson	Sarah	24
7	Patel	John	24
8	Patel	Patricia	21

Figure 16-3. *Results from a range query against a numeric column*

I don't think it's necessary to show examples of each query supported. You can see that where there is support, the query executed seamlessly. It is worth us taking a specific look at joins between tables; however, joins are going to work best where the columns we are joining on are indexed – so let's look at indexing first.

Indexes on Columns with Randomized Encryption

The ability to create indexes on our columns with randomized encryption is such an important feature. I'm sure database performance is of great importance to anyone reading this book. Imagine enabling a wider range of querying on our encrypted columns without allowing indexes. You'd be able to query against the columns, but all queries would have to scan – and decrypt – the whole table. Performance would be terrible, and the new functionality would therefore be limited in its usefulness. Implementing indexes against columns with randomized encryption was no doubt far more complex to implement than the rich querying that enclaves support – but it had to be done.

In principle creating an index on an encrypted column is a simple activity. There are however a number of considerations you need to be aware of, so we're going to look at it in some detail. There are some interesting side points – like how statistics work – that are also worth looking at.

Let's create an index on our table with the following SQL:

```
CREATE NONCLUSTERED INDEX IX_LastName
ON dbo.Person(LastName, FirstName);
```

When you execute this, you are going to get the following warning:

```
Warning: Index 'dbo.Person.IX_LastName' has an enclave-enabled key
column, however Accelerated Database Recovery is not enabled for database
'TestAlwaysEncryptedEnclaves'. Enabling it is strongly recommended to
increase the database availability during recovery.
```

This error message is strongly recommending to us that if we want to have indexes on our columns with randomized encryption, we should turn on Accelerated Database Recovery for our database. We're going to look a little bit later in detail at what this means and show what happens with and without this setting. For the moment though I'll just say I also strongly recommend that you turn on Accelerated Database Recovery for your database if you are going to have indexes on columns that use randomized encryption with enclave enabled keys.

First though, let's understand what indexes look like and how they work with enclaves. Remember with the basic version of Always Encrypted we could only have indexes on columns with deterministic encryption. Those indexes were literally indexes of the encrypted values held in the table and could therefore only be used for equality matching against, for instance, an encrypted value passed as a parameter. Ordering of the records however would be effectively random as compared to the order of the plaintext values.

With randomized encryption, we can't index based on the encrypted values as two identical plaintext values will have different encrypted values. Also, to allow indexes to support range queries, the index must be ordered in the same order as the underlying plaintext. As such the index must be an index of plaintext values, in the same order as if the column was not encrypted. To preserve security of our data, however, the details in the index must themselves be encrypted.

In general, there are a number of different types of operations that need to be able to occur against indexes:

- Reading from the index to support a query.

- Updating the index when data is modified.

- Index rebuilds.

- Rollback of uncommitted transactions in case of a service failure or restart.

When working with indexes on columns encrypted with randomized encryption, there are implications for each of these types of activities. Let's go through them in turn.

Reading from an Index

The most important type of operation that an index needs to support is being read, through scans, seeks, or lookups. All these operations will require being able to read the index in plaintext – so they must be carried out in the enclave. In general, we use an index where a query has a predicate that targets the column indexed with some form of comparison. We already know that queries with such a predicate against columns with randomized encryption require the use of the enclave, so in this case the use of an index doesn't place any extra requirement on us.

We'll look at a quick example that uses the index we've just created. We create a new query window against a connection with enclave computations enabled and then run the following query and capture the execution plan (using the Include Actual Execution Plan option in SSMS):

```
DECLARE @LastName nvarchar(50) = 'Smith';
SELECT LastName, FirstName
FROM dbo.Person
WHERE LastName = @LastName;
```

Figure 16-4 shows the execution plan:

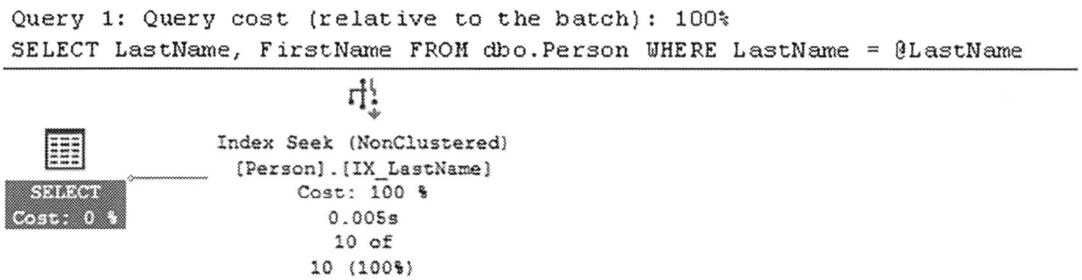

```
Query 1: Query cost (relative to the batch): 100%
SELECT LastName, FirstName FROM dbo.Person WHERE LastName = @LastName
```

Figure 16-4. Execution plan using an index on a column encrypted with randomized encryption

You can see execution plan in Figure 16-4 looks the same as if the column the index was against wasn't encrypted. There's not a lot more to say about that behavior, and such indexes work exactly as you might expect and hope.

It's interesting to also take a look at statistics against the index. Just like regular indexes, a statistics object with the same name gets created and maintained. Let's run the following DBCC command to view the statistics:

```
DBCC SHOW_STATISTICS('dbo.Person','IX_LastName');
```

Figure 16-5 shows the output:

	Name	Updated	Rows	Rows Sampled	Steps	Density	Average key length	String Index	Filter Expression	Unfiltered Rows	Persisted Sample Percent
1	IX_LastName	Apr 8 2022 2:51PM	100	100	7	0.1	136.4	NO	NULL	100	0

	All density	Average Length	Columns
1	0.1	68.2	LastName
2	0.01	136.4	LastName, FirstName

	RANGE_HI_KEY	RANGE_ROWS	EQ_ROWS	DISTINCT_RANGE_ROWS	AVG_RANGE_ROWS
1	Brown	0	10	0	1
2	Davies	0	10	0	1
3	Jones	10	10	1	10
4	Robinson	10	10	1	10
5	Taylor	10	10	1	10
6	Williams	0	10	0	1
7	Wilson	0	10	0	1

Figure 16-5. *Statistics on our encrypted index*

You can see this looks just like the statistics you would see on an unencrypted index. In particular, you can see the plaintext values from the table in the third result set and the number of rows in each step. This is different to when we looked at indexes on columns with deterministic encryption (in the section on the basic version of Always Encrypted) where both the index and related statistics object would be based on encrypted values.

Let's change our connection and disable Always Encrypted and then run the DBCC command again – making sure to select the correct database to execute the query against. Now look at just that third result set again (Figure 16-6).

	RANGE_HI_KEY	RANGE_ROWS	EQ_ROWS	DISTINCT_RANGE_ROWS	AVG_RANGE_ROWS
1	0x016855182EB71CD77235C0676E03454D7EF0605D5A833FA...	0	10	0	1
2	0x0153118E16E7CD18D48A63E21255F1CCB3882A73DFCDB5...	0	10	0	1
3	0x012F5E77C73BE2D6028A3DD208B22D540178AAED37E206...	10	10	1	10
4	0x01F8F9887CA54943A4A40F555BAAA08D5E1A5BF2710C08B...	10	10	1	10
5	0x010D8EE102C5D855ABD7BFC92F2929665833885140F7218...	10	10	1	10
6	0x010F7515FE04F3636E61602B0A68CBD708F0A79E8DAF18F7...	0	10	0	1
7	0x01A90D6ED62B6460E822539A02764CA3FB7B21A5DD432F...	0	10	0	1

Figure 16-6. *Viewing statistics on our encrypted column with Always Encrypted disabled*

This time we only see encrypted values for the RANGE_HI_KEY of each step, the statistics object itself is also encrypted. It becomes clear from this that to view this information in plaintext is another operation that requires the use of the enclave. This data is required by the query optimizer to perform cardinality estimation and find the best execution plan for a given query. In most cases, however, it's only going to be relevant where there is a predicate against our encrypted column – and therefore we are issuing a query that requires enclave computations – so the information will be available to the optimizer in those cases.

Looking at this sort of detail shows us the level of consideration and development that Microsoft had to undertake in implementing Always Encrypted with enclaves to make everything work in a seamless fashion. It's impressive that everything works just as it should – though that's also what we've come to expect with SQL Server.

Updating an Index When Data Is Modified

As we saw with the basic version of Always Encrypted, the simple updating or inserting of data doesn't require the use of the enclave. Data is encrypted on the client side before being sent over to SQL Server. Keeping the index updated however is a different matter as the index is based on the plaintext values. Such operations require the decrypted CEK, both to read the plaintext values that are being inserted or updated and to decrypt the relevant index's pages, update them, and encrypt them again. As this requires enclave computations, the data modification activity – such as in insert or update query – must be carried out over a connection that allows enclave computations. You can still insert or update values without specifying an Attestation URL in the connection if the columns aren't indexed (or use deterministic encryption). It's unlikely this causes you a problem as you're unlikely to mix connections where some specify the Attestation URL but some don't, but if you do plan to do that, then this could cause you issues. Let's look at a quick example where we attempt to insert a row into our table, over a connection with Always Encrypted enabled, but without specifying an Attestation URL. Here is the SQL for the insert:

```
DECLARE @LastName nvarchar(50) = 'McGiffen';
DECLARE @FirstName nvarchar(50) = 'Matthew';
DECLARE @Age int = 150;
INSERT INTO dbo.Person(LastName, FirstName, Age)
VALUES (@LastName, @FirstName, @Age);
```

It's no surprise that we receive an error:

```
An error occurred while executing batch. Error message is: Error occured
when reading 'sp_describe_parameter_encryption' resultset. Attestation URL
has not been specified in the connection string, but the query requires
enclave computations.  Enclave type is 'VBS'.
```

As discussed though, you don't get the error if the index doesn't exist.

Index Rebuilds

Now we come on to index rebuilds and reorganizations. These are generally carried out on a schedule, usually from a SQL Server Agent job, often running on the server itself, which means that SQL Server Agent jobs can't access your CMKs; therefore, they can't access your CEKs – therefore, how are the rebuilds going to happen? The answer is that they can still proceed – but only as long as the enclave is already hydrated with the required CEKs.

We've just been running various queries that required the use of the enclave and that required the CEK that our columns are encrypted with to be present in the enclave, so let's try an index rebuild command. In particular, let's do it over a connection that doesn't have Always Encrypted enabled. You can rebuild the index with this SQL:

```
ALTER INDEX IX_LastName ON dbo.Person REBUILD;
```

If you're following along with these examples, you'll see that executes without error. What we're going to try next is rebooting our SQL Server box which, amongst other things, will clear out the cached information in the enclave. Then we run the query again. This time we get an error:

```
Msg 33546, Level 16, State 1, Line 1
The statement triggers enclave computations, but a column encryption
key, needed for the computations, has not been found inside the enclave.
Check that: (1) column encryption and enclave computations are enabled on
connection, (2) driver is enclave-enabled. For additional reasons see:
https://go.microsoft.com/fwlink/?linkid=2086681.
```

The error is pretty clearly telling us what the problem is. The required CEK does not exist in the enclave. You don't get this error if you execute the command over a connection with Always Encrypted enabled and the Attestation URL specified and where the client the command is being executed from has access to the CMK, but as discussed, that is likely to not be possible for your SQL Server Agent jobs.

So how do you work around this problem? To be specific, how you can you ensure that the enclave is hydrated with the right CEKs before an index rebuild job needs to happen? The keys will be there if the right queries have been executed between the server restart and the job execution, but how do you guarantee that is the case?

There is a solution, but it is of necessity a bit clunky. The answer is that after a restart you can run a process from a client server (which has access to the CMKs) in order to hydrate the enclave with the keys. Microsoft provides a stored procedure to do that – *sp_enclave_send_keys* – which will cause all the CEKs which meet the following requirements to be sent to the enclave:

- Key is enclave enabled.

- Key is used to encrypt at least one column with randomized encryption.

- There is an index on at least one such column encrypted by the key.

It is perhaps an obvious point but the stored procedure must be executed over a connection with Always Encrypted enabled and the Attestation URL specified. This works after a manual restart, as long as you have a process in place so that the individual restarting the server knows there is an additional task they need to carry out once it is back up again. In case of an unexpected restart, then you need to think about how you might want to make sure it happens; if you have monitoring that triggers an alert when the server goes down, then you could use that alert to trigger an automatic action.

Once the enclave is hydrated, your index rebuild operations will be able to proceed successfully.

Database Recovery After Failure or Shutdown

The final operation we need to be able to perform on our indexes is during the database recovery process after a failure or unplanned shutdown of the SQL box. Here we might have uncommitted transactions against our tables and indexes that need to be rolled back. In the case of the tables, SQL Server can simply rollback the current encrypted value to the previous encrypted value, but for indexes, it must be able to access the plaintext values to update the index correctly. This operation happens automatically on restart of a SQL Server – but at that point in time, the enclave is empty and doesn't contain any of our keys – it won't until queries are issued against it that require those keys in the enclave. Thus, the recovery operation is blocked and so may be access to your data. You can use the stored procedure mentioned in the last section to deal with that – *sp_enclave_send_keys* – but Accelerated Database Recovery provides a more seamless option so let's look at that.

First let's understand the problem better with an example. Let's open a transaction and update the data in our Person table – this needs to be executed on a connection with Always Encrypted enabled and the Attestation URL specified:

```
BEGIN TRAN
DECLARE @LastName nvarchar(50) = 'McGiffen';
UPDATE dbo.Person SET LastName = @LastName;
```

You may receive a warning telling you that you haven't closed the transaction. Without committing the transaction, we'll now restart our SQL Server. When it comes back up, one of the activities it will need to undertake on startup is the Database Recovery process which will need to rollback this uncommitted transaction. Let's reopen our connection to the SQL box in SSMS and execute the following query:

```
SELECT *
FROM dbo.Person;
```

You should see that the query just hangs without completing. The reason why is that the index on the table is still undergoing the database recovery process. In order to roll back the changes to the index, the recovery process needs the CEK to exist in the enclave, so it is having to wait until it is hydrated. In another query window let's run a query that will cause the CEK to be sent to the enclave:

```
DECLARE @LastName nvarchar(50) = 'Williams';
SELECT LastName,FirstName
FROM dbo.Person
WHERE LastName = @LastName;
```

When this executes, the CEK gets sent to the enclave. Once that's there, the database recovery process can complete the rollback of the uncommitted changes to the index, and then the query can be executed. You may notice that the query takes a little longer than normal, and it's because the recovery process must happen before this query too can execute. Once that's done, you should also see that your original query has now completed.

Obviously, this could be problematic if queries that don't require the use of the enclave are blocked until a query that does require enclave computations with the required CEK is executed. Enabling Accelerated Database Recovery however can fix that.

Accelerated Database Recovery works through a persisted version store which maintains row versions until they are no longer required. That means that in case of recovery, we can revert to the last versions of rows that were successfully committed. The process is almost instantaneous. In the case of where we are working with encrypted indexes using enclaves, it means we still have the old version of the data, so we don't need access to the keys to be able to revert the transaction and roll back the changes to the index.

You can turn on Accelerated Database Recovery with a single command. Any open connections to the database can block the setting change, so make sure they are all closed – or pointing to other databases – first, and then execute the following:

```
ALTER DATABASE TestAlwaysEncryptedEnclaves
SET ACCELERATED_DATABASE_RECOVERY = ON;
```

Now we'll run the test again. First execute the command to update the data without committing the transaction:

```
BEGIN TRAN
DECLARE @LastName nvarchar(50) = 'McGiffen';
UPDATE dbo.Person SET LastName = @LastName;
```

Next, we restart the SQL box again, reconnect to the database, and then execute our select query:

```
SELECT *
FROM dbo.Person;
```

This time you should see that it executes instantly. Accelerated Database Recovery has allowed the recovery process to complete without the enclave needing to be hydrated with the CEK.

Joins

Finally, we'll take a look at joining between columns that are encrypted with randomized encryption and enclave enabled keys. I wanted to cover this last as we ideally want indexes on the columns we are joining. At the beginning of the chapter, I stated that joins were supported but only nested loop joins if you are on SQL Server 2019 rather than 2022 (or higher), so I want to demonstrate that specifically.

One key thing to understand about joining encrypted columns is that they can only be joined to other columns of the same data type that use the exact same CEK object. That means that cross database joins are not permitted. Even if you created identical CEKs in each database that have the same underlying key value, the join will not work.

It's possibly not that common that you are going to need to join on encrypted columns as usually you join based on Id values which are just – for instance – sequential integers or GUIDs that are sequentially or randomly assigned. These Ids do not in themselves represent personal information, so in most cases you wouldn't consider encrypting them.

Let's create some additional tables so we can work through a few examples. We'll create a second table to join to our Person table, and we'll also create unencrypted copies so we can see the differences between working with encrypted and unencrypted data. As with most of the code so far, make sure your connection specifies an Attestation URL as we'll need to encrypt data in place for our new encrypted table. You can create the extra tables and data with the following script:

```
--Create a second encrypted table
CREATE TABLE dbo.PersonSalary(Id INT IDENTITY(1,1) PRIMARY KEY, LastName
nvarchar(50), FirstName nvarchar(50), Salary DECIMAL(10,2) NULL);

INSERT INTO dbo.PersonSalary (LastName,FirstName)
SELECT LastName.Name, FirstName.Name
FROM
(VALUES ('Smith'),('Jones'),('Taylor'),('Brown'),('Williams'),('Wilson'),('
Johnson'),('Davies'),('Patel'),('Robinson')) AS LastName(Name)
CROSS JOIN
(VALUES ('David'),('John'),('Michael'),('Paul'),('Andrew'),('Susan'),('Marg
aret'),('Sarah'),('Patricia'),('Mary')) AS FirstName(Name);

UPDATE dbo.PersonSalary SET Salary = 100000 - (Id*Id*7)
GO

ALTER TABLE dbo.PersonSalary
ALTER COLUMN LastName nvarchar(50) COLLATE Latin1_General_BIN2
ENCRYPTED WITH (COLUMN_ENCRYPTION_KEY = [TestCEK], ENCRYPTION_TYPE =
Randomized, ALGORITHM = 'AEAD_AES_256_CBC_HMAC_SHA_256') NOT NULL
WITH
```

```
(ONLINE = ON);

ALTER TABLE dbo.PersonSalary
ALTER COLUMN FirstName nvarchar(50) COLLATE Latin1_General_BIN2
ENCRYPTED WITH (COLUMN_ENCRYPTION_KEY = [TestCEK], ENCRYPTION_TYPE =
Randomized, ALGORITHM = 'AEAD_AES_256_CBC_HMAC_SHA_256') NOT NULL
WITH
(ONLINE = ON);

ALTER TABLE dbo.PersonSalary
ALTER COLUMN Salary DECIMAL(10,2)
ENCRYPTED WITH (COLUMN_ENCRYPTION_KEY = [TestCEK], ENCRYPTION_TYPE =
Randomized, ALGORITHM = 'AEAD_AES_256_CBC_HMAC_SHA_256') NOT NULL
WITH
(ONLINE = ON);

CREATE INDEX IX_LastName
ON dbo.PersonSalary(LastName, FirstName);

--Create unencrypted versions of our tables
CREATE TABLE dbo.Person_Unencrypted(Id INT IDENTITY(1,1) PRIMARY KEY,
LastName nvarchar(50), FirstName nvarchar(50), Age INT NULL);

INSERT INTO dbo.Person_Unencrypted (LastName,FirstName)
SELECT LastName.Name, FirstName.Name
FROM
(VALUES ('Smith'),('Jones'),('Taylor'),('Brown'),('Williams'),('Wilson'),('
Johnson'),('Davies'),('Patel'),('Robinson')) AS LastName(Name)
CROSS JOIN
(VALUES ('David'),('John'),('Michael'),('Paul'),('Andrew'),('Susan'),('Marg
aret'),('Sarah'),('Patricia'),('Mary')) AS FirstName(Name);

UPDATE dbo.Person_Unencrypted SET Age = (Id*Id) % 100;

CREATE INDEX IX_LastName
ON dbo.Person_Unencrypted(LastName, FirstName);

CREATE TABLE dbo.PersonSalary_Unencrypted(Id INT IDENTITY(1,1) PRIMARY KEY,
LastName nvarchar(50), FirstName nvarchar(50), Salary DECIMAL(10,2) NULL);
```

237

```
INSERT INTO dbo.PersonSalary_Unencrypted (LastName,FirstName)
SELECT LastName.Name, FirstName.Name
FROM
(VALUES ('Smith'),('Jones'),('Taylor'),('Brown'),('Williams'),('Wilson'),('
Johnson'),('Davies'),('Patel'),('Robinson')) AS LastName(Name)
CROSS JOIN
(VALUES ('David'),('John'),('Michael'),('Paul'),('Andrew'),('Susan'),('Marg
aret'),('Sarah'),('Patricia'),('Mary')) AS FirstName(Name);

UPDATE dbo.PersonSalary_Unencrypted SET Salary = 100000 - (Id*Id*7);


CREATE INDEX IX_LastName
ON dbo.PersonSalary_Unencrypted(LastName, FirstName);
```

I'm going to look at joining our Person table to our PersonSalary table so that we can display the Age and Salary in a single result set. This is perhaps a bit of an artificial example and doesn't represent good database design, but it demonstrates well the points we need to understand. Let's execute the following query that joins on our encrypted LastName and FirstName columns:

```
SELECT p.LastName, p.FirstName, p.Age, ps.Salary
FROM dbo.Person p
INNER JOIN dbo.PersonSalary ps
    ON p.LastName = ps.LastName
  AND p.FirstName = ps.FirstName;
```

The query executes successfully. Figure 16-7 shows the first few rows of results.

	LastName	FirstName	Age	Salary
1	Smith	David	1	99993.00
2	Smith	John	4	99972.00
3	Smith	Michael	9	99937.00
4	Smith	Paul	16	99888.00
5	Smith	Andrew	25	99825.00
6	Smith	Susan	36	99748.00
7	Smith	Margaret	49	99657.00
8	Smith	Sarah	64	99552.00
9	Smith	Patricia	81	99433.00
10	Smith	Mary	0	99300.00

Figure 16-7. *Results from our query joining on encrypted columns*

Now let's look at the execution plan, which you can see in Figure 16-8.

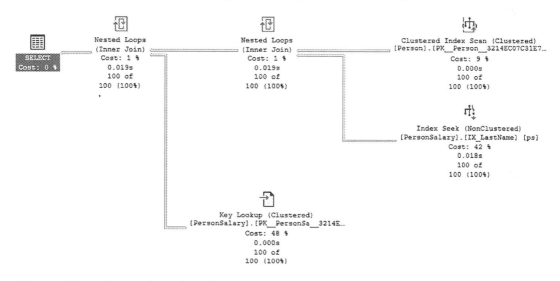

Figure 16-8. *Execution plan for our query joining on encrypted columns*

We can see the plan scans the Person table and for each row it finds the matching row in the index on the PersonSalary table. Finally, it does a key lookup to get the Salary from the PersonSalary table as the Salary isn't included in the index. Nested loop joins are used to achieve all that. Now let's look at the equivalent query against our unencrypted versions of the same table:

```
SELECT p.LastName, p.FirstName, p.Age, ps.Salary
FROM dbo.Person_Unencrypted p
```

```
INNER JOIN dbo.PersonSalary_Unencrypted ps
    ON p.LastName = ps.LastName
  AND p.FirstName = ps.FirstName;
```

Again, let's look at the execution plan as shown in Figure 16-9.

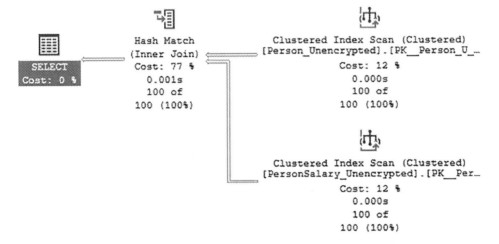

Figure 16-9. *Execution plan for the query against unencrypted tables*

Here we can see the optimizer has decided it's more efficient to scan both tables, ignore the indexes, and join the results via a hash match join. Remember, for the encrypted versions of the tables, hash match joins are not supported so the optimizer doesn't have the option to use them. Let's capture the execution statistics using the following command and run both queries again:

```
SET STATISTICS IO, TIME ON;
```

Here's the output I get for the encrypted version that uses nested loops:

```
Table 'PersonSalary'. Scan count 100, logical reads 402, physical reads 0,
page server reads 0, read-ahead reads 0, page server read-ahead reads 0,
lob logical reads 0, lob physical reads 0, lob page server reads 0, lob
read-ahead reads 0, lob page server read-ahead reads 0.
Table 'Person'. Scan count 1, logical reads 5, physical reads 0, page
server reads 0, read-ahead reads 0, page server read-ahead reads 0, lob
logical reads 0, lob physical reads 0, lob page server reads 0, lob read-
ahead reads 0, lob page server read-ahead reads 0.
```

(1 row affected)

```
 SQL Server Execution Times:
   CPU time = 15 ms,  elapsed time = 23 ms.
```

We have a little over 400 logical reads in total and 15ms of CPU consumed. Now let's look at the same capture for the query against the unencrypted tables that uses a hash match join:

```
Table 'Workfile'. Scan count 0, logical reads 0, physical reads 0, page
server reads 0, read-ahead reads 0, page server read-ahead reads 0, lob
logical reads 0, lob physical reads 0, lob page server reads 0, lob read-
ahead reads 0, lob page server read-ahead reads 0.
Table 'Worktable'. Scan count 0, logical reads 0, physical reads 0, page
server reads 0, read-ahead reads 0, page server read-ahead reads 0, lob
logical reads 0, lob physical reads 0, lob page server reads 0, lob read-
ahead reads 0, lob page server read-ahead reads 0.
Table 'PersonSalary_Unencrypted'. Scan count 1, logical reads 4, physical
reads 0, page server reads 0, read-ahead reads 0, page server read-ahead
reads 0, lob logical reads 0, lob physical reads 0, lob page server reads
0, lob read-ahead reads 0, lob page server read-ahead reads 0.
Table 'Person_Unencrypted'. Scan count 1, logical reads 4, physical reads
0, page server reads 0, read-ahead reads 0, page server read-ahead reads
0, lob logical reads 0, lob physical reads 0, lob page server reads 0, lob
read-ahead reads 0, lob page server read-ahead reads 0.
```

(1 row affected)

```
 SQL Server Execution Times:
   CPU time = 0 ms,  elapsed time = 2 ms.
```

Here we have less than 10 logical reads in total, and less than a milli-second of CPU consumption, the hash match was a lot more performant. You can see this has potential impact for you if you are joining on encrypted columns and your queries would work best with a hash match. Nested loops generally work best where you end up with only a small set of records as the parent of the loop and then each of those is looked up in the child table. Hash match is generally best where there are a large number of records on both sides.

To close off, let's just look at what happens if you try to force a hash match join against your encrypted tables as shown in the following query:

```
SELECT p.LastName, p.FirstName, p.Age, ps.Salary
FROM dbo.Person p
INNER HASH JOIN dbo.PersonSalary ps
    ON p.LastName = ps.LastName
  AND p.FirstName = ps.FirstName;
```

We get an error:

```
Msg 8622, Level 16, State 1, Line 202
Query processor could not produce a query plan because of the hints defined
in this query. Resubmit the query without specifying any hints and without
using SET FORCEPLAN.
```

If you are using SQL Server 2019, then you need to be aware of this if you are implementing encryption against an existing application and you use such query hints, or other methods of attempting to force a plan, where they might target columns you want to encrypt. From SQL Server 2022, all join types are supported so this is not an issue.

Summary

In this chapter, we've looked at rich queries, indexes, and joins against columns with randomized encryption. In general, all these things work as seamlessly as you expect.

Key things to remember about rich querying:

- With enclaves you can perform range and equality queries against columns with randomized encryption.

- Range queries however still cannot be executed against columns using deterministic encryption.

Key things to remember about indexes:

- Indexes (and associated statistics objects) on columns with randomized encryption are based on the plaintext values in the column but are themselves encrypted so they can only be read inside the enclave.

- When working with indexes on columns with randomized encryption, you should turn Accelerated Database Recovery on.

- When you have an index on a column with randomized encryption, you can only insert or update data on a connection that allows enclave computations.

- In order to perform index maintenance, the enclave must already be hydrated with any CEKs relating to the columns in the index.

Key things to remember about joins:

- Joins are supported between columns encrypted with randomized encryption, but the columns must be encrypted using the same CEK object.

- Only nested loop joins are supported in SQL Server 2019; in some cases, this may have performance impact on your queries. In SQL Server 2022, the full set of join types is supported so this is not a problem.

That closes this look at the extra functionality offered when using Always Encrypted with enclaves. In the next chapter we'll look at how you go about setting up the more secure form of attestation.

CHAPTER 17

Setting Up TPM Attestation

In Chapter 14 we looked at setting up Always Encrypted with secure enclaves using host key attestation. Microsoft recommends using host key mode in dev/test scenarios or where you don't have a physical TPM (Trusted Platform Module) – though you can use TPM mode in some virtualized scenarios. A TPM is usually a physical chip that sits on the motherboard of your computer, but you can have virtualized TPMs on VMs.

TPM attestation is the more secure form of attestation and allows HGS to verify that your SQL Server hasn't been tampered with. In TPM mode we are protected against even sophisticated hardware and software attacks, though it is important to understand that if you are using TPM mode in a virtualized scenario, HGS can only attest to the security of the virtual machine and not the underlying host. That might mean that the memory of the VM was accessible from the virtual host and that plaintext queries or data might therefore be retrievable from the enclave.

The underlying principle of Always Encrypted with secure enclaves is that the enclave is a trusted and secure portion of memory where cryptographic operations can be carried out and plaintext data and keys can be interacted without it being possible to access them from the outside. The technology that supports enclaves is known as virtualization-based security (VBS) and is based on Windows Hypervisor, using the same principles that prevent two VMs running on the same host to access each other's memory.

In order for a client to know that it's talking to a legitimate instance of VBS, it must be able to verify that both the hardware and software are legitimate and haven't been tampered with. The TPM is used for that. Among other functions the TPM captures measurements during the boot process that can be used to verify the health of the server from security standpoint. As part of that, the unique identifier for the VBS instance is captured which means that it cannot be impersonated. Secure boot is also

© Matthew McGiffen 2022
M. McGiffen, *Pro Encryption in SQL Server 2022*, https://doi.org/10.1007/978-1-4842-8664-7_17

recommended to be enabled for your SQL Server, and that can be used to verify that the boot processes are the legitimate Microsoft ones and have not been intercepted or hacked.

Prerequisites for Your SQL Server to Support TPM Attestation

Your SQL Server must satisfy a number of requirements to use TPM attestation in addition to having SQL Server 2019 or higher installed.

- The server OS must be Windows 10 Enterprise edition version 1809 or higher or Windows Server 2019 or higher.

- It must have a TPM chip with version 2.0 rev 1.16, and the TPM must have a valid Endorsement Key Certificate.

- The CPU must have support for the correct virtualization technologies. This should be Intel VT-x with Extended Page Table or AMD-V with Rapid Virtualization Indexing.

If you are attempting to use enclaves with TPM attestation on a virtual server, then you need to make sure the VM supports nested virtualization. If you're using Hyper-V (2016 or later) or Azure, then it's recommended you use a Generation 2 VM to support this. One place you may run into issues with a virtualized server is whether the endorsement key certificate for the virtual TPM is trusted. You may need to contact your hypervisor vendor to obtain the root and intermediate certificates to install on your HGS box so that it can trust this certificate.

Artifacts That Are Required by Attestation

There are a few items that we need to collect from our SQL Server and register with HGS. The attestation server will use these for verifying the ongoing health and security of the database server. We'll look at how you collect and register them when we go over setting things up, but for now let's just look at what each of them are.

TPM Endorsement Key Certificate

Every TPM chip has a certificate with a unique asymmetric key. We capture the certificate and public key from the SQL Server's TPM and register these with HGS. These can be used to verify the identity of the server. They are sometimes referred to as the platform identifier.

TPM Baseline

TPM captures a number of items known as platform control registers (PCRs) during the boot process. These measure the firmware and OS configuration. We capture this information and register it as a baseline with HGS. This baseline is often referred to as a "fingerprint." If any of the boot characteristics change, then that will alter the fingerprint so HGS can check that to identify if there has been any tampering. Items captured include the VBS configuration.

Code Integrity Policy

TPM attestation requires that we have a code integrity policy defined and implemented on our SQL box. Code integrity is a feature that makes sure drivers and system files on the server are trusted before allowing them to run. We collect this from the SQL Server and register it with HGS. HGS can then use this during attestation to verify that the code integrity policy is still in place and hasn't been tampered with.

Through the combination of these three items, the attestation process is able to verify that:

- The SQL Server is who is it says it is. It is definitely the same server that we registered with HGS in the first place.

- The hardware hasn't been tampered with.

- The software hasn't been tampered with.

Installing and Configuring HGS

We looked at setting up HGS for our demo environment in Chapter 14. For production usage you'll want an HGS cluster to maintain high availability. It's beyond the scope of this book to go into details about setting up an HGS cluster, but Microsoft provides plenty of documentation on how you can achieve the required tasks.

Once the cluster is set up, we are ready to perform the extra configuration required for Always Encrypted with enclaves using TPM attestation.

First we need to switch to TPM attestation; to do that, we open an elevated PowerShell module and execute the following on the HGS host machine:

```
Set-HgsServer -TrustTpm
```

All HGS servers in your cluster will now use TPM attestation with SQL Server.

The last step we need to take with HGS is to import TPM vendor root (and intermediate) certificates into the HGS server's Trusted TPM Root Certificate store. Each TPM has a certificate with an endorsement key. The certificate is signed by the manufacturer of the TPM module. In order for HGS to know that the TPM can be trusted, it must be able to verify that it is signed by a trusted source.

Microsoft maintains a package which holds a list of known and trusted TPM vendor root certificates. You can find and download it by searching for "Install trusted TPM root certificates" and following the instructions in the documentation for the package.

The package contains the required certificates for most vendors. By default it will install all of them, but you can remove any you don't require before running the included setup command. You may however find that the required certificates for the hardware vendor of your SQL Server machine don't exist, in which case you will need to contact them directly to obtain them. This may also occur if you are working with your database server virtualized, either within an on-premises hypervisor or in the cloud.

The package installs required root certificates to the TrustedTPM_RootCA certificate store and intermediate certificates to the TrustedTPM_IntermediateCA certificate store.

Configuring the SQL Server

There are a number of steps we need to take to configure our SQL Server and register it with HGS. Some of these steps are the same as when we were setting things up in host key mode to create our demo environment. I'll go over these here again and provide a little more detail as you are more likely to run into issues when you are setting things up for TPM attestation.

Install the Attestation Client Components

In order for SQL Server to talk to HGS as part of the attestation process, we need to install the Host Guardian Hyper-V support feature, so let's do that on our SQL box. Open a PowerShell console with administrative privileges and run the following command (the installation will require a reboot to complete):

```
Enable-WindowsOptionalFeature -Online -FeatureName HostGuardian -All
```

The installation will also configure and enable VBS if necessary.

Making Sure VBS Is Configured Correctly

To be able to register our SQL Server with HGS, it must have a permitted configuration of VBS. Remember VBS is used to host the enclave, so we want to be sure that it is set up in a secure manner. There are a number of properties of VBS that we are particularly interested in in the context of running secure enclaves:

- **Base Virtualization Support** – this represents the hardware features required to run a hypervisor, and therefore an enclave, so this must exist.

- **Secure Boot** – this requires that the boot loader for your system is one that has been digitally signed by Microsoft. We can run Always Encrypted with enclaves without secure boot enabled, but it is recommended that we do use it.

- **DMA (Direct Memory Attack) Protection** – this protects our enclave memory from direct attacks. We really want to have this enabled in our production environments, but in some cases it will not be available where we are running SQL Server on a VM.

We can check our VBS configuration through the Windows System Information tool which we can launch through the Run dialog by typing *msinfo32.exe*. Figure 17-1 shows the VBS configuration on my system.

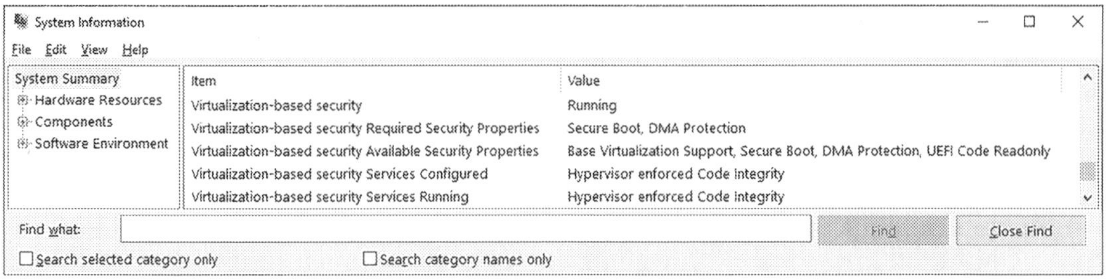

Figure 17-1. *Viewing our VBS configuration in the System Information Tool*

You find the virtualization-based security settings in the system summary page by scrolling down. The most important setting is that VBS is running. If it's not, then it's likely that one or more of the "Required Security Properties" aren't listed in the "Available Security Properties." In this case, your first port of call should be to see if you can enable the missing features, and you may need to contact your hardware vendor to see if that is possible. If the feature can't be enabled, then you can lower the requirements for VBS to remove Secure Boot and/or DMA Protection. You do this via a registry key which you can modify via PowerShell (running as an administrator):

```
Set-ItemProperty -Path HKLM:\SYSTEM\CurrentControlSet\Control\DeviceGuard
-Name RequirePlatformSecurityFeatures -Value 0
```

The value you set for the registry key depends on which properties you wish to be required:

0 – no security features are required.

1 – only Secure Boot is required.

2 – only DMA is required.

3 – both Secure Boot and DMA are required.

You will need to reboot after changing this setting, after which you can then go and check again whether VBS is running.

Configure the Attestation URL

This is the same step we carried out previously for host key attestation. The only difference is that in this case you will use your production attestation URL for HGS (which is likely to be a cluster name). Execute the following command in an elevated PowerShell console.

```
Set-HgsClientConfiguration -AttestationServerUrl "https://MyHGSCluster/
Attestation" -KeyProtectionServerUrl http://localhost
```

If you're not certain what your attestation URL is, you can run Get-HgsServer on any HGS server to get the cluster name.

Note that the KeyProtectionServerUrl parameter is used for key protection, but Always Encrypted doesn't use this so we are effectively setting it to a dummy value.

Configuring a Code Integrity Policy

HGS requires that all computers registered for TPM attestation have a code integrity policy in place. The policy should be implemented via Windows Defender Application Control (WDAC). WDAC polices prevent software from running on the machine if it is not from a trusted publisher or if the files used don't match the registered hashed values for the software. This prevents hacked versions of software from being installed or executed. If you already have a WDAC code integrity policy defined on your SQL box, then you can skip this step.

Windows has sample policies you can use. You will need to convert the sample policy to a binary format that can be understood by the OS and HGS. This example is based on the AllowAll sample policy and disables enforcement and user mode code protection which are not required for our purposes and put extra restrictions on the system:

```
$tempolicyfile = "C:\Temp\AllowAll_Temp.xml"
Copy-Item -Path "$env:SystemRoot\schemas\CodeIntegrity\ExamplePolicies\
AllowAll.xml" -Destination $tempolicyfile
Set-RuleOption -FilePath $tempolicyfile -Option 0 -Delete
Set-RuleOption -FilePath $tempolicyfile -Option 3

ConvertFrom-CIPolicy -XmlFilePath $tempolicyfile -BinaryFilePath "C:\Temp\
MyCIPolicy.bin"
```

Here we copy the sample policy to our C:\Temp folder (make sure you use a destination that exists), make the required edits, and then create a binary version of the file. The binary file can be used to deploy the policy to your SQL Servers using group policy.

It's beyond the scope of this book to go into WDAC policies and using Group Policy in any detail, so you may want to work with your security team and system administrators to fulfill this requirement.

Collect and Register Attestation Artifacts

We now have everything set up, and we are ready to collect the required artifacts in order to be able to register the SQL Server with HGS in TPM mode.

Remember there are three things we need to collect:

- The TPM Endorsement Key certificate and public key

- The TPM baseline

- The applied code integrity policy

We can collect them all with the following script (again we are saving them to C:\Temp):

```
# Collect the Endorsement Key certificate and public key
$ComputerName = $env:computername
$OutputPath = "C:\Temp"
(Get-PlatformIdentifier -Name $ComputerName).Save("$OutputPath\
$ComputerName-EK.xml")

# Collect the TPM baseline
Get-HgsAttestationBaselinePolicy -Path "$OutputPath\$ComputerName.tcglog"
-SkipValidation

# Collects the applied code integrity policy
Copy-Item -Path "$env:SystemRoot\System32\CodeIntegrity\SIPolicy.p7b"
-Destination "$OutputPath\$ComputerName-CIpolicy.bin"
```

You then need to copy them to the HGS box where you can register them by running the following commands in an elevated PowerShell console:

```
# Register the unique TPM Endorsement Key
Add-HgsAttestationTpmHost -Path "C:\Temp\MySQLServer-EK.xml"

# Register the TPM baseline
```

```
Add-HgsAttestationTpmPolicy -Name "MySQLServerHardwareAndSoftwareConfig"
-Path "C:\Temp\MySQLServer.tcglog"

# Register the code integrity policy
Add-HgsAttestationCiPolicy -Name "AllowAll" -Path "C:\Temp\MySQLServer-
CIpolicy.bin"
```

You may get an error when registering the Endorsement Key, saying that the key is untrusted due to a "partial chain" or "untrusted root." This can happen when required root or immediate certificates relating to your TPM's manufacturer do not exist in the correct place in your certificate store. We went over this briefly when we looked at setting up HGS earlier in the chapter, so go back and make sure you have imported the trusted TPM root certificates correctly.

For clustered or other high-availability scenarios, you are likely to have at least two SQL Servers. They will definitely have different TPM Endorsement Keys, so you will need to register this for each of them. If they have an identical hardware and software configuration, then you only need to register the TPM baseline once as it will be identical; otherwise, you may have to register this for each server. It's likely you will use a common code integrity policy, so you should only need to register this once.

HGS also has some built-in policies that are enforced in TPM mode. Specifically, there is an IOMMU (input-output memory management unit) policy which you will need to disable if your server doesn't have an IOMMU present. You can do that with the following PowerShell:

```
Disable-HgsAttestationPolicy Hgs_IommuEnabled
```

Check SQL Server Can Attest Successfully

We now should have everything set up to support SQL Server being able to attest successfully with HGS and therefore to use enclaves with Always Encrypted. Before we proceed though, we should check that attestation works (we should do this for all our

SQL Servers that may be required to attest). We can make an attestation attempt from our SQL Server with the following PowerShell command (we used the same command when we looked at Host Key attestation):

```
Get-HgsClientConfiguration
```

The most important field in the output is AttestationStatus. If this returned "Passed," then we are all good. If it fails, then you'll need to troubleshoot. Other than Passed, the most common responses are:

- **Expired** – the health certificate has expired – this can be caused if the system time is out of synch between your SQL Server and HGS.

- **InsecureHostConfiguration** – attestation has failed because of one of the policies defined. We can check the AttestationSubStatus field in the output to get more information.

- **NotConfigured** – the computer hasn't been configured with an AttestationURL.

- **TransientError** – this could be related to a network issue.

- **TpmError** – the computer TPM has reported an error. You may need to delve into your TPM logs and potentially clear the TPM, but you must pause other services that rely on the TPM before doing this.

- **UnauthorizedHost** – you don't get this in TPM mode, but rather in Host Key mode. The error is telling you the Host Key isn't registered.

Where we get the InsecureHostConfiguration error, we need to check the AttestationSubStatus to see what failed. Likely values we'll see are:

- **CodeIntegrityPolicy** – a code integrity policy isn't defined – or it isn't registered with HGS.

- **DumpsEnabled** – the computer allows crash dumps but the default HGS policy doesn't allow this as the dump files could contain sensitive information. You either disable dumps or disable the Hgs_DumpsEnabled policy.

- **FullBoot** – the computer has resumed from sleep or hibernation, so the TPM logs don't match that which would be captured for a full restart. You need to restart the computer.

- **HibernationEnabled** – the computer has hibernation enabled with unencrypted hibernation files. You need to disable hibernation.

- **Iommu** – the computer doesn't have an IOMMU device enabled. We looked above at how you disable this policy.

- **SecureBoot** – Secure Boot isn't enabled; you need to enable it on the server or disable the HGS policy.

- **VirtualSecureMode** – VBS isn't running; we looked earlier in the chapter at how you check this and troubleshoot.

Configure the Enclave Type in SQL Server

Configuring enclaves within SQL Server is the same step we carried out with host key attestation. From SSMS, we execute the following command:

```
EXEC sys.sp_configure 'column encryption enclave type', 1;
RECONFIGURE;
```

We need to restart SQL Server for that change to take effect. Once that's complete, we can connect again from SSMS and check that the setting has been changed:

```
SELECT [name], [value], [value_in_use] FROM sys.configurations
WHERE [name] = 'column encryption enclave type';
```

You should see that the value of the setting is now 1.

Always Encrypted is now set up with secure enclaves and TPM attestation.

Summary

TPM mode is the more secure form of attestation. Using TPM mode means that we are protected even from sophisticated hardware and software attacks.

In order to be able to verify that your SQL Server has not been tampered with – and that the enclave can therefore be trusted as secure – we register three items from our SQL Server with the HGS service. These items can then be verified during the attestation process:

- The TPM Endorsement Key certificate and public key. This is used to confirm the computer's identity and cannot be faked.

- The TPM baseline. This shows that the boot processes are secure.

- The applied code integrity policy.

Setting up attestation in TPM mode can be complex, and you may run into unforeseen issues; in those cases, you may need additional support from your hardware vendor or from Microsoft.

If the requirements of TPM mode are daunting, or your available hardware simply won't support them, you should consider whether using Host Key attestation instead would provide enough security for your purposes.

PART V

Completing the Picture

## CHAPTER 18

Encryption In Transit Using Transport Layer Security

When we talk about encryption in transit, we are talking about encrypting data as it is transferred across the network from one machine to another. This is an important aspect of encryption to implement as unencrypted data could be intercepted. The so-called "man in the middle" attack is an example of this, where an attacker might position themselves in the middle of the communication between an application and SQL Server, perhaps impersonating a network router, in order to intercept messages passed between the two. In addition to data, this would also include queries passed, which would give the attacker information about the database design that could allow them to fashion further attacks.

It's important to protect ourselves against this sort of exploit. Transport Layer Security, more commonly referred to as TLS, does just that. With TLS implemented, all traffic between the client and server is securely encrypted. There is no real downside in implementing TLS, except for a possible performance impact in rare edge cases, so it should be something you consider doing by default for your production servers. If you've not heard of TLS, then you may have heard of SSL (Secure Sockets Layer) in the context of encrypting Internet traffic. TLS is simply the more secure descendent of SSL, and in fact although we still commonly hear of Internet traffic being protected by SSL, in most cases it is TLS that is actually being used; it just gets referred to as SSL as that is the term more people are familiar with.

© Matthew McGiffen 2022
M. McGiffen, *Pro Encryption in SQL Server 2022*, https://doi.org/10.1007/978-1-4842-8664-7_18

All modern versions of SQL Server use TLS 1.2 which is more secure than predecessors. In this chapter we're going to look at how you enable TLS with SQL Server in order to make sure that all communications between the client and the database server are securely encrypted.

How TLS Works

TLS depends on the server, in this case SQL Server, having a certificate and associated asymmetric key pair that can be used to encrypt data. When a connection is opened that needs to be encrypted, first there is an initial handshake between the client and server. During this process the version of TLS to be used is agreed, and the server provides its certificate and associated public key back to the client for verification. Assuming the verification is successful, then a secure connection can be created.

The client generates a symmetric encryption key that will be used to encrypt the messages sent between the client and server in both directions. The client then encrypts this key with the server's public key and sends this back to the server. The server then decrypts this with its own private key. The client and server now have secure channel over which they can communicate.

It's worth noting that logons get encrypted even if you haven't enabled TLS. Whenever SQL starts, it generates a new self-signed certificate and key pair to be used while it is running. This is used to encrypt logons so they are always protected.

Obtaining a Certificate to Use for TLS

The certificate can either be self-signed certificate or one issued by a recognized certification authority (CA). Self-signed certificates are fine for development and testing purposes, but for production usage, you should request one from a valid CA. The CA could be an internal one to your organization or an external provider. Every CA has a certificate that is used to verify certificates issued by that CA. These certificates are installed in a machine's local certificate store. We can see them if we open up the "Manage Computer Certificates" Control Panel app. Trusted CA certificates are found either as Trusted Root Certification Authorities or Intermediate Certification Authorities (which themselves have generally been issued by a trusted root CA). Figure 18-1 shows the trusted root certification authorities on my system.

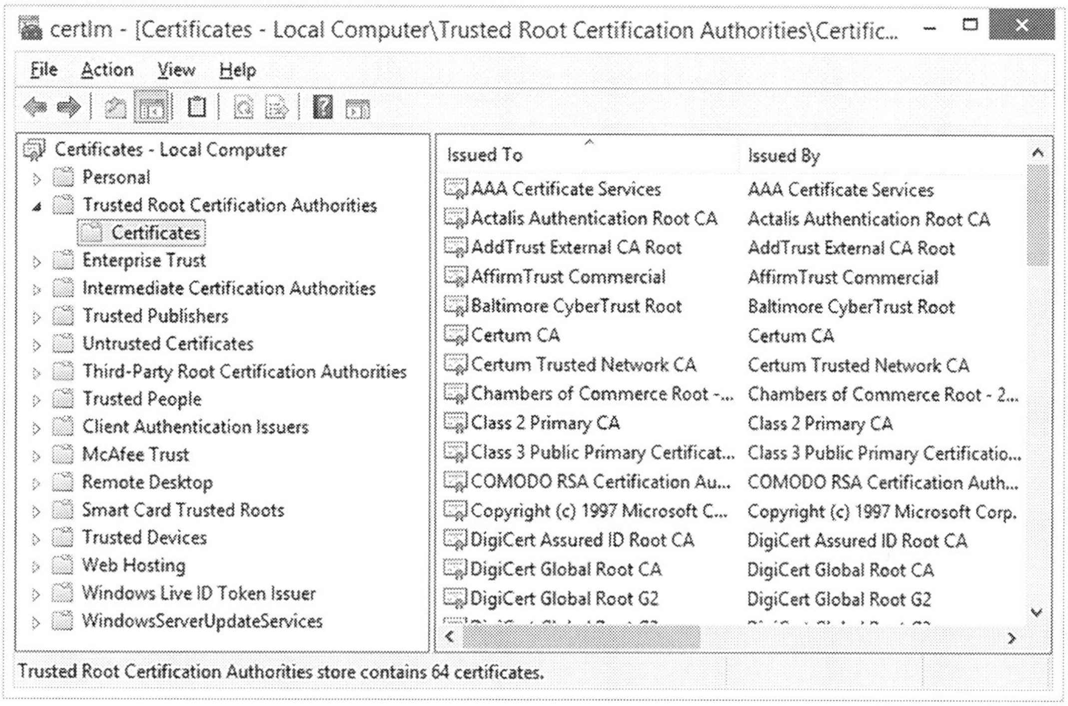

Figure 18-1. *Viewing trusted root certification authorities*

If the CA that is issuing your TLS certificate does not exist in your certificate store as a trusted CA, then that CA's certificate needs to be imported.

When requesting a certificate from a CA, the certificate must meet a number of requirements in order for SQL Server to be able to use it for TLS. These are:

- The *Subject* property *CN* field must be the host name or fully qualified domain name (FQDN) of the SQL Server. Note though that where you are using a failover cluster instance this should be instead the SQL Server Virtual Network Name.

- The *Subject Alternative Name* property *DNS* field must contain both the host name and the FQDN.

- The certificate must be created by using the *KeySpec* option of "AT_KEYEXCHANGE."

261

- The *Intended Purpose* must be "Server Authentication."

- The certificate must be valid at the point it is added to SQL Server. That means the current system time must be greater than the certificate's *Valid From* and less than the certificate's *Valid To*.

The certificate should then be installed in the SQL Server's Local Machine certificate store.

If you wish to simply create a self-signed certificate, which is what we will do here and use for our demo, then you can do so with a PowerShell command similar to the following. This command will automatically import the certificate into the local store, so it's best to run it on your SQL Server, and you'll need to open PowerShell with administrative privileges for that to work:

```
New-SelfSignedCertificate -Type SSLServerAuthentication `
    -Subject "CN=matthewmcgiffen.com" -FriendlyName 'matthewmcgiffen.com' `
    -DnsName "matthewmcgiffen.com",'localhost.' `
    -KeyAlgorithm 'RSA' -KeyLength 2048 -Hash 'SHA256' `
    -TextExtension '2.5.29.37={text}1.3.6.1.5.5.7.3.1' `
    -NotAfter (Get-Date).AddMonths(36) `
    -KeyExportPolicy Exportable -KeySpec KeyExchange `
    -Provider 'Microsoft RSA SChannel Cryptographic Provider' `
    -CertStoreLocation Cert:\LocalMachine\My `
| fl -Property Thumbprint,FriendlyName,DnsNameList,NotAfter,PrivateKey,
  SerialNumber,Subject,Issuer
```

Now we have a certificate – shown in Figure 18-2 – we're ready to configure our SQL Server to use TLS.

Figure 18-2. *Viewing our new certificate in the certificate store*

Setting Up TLS on Your SQL Server

Setting up TLS requires only a few simple steps. The first is to ensure that your SQL Server service account has access to the private key for the certificate. We do this by right-clicking the certificate in the certificate store and selecting All Tasks and then Manage Private Keys. Then you add the service account for your SQL Server and give it Read permissions. In my case the service account is NT Service\ MSSQL$MSSQLSERVER01, as you can see from Figure 18-3.

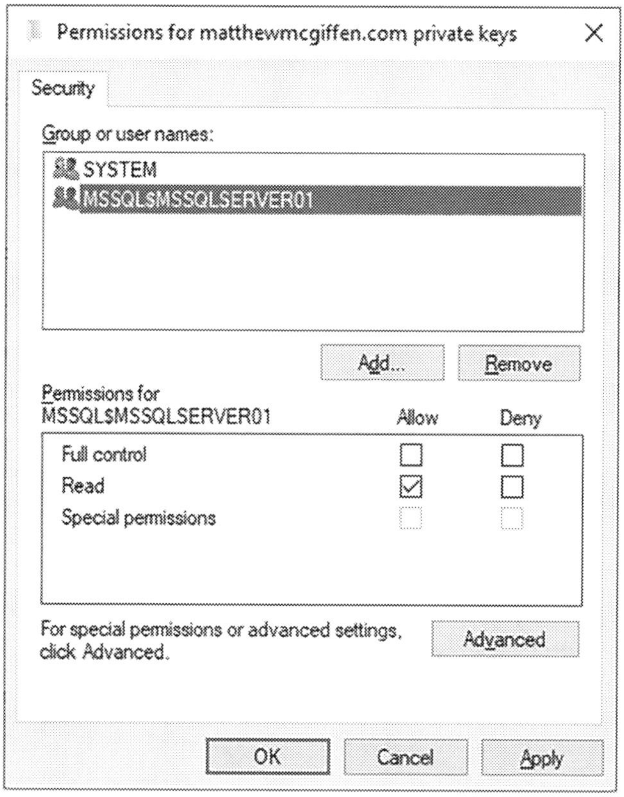

Figure 18-3. *Giving your SQL Server service account permissions to the key*

Next, we configure TLS using the SQL Server Configuration Manager on our SQL Server.

In earlier versions of SQL Server and Windows we always saw Microsoft SQL Server Configuration Manager as an item in our Start Menu. This has been replaced with a snap-in for the Microsoft Management Console (MMC) program. To open it from MMC you can go to the Start menu and then Run. Then type "mmc" in the Run dialog. Once MMC has opened you can go to File and select Add/Remove Snap-in. SQL Server Configuration Manager (Figure 18-4) should appear in the list of available snap-ins, and it is then a simple task to add it to your console.

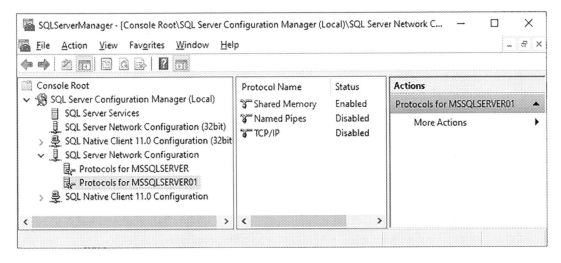

Figure 18-4. *SQL Server Configuration Manager*

I have two SQL Server instances on this machine. It's the MSSQLSERVER01 instance that I want to configure TLS on, so I right-click "Protocols for MSSQLSERVER01" in the left-hand pane and select Properties.

The dialog that opens (Figure 18-5) shows a first tab entitled Flags. Here we can configure the Force Encryption option. If we set Force Encryption to "Yes," then that will force all connections to our SQL instance to use TLS.

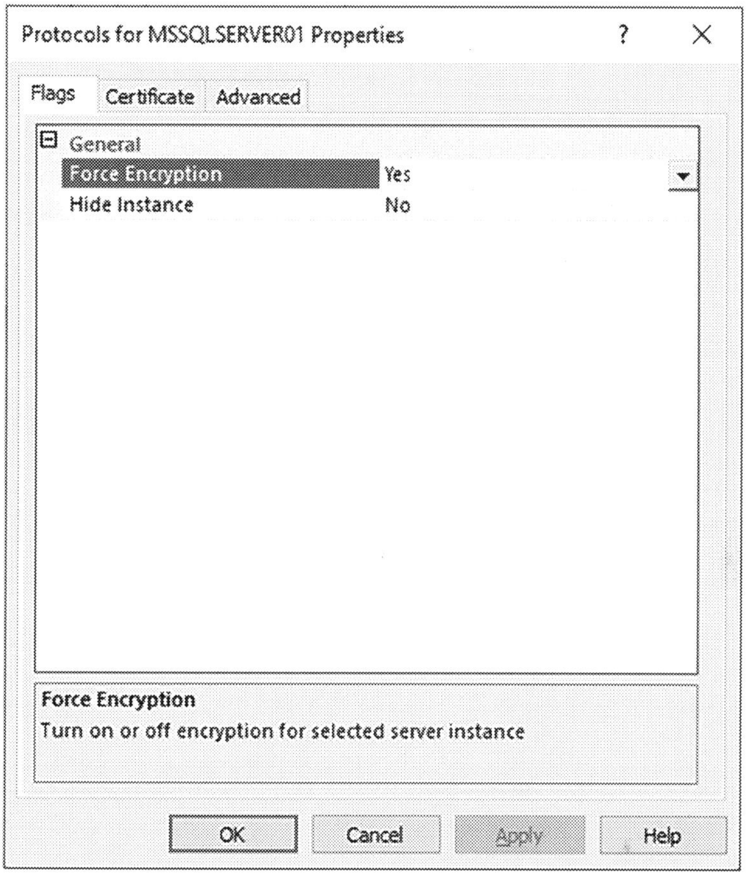

Figure 18-5. *Setting the Force Encryption option for TLS*

If you don't set Force Encryption to "Yes," then the connection will only be encrypted using TLS if the client requests that through the connection string. It's highly recommended that you do have this set to "Yes."

In the Certificate tab we select the certificate to be used for TLS, as shown in Figure 18-6.

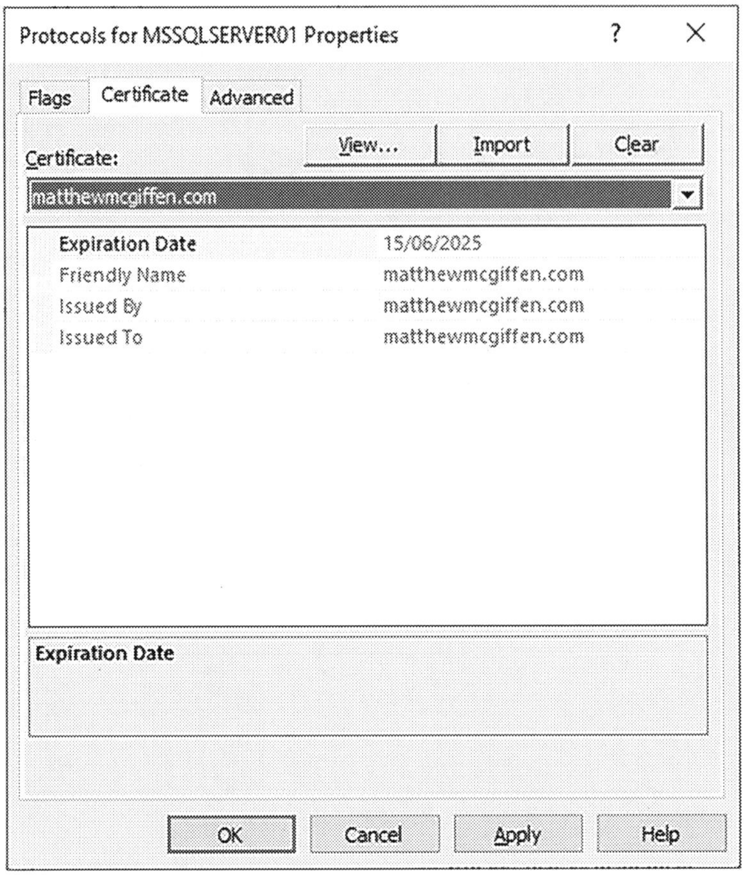

Figure 18-6. *Selecting the certificate to be used for TLS*

The certificate I created is available to select from the drop-down. If you have loaded a certificate from a valid CA, you should also be able to see and select that. If you can't see the certificate in the list, then that means that the certificate does not have the right properties to be used for TLS or exists in the wrong location. You can view the certificate in the certificate store and check all the properties are correct according to the requirements we specified in the previous section.

Once you've selected the certificate you can click OK. SQL Server Configuration Manager will pop up a message to tell you that your SQL Server instance will need to be restarted before the change takes effect. Simply restart the instance and TLS is now configured.

If your SQL Server instance refuses to start after making these changes, the most likely cause is that you haven't configured permissions over the certificate correctly. The SQL Server service account must have a minimum of read permissions over the private key or it will fail to start, so go back and check the permissions are correct and that you have specified the correct account.

Once we're back up and running, we're ready to connect to SQL Server from our client, in this case SSMS, and check that connections are now being encrypted with TLS.

Open SSMS and connect to the server, and then open a new query window. When you open a new query window, this is creating a connection to the SQL instance. Each connection has a SPID (Server Process ID), and we can use that to check whether the connection is encrypted. You can see the SPID in the status bar of your query window appended to your login name. Or you can retrieve it using the @@SPID global variable with the following code:

```
SELECT @@SPID;
```

We can see the encryption status for the connection by querying the sys.dm_exec_ connections dynamic management view with the following SQL:

```
SELECT session_id, encrypt_option, connect_time
FROM sys.dm_exec_connections
WHERE session_id = @@SPID;
```

You should see something like that in Figure 18-7.

	session_id	encrypt_option	connect_time
1	58	TRUE	2022-06-16 08:40:59.403

Figure 18-7. Viewing the encryption status for our connection

If the encrypt_option is TRUE, then TLS is set up successfully, and all our messages to and from the server will be securely encrypted. That includes both queries sent and data received back.

Performance

Nothing comes totally for free, and there is going to be some increased CPU usage from the requirement to encrypt data. Queries sent over from the client are comparatively small so the overhead here should not be too large.

Where you could see a hit however is in the data being sent back from SQL Server. If the result set is large, for instance, MBs in size, then that may slow down the query time and increase CPU by a noticeable amount. In most cases it's not going to be enough to worry you, but there could be situations like large reporting or data warehouse loads where you see an issue.

In that case you could consider allowing some connections to go unencrypted. You would do this by configuring TLS with Force Encryption set to "No." Then you would need to specify the encryption option for connections in the connection strings from the client applications.

Summary

Encryption in transit is an important part of your overall encryption strategy. As TLS is simple to set up and has minimal downside, you should consider enabling it by default for your production database servers.

Key points to remember are:

- TLS ensures that both queries sent from the client and data received back are both securely encrypted.

- TLS doesn't cover logins which are automatically encrypted out of the box by SQL Server.

- TLS can use a self-signed certificate or one issued by a trusted certification authority (CA). The latter is more secure and is what you should be considering for production usage.

- The only potential downside with TLS is performance impact, and this is only likely to occur if you are returning very large result sets back to a client. In this case you could consider having encryption on for some workloads but not others.

In the next chapter we're going to look at how you should securely store passwords in your database, for instance, those associated with logons for your application.

## CHAPTER 19

Hashing and Salting of Passwords

In this chapter we're going to look at how you should go about securely storing passwords in your database. In most cases these will be passwords related to user logons for your application. In many ways a password is the most sensitive piece of information that we might store. If a user's password is obtained by an attacker, then it is likely they can access all of the other information we hold about a user. Worse than that, despite recommendations to the contrary, most users reuse the same password across multiple services that they use. That means that if their password is breached in our application, then that may give an attacker access to accounts the user holds with other organizations.

Hashing

The best practice for storing passwords is that we shouldn't even store the password encrypted. Instead, we store what's known as a hash value created using a hash function. A hash function is one that takes an input and generates a seemingly randomized fixed length string that cannot be reverse-engineered to find the original value. Hash functions have a few key properties:

- They are deterministic. This means that the same value passed in will always return in the same output.

- Small changes in the input value will cause large changes to the output. There is no way of comparing the two output values and understanding that the inputs were similar. This is known as the Avalanche effect.

© Matthew McGiffen 2022
M. McGiffen, *Pro Encryption in SQL Server 2022*, https://doi.org/10.1007/978-1-4842-8664-7_19

- Functions are one-way. This means that there is no way to take the output value and reverse-engineer it to find the input. There is one exception to this that we will look at next when we discuss the concept of salting.

- Hash functions are generally engineered to minimize the chance that two different inputs will produce the same output, though it is always theoretically possible that such an event – known as a collision – should occur.

In the case of passwords, we don't need to store the password or be able to decrypt it. When a user attempts to logon, we simply run the entered password through the hash function and verify that the output matches what we have stored in the database. As we don't store the actual password in the database, even our most privileged administrators – or an attacker who manages to gain those privileges – can't view the actual password value.

Salting

I've just stated that it shouldn't be possible to reverse-engineer a hashed value; however, there is one method an attacker might attempt. As hash functions are deterministic and collisions are rare, if you know the hashed output for a given input, and you see that same output again, then you can have some confidence that the same input value was used.

An attacker can attempt to exploit that by using a database that contains the hashed values of a large number of common passwords, each hashed by the most common hashing functions/algorithms. They can then compare those values to a given hash value and see if it is one they recognize. This is known as a dictionary attack.

Let's look at an example. Values like "password," "Password," and "password1" probably exist as user passwords far more than they should, and they will certainly exist in databases of commonly hashed values. Let's say an attacked has managed to get hold of your user table where hashed passwords are stored. It will be fairly trivial to identify accounts that use those passwords and be able to access them.

In practice a database of hashed values used by a hacker could contain a large number of items, possibly even all possible string values up to a certain length. So, it's important that we try and protect against this sort of attack in case our users have chosen their passwords unwisely.

This is where the concept of salting comes in. A Salt is a random value that is generated each time we want to store a hashed value. Rather than just hashing the input value, we combine the salt with the input before running through the hash function. We then store the salt alongside the hashed value in the database. By combining a random value with the input in this manner, we make dictionary-type attacks all but impossible.

Then when a user logs on, we take the entered password, add the salt, and then hash the combined value. We compare that against the stored hashed value to see if they match. This is known as hashing and salting and is what SQL Server does internally to protect passwords where you have SQL Authentication enabled – though the fine details of exactly how it is done are kept confidential by Microsoft.

Hashing and salting are often carried out in the application itself which is the preferred approach as it removes the need to transmit unhashed passwords across the network to be stored or for verification. It is perfectly possible to do it in SQL; however, remember that means you are passing the raw passwords from the application to your database server across the network, so make sure you have TLS enabled as described in the last chapter to ensure your network traffic is encrypted.

In SQL Server there are a few functions that provide hashing capabilities; the main ones are HASHBYTES, CHECKSUM, and BINARY_CHECKSUM. We'll focus here on looking at HASHBYTES which is the most secure by far.

Using the HASHBYTES Function

HASHBYTLES returns the hashed value of a given input using a specified algorithm. The input can either be a string or binary value. You have a choice of algorithms to use, but most that are allowed for use with the function are deprecated so you should pick either SHA2_256 or SHA2_512. The number at the end of the algorithm name refers to the number of bits in the binary hashed output, so SHA2_256 is 256 bits (32 bytes) and SHA2_512 is 512 bits (64 bytes). Unlike encryption, the increase in the bit size of the algorithm doesn't make it orders of magnitude more infeasible to crack, mainly because an attacker is unlikely to try a brute force approach, but the 512-bit version is still more secure than the 256-bit, so that's what I'd recommend you use in practice.

Let's look at some examples of using the function and the output we get to see how it works. First we'll execute this SQL:

```
SELECT HASHBYTES ('SHA2_512','Password');
```

Our output here is:

```
0xE6C83B282AEB2E022844595721CC00BBDA47CB24537C1779F9BB84F04039E1676E6BA857
3E588DA1052510E3AA0A32A9E55879AE22B0C2D62136FC0A3E85F8BB
```

This is a seemingly random binary string, but if you run it on your machine, you should see you get exactly the same value. As mentioned earlier, hashing functions are deterministic and always produce the same output for the same input.

Now let's make a small change to our input value and run the function again with the following SQL:

```
SELECT HASHBYTES ('SHA2_512','Password1');
```

Our output here is:

```
0xCBE0CD68CBCA3868250C0BA545C48032F43EB0E8A5E6BAB603D109251486F77A91E46A31
46D887E37416C6BDB6CBE701BD514DE778573C9B0068483C1C626AEC
```

You can see there is no discernible pattern or similarity between the two strings, hash functions produce large changes in the output for small changes in the input – so there is no way to tell that two separate inputs were similar.

You can see the HASHBYTES function is simple to use; let's look at an example of how we could use it in practice to store passwords.

Storing Passwords Using HASHBYTES and a Salt Value

I have a database called Test; within that I'm going to create a table called Users to store usernames and hashed passwords as well as the salt value that we combine with the password before hashing. The following SQL creates the table.

```
USE Test;
CREATE TABLE dbo.Users (
    Id int IDENTITY(1,1),
    UserName varchar(50),
    Salt varbinary(16),
    HashedPassword varbinary(64)
);
```

To generate the salt, I'm going to use the CRYPT_GEN_RANDOM function which returns a binary value and is the most suitable function for providing a random value to be used for cryptography. The only parameter is the length in bytes that we want our randomly generated value to be. The best practice for a salt value is that it should be 128 bit (16 bytes) or longer, so 16 bytes is what we shall use.

Here is an example taking a passed username and password, generating a salt value, then hashing the password with the salt value, and storing the new user record in the Users table. In practice you would do this within a stored procedure:

```
--Store New User and Password
DECLARE @UserName varchar(50) = 'matt.mcgiffen';
DECLARE @PassWord varchar(50) = 'SomePassword';
DECLARE @Salt varbinary(16);
DECLARE @HashedAndSaltedPassword varbinary(64);

SET @Salt = CRYPT_GEN_RANDOM(16);

SET @HashedAndSaltedPassword = HASHBYTES('SHA2_512', @Salt + CAST(@Password AS varbinary(50)));

INSERT INTO dbo.Users (UserName, Salt, HashedPassword)
VALUES (@UserName, @Salt, @HashedAndSaltedPassword);
```

Let's look at what we end up with stored in the database with the following query:

```
SELECT * from dbo.Users;
```

We can see the results in Figure 19-1.

Id	UserName	Salt	HashedPassword
1	matt.mcgiffen	0x188971CF598A7E2FD34EC3FEA142DD23	0x03BC901832B1F533711197122C94BEC4A1D4C9D8BBBFE52...

Figure 19-1. *Viewing the hashed password stored in the database*

We can run the same code again to add a second user. I'll call this user matthew. mcgiffen. I'm going to use the same password so we can see that, because we use a salt value, the hashed password that gets stored is different. We can see both records in Figure 19-2.

273

	Id	UserName	Salt	HashedPassword
1	1	matt.mcgiffen	0x188971CF598A7E2FD34EC3FEA142DD23	0x03BC901832B1F533711197122C94BEC4A1D4C9D8BBBFE52E...
2	2	matthew.mcgiffen	0x60D1AC5BA42048D6532CF1641D9974FB	0xDA2B4C2EEDF20B94F888C8E3EADC36CEEA3F6D41C4FB9D...

Figure 19-2. *Different hashed values get stored for the same password*

When we want to verify a password in the case of a User Login, we simply retrieve the salt and hashed password from the database. Then we combine the salt with the password the user has entered and run it through the same HASHBYTES function. Finally, we check that the resulting hashed value matches what is stored in the database. The following SQL shows that in practice:

```
--Verify User's Password
DECLARE @UserName varchar(50) = 'matt.mcgiffen';
DECLARE @PassWord varchar(50) = 'SomePassword';
DECLARE @Salt varbinary(16);
DECLARE @HashedAndSaltedPassword varbinary(64);

SELECT
      @Salt = Salt,
      @HashedAndSaltedPassword = HashedPassword
FROM dbo.Users
WHERE UserName = @UserName;

IF HASHBYTES('SHA2_512', @Salt + CAST(@Password AS varbinary(50))) =
@HashedAndSaltedPassword
BEGIN
      PRINT 'Password is correct'
END
ELSE BEGIN
      PRINT 'Password is incorrect'
END;
```

Run the code and check your messages tab; you should see you get the confirmation message "Password is correct."

Summary

Where we need to store passwords in the database, it's best practice to not even store the password encrypted, but to store a hashed value instead. The hashed value can be used to verify an entered password is correct but cannot be reverse-engineered, so even someone who has or gains administrative access will not be able to view the actual password. In practice we should also combine the password with a salt value before hashing. This protects us from dictionary-type attacks. The salt value is stored in the database alongside the hashed value.

The best approach is to manage the hashing and salting in your application; this removes the need to transmit unhashed passwords across the network. You can however do it at the SQL end if you need to. In that case, make sure network traffic is encrypted with TLS.

Key Points to Remember

- Hashing functions are one way; they provide a thumbprint that can be used to verify a piece of information but cannot be used to obtain the piece of information itself.

- Hashing functions are deterministic; the same input will always result in the same output.

- Small changes in the input will result in large changes in the output. This means you can't compare two hash values to identify if the original values are similar.

- You can use the HASHBYTES function in SQL Server for hashing and the CRYPTO_GEN_RANDOM function to generate suitable values for use as salts.

In the next chapter we'll look at how you can manage your encryption keys using an external key store. This is known as Extensible Key Management (EKM).

## CHAPTER 20

Extensible Key Management (EKM)

EKM is functionality that exists in SQL Server to allow you to store your keys in a secure repository away from your database or application servers. Traditionally this repository would have been a piece of hardware known as a Hardware Security Module (HSM) which would sit in a rack in your server room. These days we're much more likely to use an HSM backed cloud service such as Azure Key Vault.

The advantages are twofold. Firstly, security can be greatly improved as the ability to manage keys in a central location means that you can limit who has access to the keys. Secondly, management of keys is much improved. You can store keys from multiple application and database servers in a centralized resource, and this is much easier to manage than having them all over the place with no guarantee that we actually know all the keys that we have in use. In the case of TDE, I stressed a number of times that you must not lose the keys; this is much less likely to happen if you take an approach of centralized management. It's also easier to make sure that common policies are applied and that expiry of keys and rotation is handled appropriately.

HSMs can also be used to offload encryption workloads to a separate piece of hardware; that's less commonly used though, so in this chapter we're just going to focus on using EKM for key storage.

You have a lot of choices of services and hardware you can work with using EKM. When SQL Server needs to access keys using EKM, it does so via an installed module from the provider that allows it to connect to the key store. In the examples in this chapter, we're just going to focus on using Azure Key Vault, and we'll look in brief at how you set things up in Azure for the sake of our demos. It is beyond the scope of this book however to go into full detail of how you should work with a provider such as Azure Key Vault in production. If you're using a different provider, then you should be able to follow their documentation to perform the equivalent tasks. The actions you take at the

© Matthew McGiffen 2022
M. McGiffen, *Pro Encryption in SQL Server 2022*, https://doi.org/10.1007/978-1-4842-8664-7_20

SQL end should be quite similar regardless of provider. We'll look at how you work with Azure Key Store to store keys for use by TDE as well as Always Encrypted, though you can also use it to store other keys you may have on your database server.

It's probably worth mentioning that one provider you may think of using, AWS Key Management Service (KMS), doesn't at the time of writing support using it for TDE on-premises or even if you are running SQL Server on an AWS virtual machine (EC2). You can however use it if you are running SQL Server on AWS Relational Database Service. The reason for this is that AWS do not share a module you can install to connect SQL Server to KMS.

Creating the Required Objects in Azure

For the examples in this chapter, you'll be able to use a free subscription to Azure, so go ahead and create one if you don't have one already and sign in. We're going to need to create the same set of objects in Azure whether we're working with TDE or with Always Encrypted:

- An Azure Resource Group

- An Azure Active Directory App Registration

- An Azure Key Vault

Creating the Resource Group

The first thing we need to do, assuming this is a fresh subscription, is to create a resource group. Search for resource groups using the search bar and click to create a new one (shown in Figure 20-1):

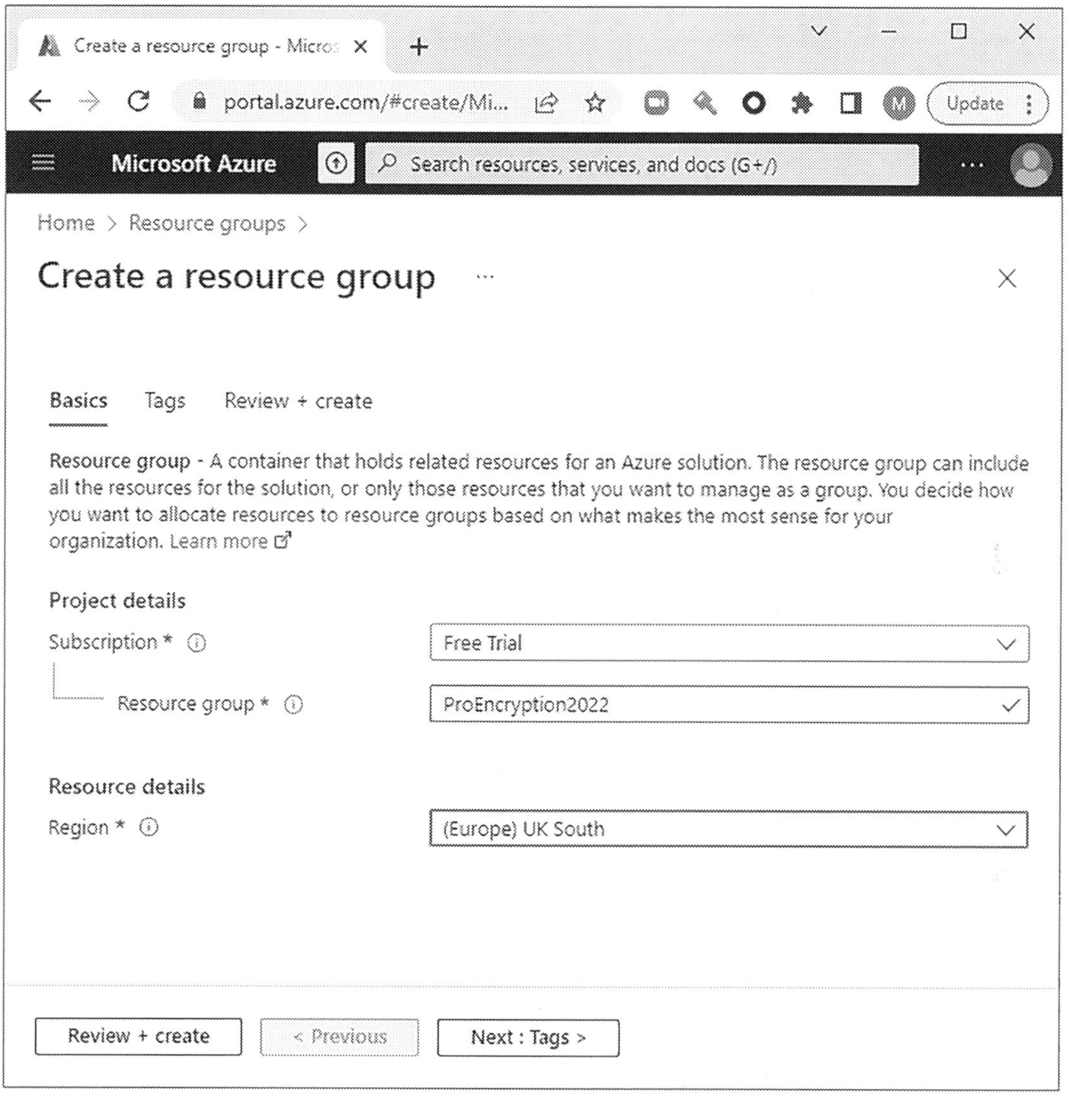

Figure 20-1. *Creating a new Resource Group*

I've called mine ProEncryption2022; give yours whatever name you want and select a region, and click "Review + create" and then "Create."

Creating the Azure Active Directory App Registration

Next, we need to create an application registration in Azure Active Directory which SQL Server will use to authenticate with Azure Key Vault. Go to Azure Active Directory, open App registrations, and click to create a new one; we'll call this ProEncryption2022 again. The rest of the settings you can leave as default (Figure 20-2):

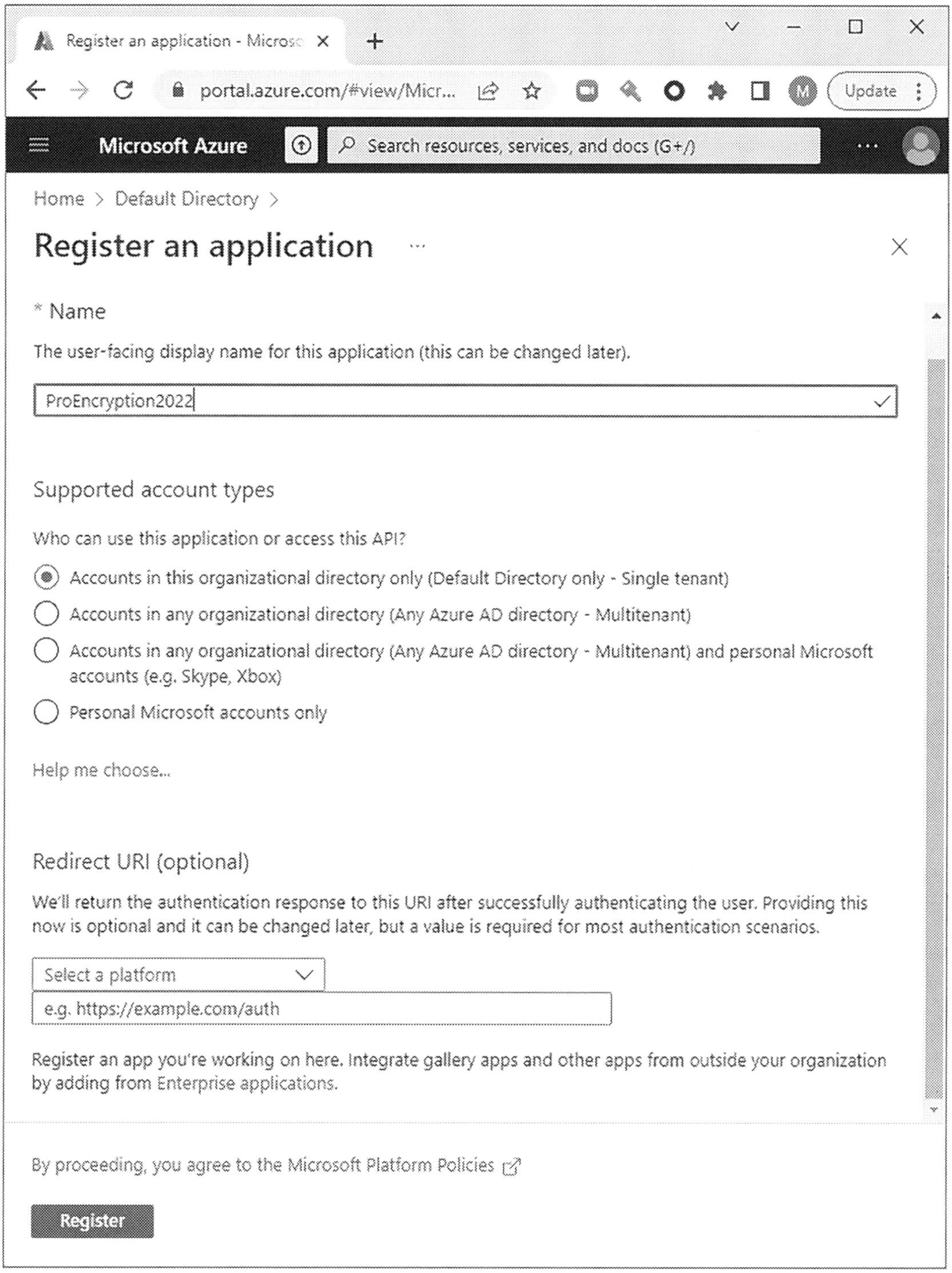

Figure 20-2. *Registering an application for authentication purposes*

Once you register the application, a summary screen is displayed (Figure 20-3):

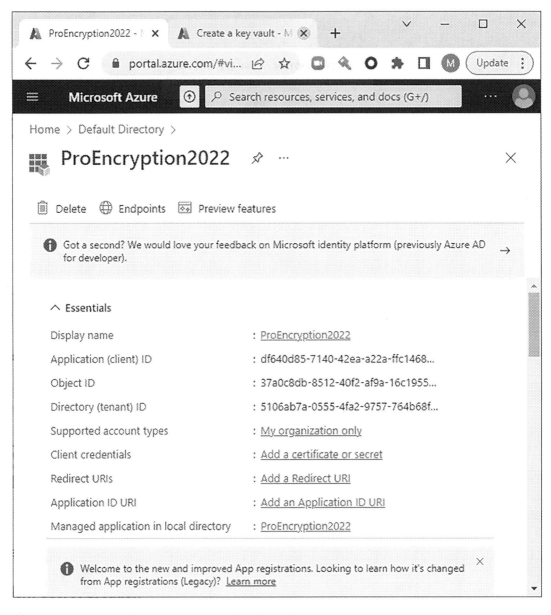

Figure 20-3. *Application registration details*

You need to capture the Application (client) ID as we'll use that as part of the credentials we use to connect to the key vault; mine is df640d85-7140-42ea-a22a-ffc1468d809c. You can make a note of yours now – but you can come back and get it later.

Now we need to create a client secret that will be used to authenticate. On the left you will see "Certificates & secrets." Open this, and then click to create a new client secret. You need to give a description and can specify an expiry period, and then click Add (Figure 20-4):

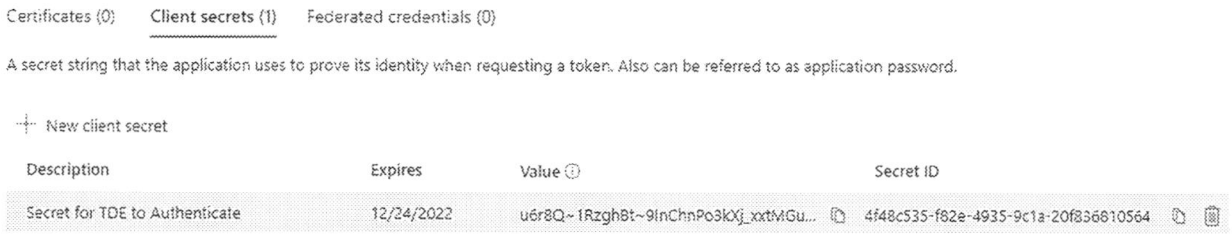

Certificates (0)   **Client secrets (1)**   Federated credentials (0)

A secret string that the application uses to prove its identity when requesting a token. Also can be referred to as application password.

╬ New client secret

Description	Expires	Value ⓘ	Secret ID
Secret for TDE to Authenticate	12/24/2022	u6r8Q~1RzghBt~9InChnPo3kXj_xxtMGu...	4f48c535-f82e-4935-9c1a-20f836810564

Figure 20-4. *Viewing our created client secret*

This takes us back to the previous screen where we can see our newly created secret. It is important at this stage to capture the Value as, for security reasons, the value will not be shown once you leave and come back. My value is u6r8Q~1RzghBt~9InChnPo3kXj_xxtMGuEMH.bxv.

Creating the Key Vault

Now we can go ahead and create the key vault. Microsoft recommendations are that you should use a separate key vault for each application you are working with. Browse to key vaults and again click to create a new one. You need to select the resource group we created, give it a name, and select a region. The rest of the settings on the first page can be left at default values (Figure 20-5):

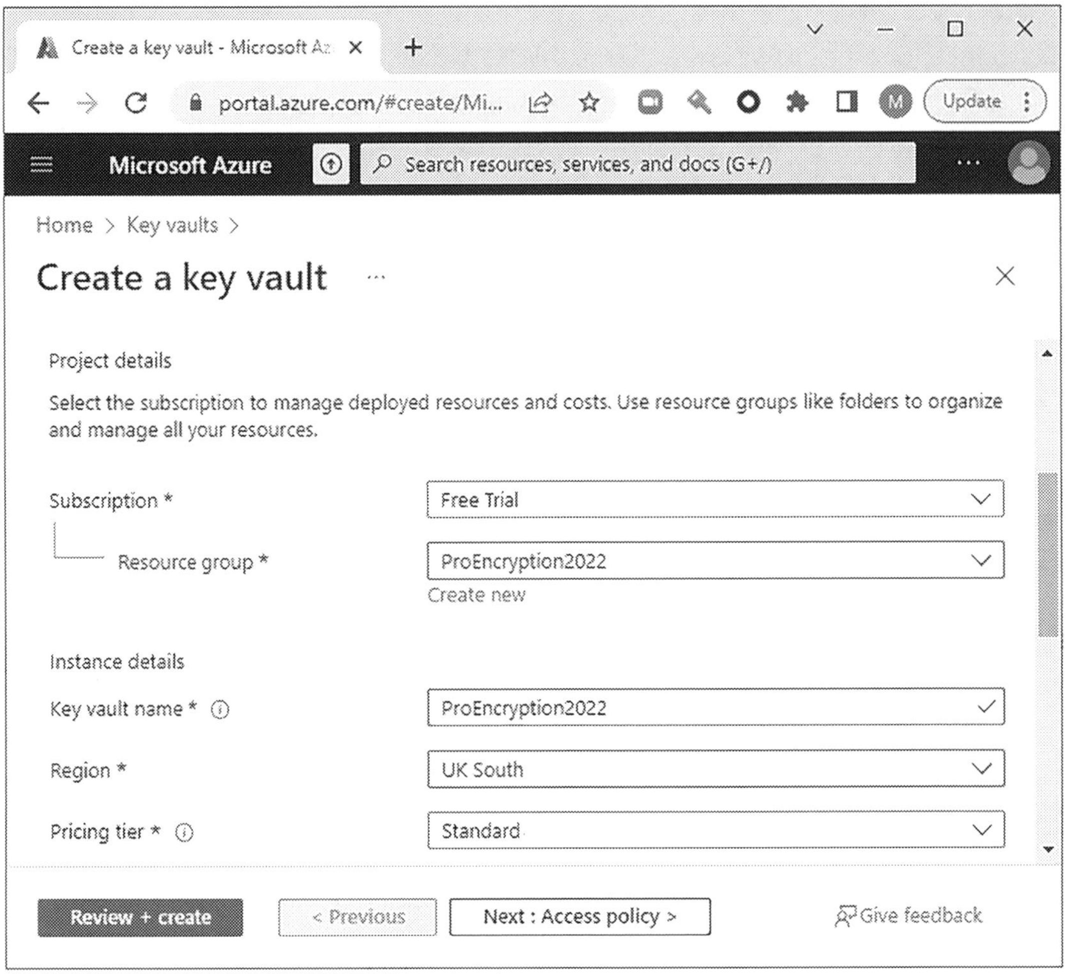

Figure 20-5. *Creating a key vault*

Click Next to configure the Access policy. On the page that opens, you need to click Add Access Policy. We are going to give permissions to the app registration we created. First, in the "Configure from template" dropdown, select SQL Server Connector; this just assigns the default set of permissions for the access policy. Then click to select a principal, and, using the search box that opens, find your app registration (Figure 20-6):

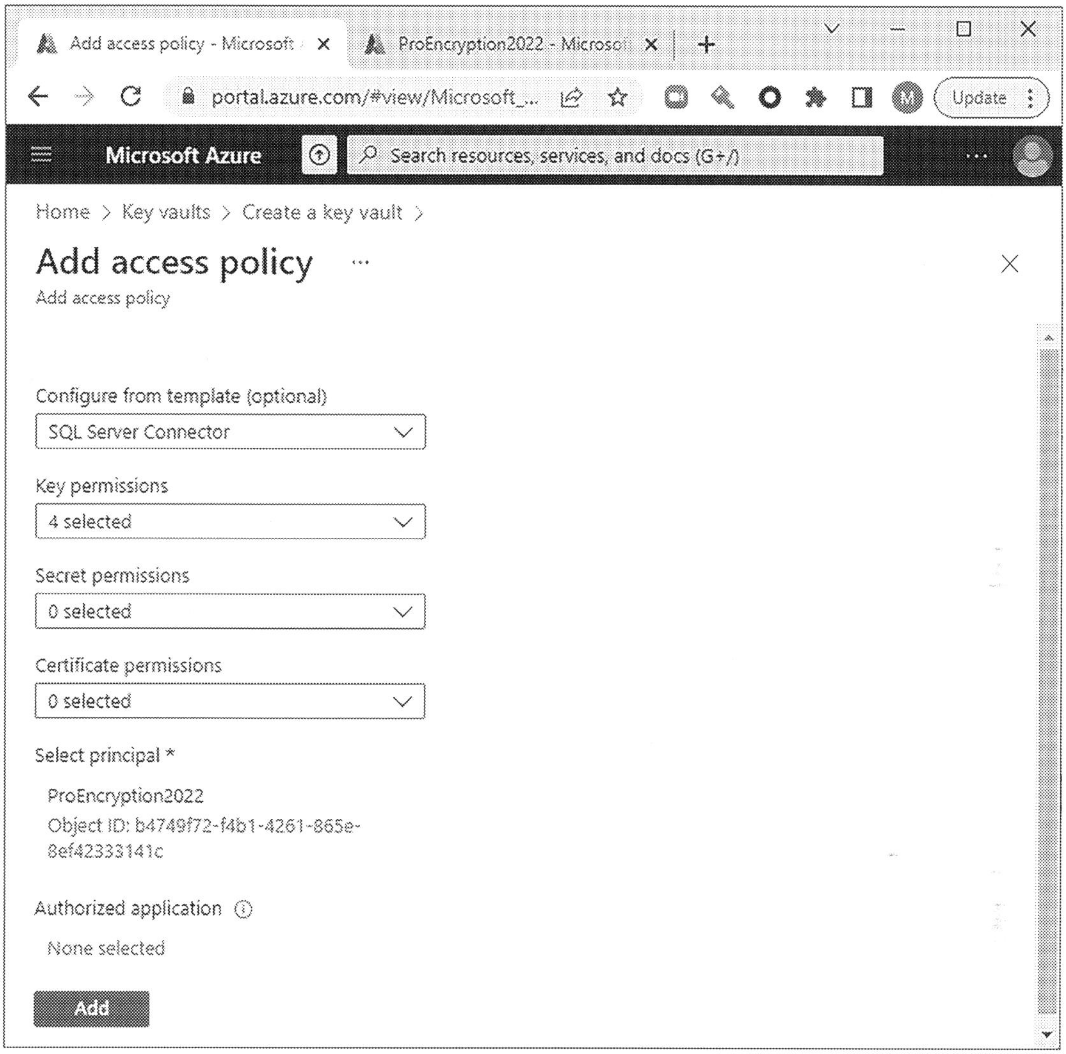

Figure 20-6. *Adding an access policy*

Click Add and we are taken back to the Create key vault, Access policies page. We can see the application we have added listed under current access polices. Check the correct key permissions are selected; these should be Get, List, Wrap Key, and Unwrap Key.

When we click Next, we are taken to the networking page; for this demo, the default, which will use a public endpoint, is fine so just click. Next again, and then click Next through the remaining pages to create the key vault. Once creation is complete, click to go to the resource.

We now have the basic set of objects in place that we will need when working with either TDE or Always Encrypted.

Setting Up TDE to Use Azure Key Vault
Creating the Key for TDE

When we set up TDE in an earlier chapter, and didn't use EKM, we had a database encryption key in our TDE enabled database that was itself encrypted by the asymmetric key associated with a server-level certificate. With EKM we instead are able to have the database encryption key protected by a key stored with our EKM provider.

Before we set things up on our SQL box, let's create the key we're going to use in our key vault. Browse to your key vault in the Azure Portal, and go to Keys and then click "Generate\Import." We need to give the key a name, in this case TestTDEKey. The key should have a key type of RSA and an RSA key size of 2048. Check these values and click Create (Figure 20-7):

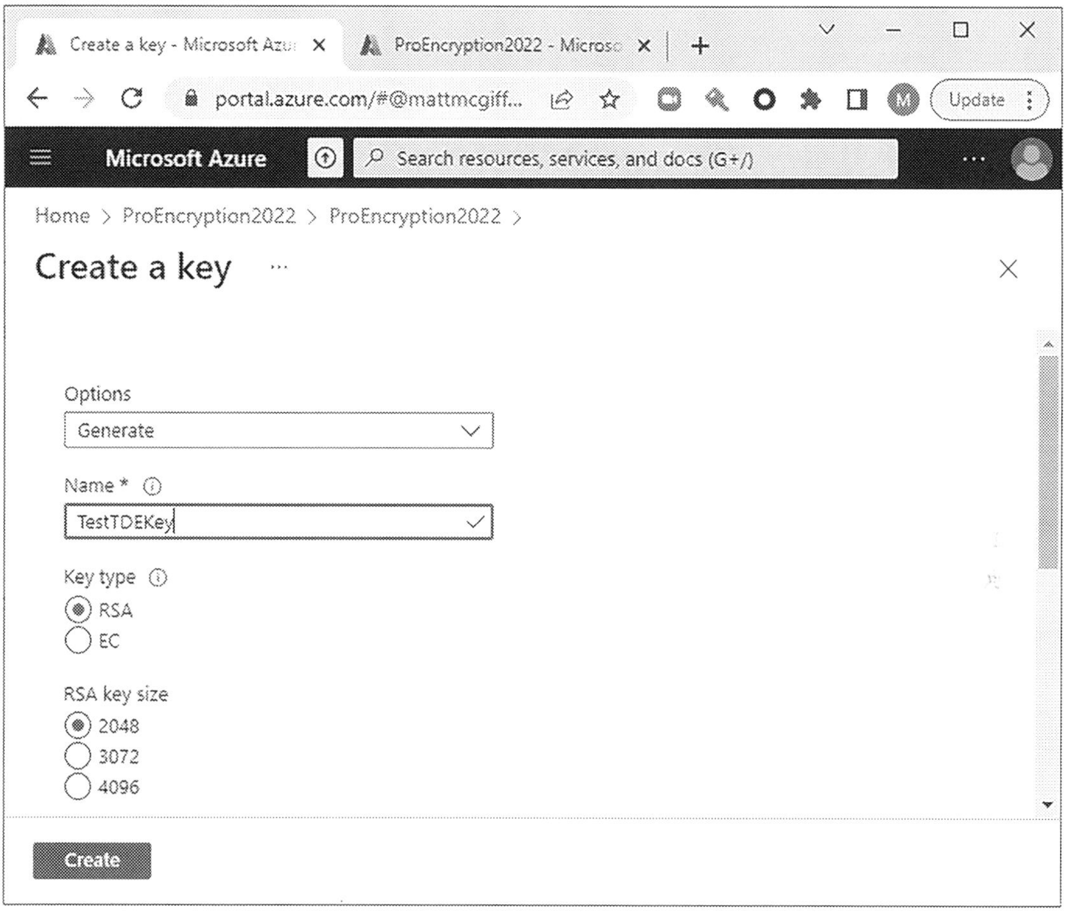

Figure 20-7. *Creating a key in Azure Key Vault*

An asymmetric key is created; we're now ready to configure things at the SQL end.

Setting Up the SQL Server

We mentioned earlier that SQL Server uses a provider connector in order to be able to connect to the key store. In the case of Azure this is called the SQL Server Connector for Microsoft Azure Key Vault. Download and install that on your SQL Server box.

Then we set things up within SQL Server via SSMS. First, configure SQL to use EKM and register the SQL Server connector as a cryptographic provider with the following SQL:

```
USE master;
```

```
GO
sp_configure 'show advanced options', 1;
GO
RECONFIGURE;
GO
sp_configure 'EKM provider enabled', 1;
GO
RECONFIGURE;

CREATE CRYPTOGRAPHIC PROVIDER AzureKeyVault_Provider
FROM FILE = 'C:\Program Files\SQL Server Connector for Microsoft Azure Key
Vault\Microsoft.AzureKeyVaultService.EKM.dll';
```

Next, we have to create a credential that will be used to connect to Azure Key Vault. You can do that with the following code:

```
USE master;
CREATE CREDENTIAL AzureKeyVault_Credential
WITH IDENTITY = 'ProEncryption2022',
SECRET = 'df640d85714042eaa22affc1468d809cu6r8Q~1RzghBt~9InChnPo3kXj_
xxtMGuEMH.bxv'
FOR CRYPTOGRAPHIC PROVIDER AzureKeyVault_Provider;
```

There are a number of pieces of information you need to supply:

- IDENTITY is the name of your key vault in Azure.

- SECRET is the Client ID for your app registration, with the hyphens removed, concatenated with the secret value we captured earlier. Even if you're following this demo exactly, you will have your own values so use those. My Client ID was df640d85-7140-42ea-a22a-ffc1468d809c, so this becomes df640d85714042eaa22affc1468d809c and then we add the secret value u6r8Q~1RzghBt~9InChnPo3kXj_xxtMGuEMH.bxv at the end.

- CRYPTOGRAHPIC PROVIDER is the one we just created.

Now we need to add the credential to the login we are currently using in order for us to be able to add a reference to the asymmetric key we have created in Azure. You'll need to set your own account name in the following code before executing:

```
ALTER LOGIN [Your Administrator Account]
ADD CREDENTIAL AzureKeyVault_Credential;
```

Now we can set up the key object which is just a pointer to tell SQL Server where to access the key from our EKM provider. You can do that with the following code – you just need to specify the key name as the one you created in your key vault:

```
USE master;
CREATE ASYMMETRIC KEY AzureKeyVault_TestTDEKey
FROM PROVIDER AzureKeyVault_Provider
WITH PROVIDER_KEY_NAME = 'TestTDEKey',
CREATION_DISPOSITION = OPEN_EXISTING;
```

If this fails, it is likely that your credential isn't set up correctly. Either it hasn't been added to your account (the previous step), or the SECRET value isn't right, so check these carefully and try again.

The final steps are to create a login from the key object that SQL Server can use to connect to Azure Key Vault and retrieve the actual keys. This login will need the same credential we already created in order to connect, but a credential can only be associated with one account at a time, so we must first remove it from our own login. You could create a second credential with the same details, but we no longer need it, and it is more secure to remove it using the following SQL:

```
ALTER LOGIN [Your Administrator Account]
DROP CREDENTIAL AzureKeyVault_Credential;
```

Now we can create a new login from the asymmetric key and add the credential to it with this code:

```
CREATE LOGIN AzureKeyVault_TestTDEKey_Login
FROM ASYMMETRIC KEY AzureKeyVault_TestTDEKey;

ALTER LOGIN AzureKeyVault_TestTDEKey_Login
ADD CREDENTIAL AzureKeyVault_Credential;
```

We're now ready to create a database and set it up to use TDE just as we did when we talked about TDE earlier in the book. I'm going to call my database TestEKM; we'll reuse it when we look at Always Encrypted next. This SQL creates the database:

```
CREATE DATABASE TestEKM;
```

Then we simply create a Database Encryption Key (DEK) with this SQL:

```
USE TestEKM;
CREATE DATABASE ENCRYPTION KEY
WITH ALGORITHM = AES_256
ENCRYPTION BY SERVER ASYMMETRIC KEY [AzureKeyVault_TestTDEKey];
```

If you get any errors from this command, it is again likely that it has to do with permissions, so check you created the login correctly and associated the right credential with it. Finally, we can turn TDE on with this SQL:

```
ALTER DATABASE TestEKM SET ENCRYPTION ON;
```

You now have your database set up with TDE using EKM and with your Database Master Key encrypted by the key stored in Azure Key Vault.

Working with Always Encrypted and EKM

Working with EKM when using Always Encrypted is quite similar in practice but it is different. With Always Encrypted, we store our Column Master Keys (CMKs) on our application servers, and SQL Server can't access them directly. It is those CMKs that we are going to store with our external key management provider. Thus, with Always Encrypted, it is actually our application servers that are connecting to Azure Key Vault to retrieve the keys. As such this isn't really using SQL Server EKM, though we generally continue to refer to it as EKM even though that is specifically a SQL Server feature.

What this means for us is that we don't have to perform the same setup in SQL Server to access Azure Key Vault; instead we need to connect through our application code.

Creating a CMK in Azure Key Vault

SSMS provides the functionality for you to create your CMKs in Azure through the same GUI that we've looked at before to create a CMK. We'll use the same database we created for TDE, or if you haven't followed that demo, you can just create it with this SQL:

```
CREATE DATABASE TestEKM;
```

Now we go to the Security folder for the database in the SSMS object explorer, expand that, expand Always Encrypted Keys and then right-click "Column Master Keys," and select to create a new one. In the page that opens up there is a Key Store dropdown from which you can select Azure Key Vault. When you select that, you will be prompted to log in to your Azure account. You may get an error similar to that shown in Figure 20-8 at this stage:

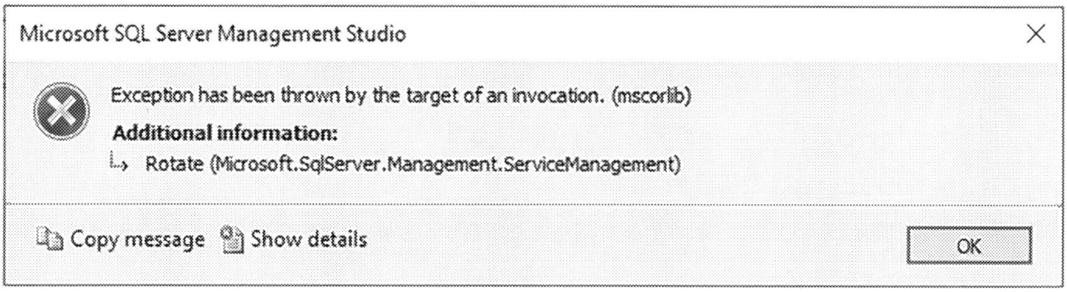

Figure 20-8. *Error logging in to Azure Key Vault*

This is because the account you are logging into Azure with doesn't have the correct permissions; in particular it should NOT have permissions around key rotation. Go into the Azure Portal and browse to Access Polies for your Key Vault, find the user you are logging in with, and make sure Rotate, Get Rotation Policy, and Set Rotation Policy are unticked. You then should be able to log in okay.

Once in, you can see your key vaults and any existing keys (Figure 20-9):

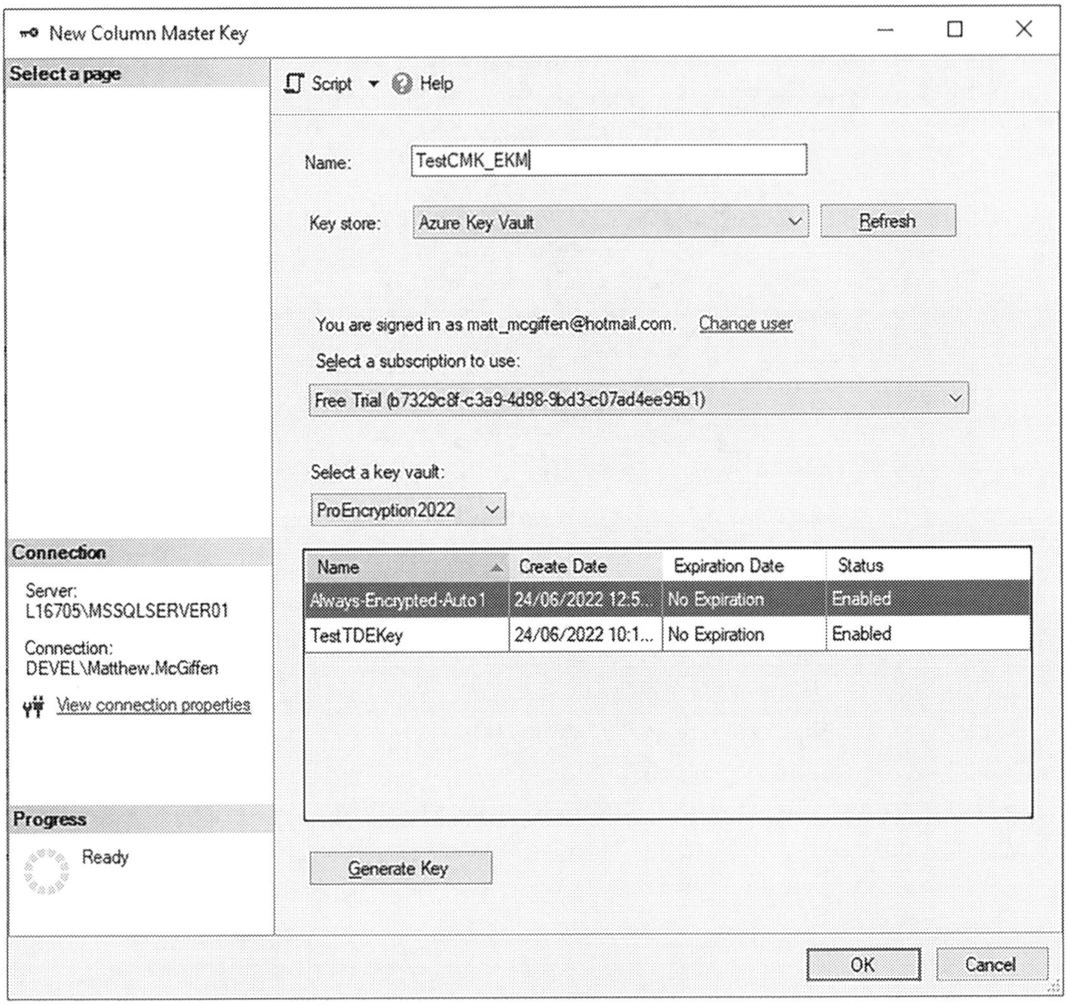

Figure 20-9. *Creating a New CMK in Azure Key Vault*

If you have more than one key vault, you can select the correct one and view any existing keys. If you want to generate a new one, you can do that through the GUI also, but you're not able to choose the name; you can see mine has been called Always-Encrypted-Auto1. If you want to name it yourself, then you can create the key through the Azure Portal as described for TDE and then select that in the SSMS GUI. Give your CMK object that will be stored in the database a name – I've called mine TestCMK_EKM – then click OK.

We can script out the definition of our new CMK in SSMS to view the properties. We see something like this:

```
CREATE COLUMN MASTER KEY [TestCMK_EKM]
WITH
(
     KEY_STORE_PROVIDER_NAME = N'AZURE_KEY_VAULT',
     KEY_PATH = N'https://proencryption2022.vault.azure.net/keys/Always-
Encrypted-Auto1/5df19d2080d74fb3a2f7d5537f803d79'
)
GO
```

We can see that the CMK object specifies the Key Store Provider as Azure Key Vault, and the KEY_PATH is the URL to the key itself.

Encrypting Columns and Working with Data

Once our CMK is set up in Azure, working with Always Encrypted is pretty much the same as when our CMK is stored on our client machine. First we create a new CEK through the GUI in SSMS. We do that by again going to the Security folder for the database in the object explorer, expanding the Always Encrypted Keys folder, and then right-clicking Column Encryption Keys and selecting to create new one.

We'll call our key TestCEK_EKM and we must select the CMK that we just created before clicking OK. Again, you may run into permission issues and receive a "Forbidden" error. When creating a CEK, it is the logged on user who needs permissions to be able to carry out the required actions in Azure Key Vault. Make sure you are signed into Azure and your account has the following permissions in the key vault (in the Access policies page for the key vault):

- Decrypt
- Encrypt
- Unwrap Key
- Wrap Key
- Verify
- Sign

One we have the CEK, we can create a table and add a row as we did earlier in the book when we first looked at Always Encrypted. Remember to make sure your connection has Always Encrypted enabled and Parameterization for Always Encrypted is enabled for your query window. You can then create the table with this SQL:

```
USE TestEKM;
CREATE TABLE dbo.EncryptedTable(
Id INT IDENTITY(1,1) CONSTRAINT PK_EncryptedTable PRIMARY KEY CLUSTERED,
LastName nvarchar(50) COLLATE Latin1_General_BIN2 ENCRYPTED WITH (
COLUMN_ENCRYPTION_KEY = TestCEK_EKM,
ENCRYPTION_TYPE = DETERMINISTIC,
ALGORITHM = 'AEAD_AES_256_CBC_HMAC_SHA_256'
) NULL,
FirstName nvarchar(50) COLLATE Latin1_General_BIN2 ENCRYPTED WITH (
COLUMN_ENCRYPTION_KEY = TestCEK_EKM,
ENCRYPTION_TYPE = RANDOMIZED,
ALGORITHM = 'AEAD_AES_256_CBC_HMAC_SHA_256') NULL
);
```

Now we can try inserting a row of data with this SQL:

```
DECLARE @LastName nvarchar(50) = 'McGiffen';
DECLARE @FirstName nvarchar(50) = 'Matthew';

INSERT INTO dbo.EncryptedTable (LastName, FirstName)
VALUES (@LastName, @FirstName);
```

Note that for all operations, including running queries over a connection with column encryption enabled, we must be signed into Azure. For instance, if I sign out of Azure and try to run a simple select query against the table, I will generally be prompted to sign into Azure and if my sign-in fails, or I cancel it, I will get an error:

```
Failed to decrypt a column encryption key using key store provider: 'AZURE_
KEY_VAULT'.
```

Working with Azure Key Vault from Your Application

Within your application code you could sign into Azure using a valid account with the correct permissions over Azure Key Vault in order to be able to access the CMKs required; however, this is not ideal from a security standpoint. Better is to authenticate using the app registration we created earlier.

In order to achieve that from your application, there are three main things you will need to do:

- Install the modules for Azure Key Vault Provider and Active Directory.

- Create a credential based on the client id and secret value from your Azure AD app registration.

- Initialize your connection to the Azure Key Vault Provider.

After doing that, your application will be able to access the required keys straight from Azure Key Vault. The rest of your code, and how you interact with a database with Always Encrypted enabled, remains the same as if you were accessing keys from your local certificate store.

If you're working with C# and Visual Studio, then Microsoft provides code samples you can use to perform the required tasks.

Summary

Extensible Key Management (EKM) is functionality within SQL Server that allows you to store your encryption keys off your SQL server in a centralized repository. This could be a physical hardware module or, more often, a cloud service such as Azure Key Vault.

Key things to remember when working with TDE and EKM:

- For TDE we use an asymmetric key stored with our EKM provider that is used to encrypt the database encryption key. This replaces the certificate we would otherwise use for the same function.

- We need to register our EKM provider with SQL Server using a provider module that we install.

- We create an asymmetric key object in our master database that is a pointer to the actual key stored with our provider. We associate that with a login that has a credential that allows it to authenticate with the provider.

Key points relating to Always Encrypted:

- With Always Encrypted, it is our Column Master Keys that we store externally.

- Even though we usually still refer to this as EKM, it doesn't require the functionality built-in to SQL Server, so we don't need to install and register a provider module on the SQL box.

- Your application code needs to manage connecting and authenticating to the provider.

- We can set up the keys using SSMS. SSMS requires you to log in to Azure in order to perform the required actions.

## CHAPTER 21

Other Methods of Column Encryption

We've talked a lot in this book about using Always Encrypted to encrypt columns of data, and in general I feel that should be the default tool you choose when wanting to perform such actions. SQL Server does however have other methods you can use to encrypt data and has done since the 2005 version of the product. In my opinion these older methods are less secure and more limiting to work with than Always Encrypted – but you may have edge cases where you want to use them. As such we'll cover them here, but as Always Encrypted is the main recommendation of this book, we will only cover them in brief. You can of course also choose to encrypt data in your application before sending it to SQL Server; we don't need to discuss that here as it's not SQL functionality, except perhaps to say that Always Encrypted again will generally offer better security than such methods.

The security gains from Always Encrypted come first from the fact that data is "always" encrypted: that means in the database and in memory as well as in transit across the network. When using other methods, data must be decrypted at the SQL end before being sent across the network in plaintext; of course, we can use TLS, as discussed in Chapter 18, to encrypt our network traffic, but that's still not as secure as using Always Encrypted and TLS. The second reason Always Encrypted is more secure is due to the separation of keys and roles. You can't access encrypted data without access to both the application and database servers. With other methods we are going to encrypt data with either keys or pass phrases, so it will only require access to the root key or pass phrase in order to access your data. As a final point, Always Encrypted also has the potential to allow you to implement encryption without code change in many cases, whereas other methods will always require code changes.

© Matthew McGiffen 2022
M. McGiffen, *Pro Encryption in SQL Server 2022*, https://doi.org/10.1007/978-1-4842-8664-7_21

All that caveat aside, you may want to use other methods for encrypting your columns of data, so let's discuss how.

SQL offers two methods of encryption, doing so using keys or using passphrases. Let's look at keys first.

Encryption Using a Symmetric Key

There are two types of encryption keys, symmetric and asymmetric. Symmetric keys are a single key, whereas asymmetric keys consist of a key pair, one which is public and can be used to encrypt data and one which is private and can be used to decrypt data. In general, asymmetric encryption is much more resource intensive, so we save using that for protecting other objects and just use symmetric keys for protecting our actual data. Asymmetric keys are more useful where we need to be able to share the public key with another process in order for it to encrypt data before sending to us; only we can decrypt the data because only we have access to the private key.

Your Key Hierarchy

When we looked at TDE, we saw that TDE uses a symmetric key stored in the database itself in order to encrypt the data. That key is itself protected (encrypted) by an asymmetric key associated with a certificate, and then we had a chain of protection going all the way up to our Service Master Key (SMK).

When we use symmetric keys to encrypt our data directly, then we can have a similar key hierarchy. We want our symmetric key protected, as otherwise anyone who can access to it will be able to decrypt our data. You can choose to have your symmetric key protected by any of the following:

- Another symmetric key

- An asymmetric key

- A certificate (which has its own asymmetric key)

- A password

It's common that we will use a hierarchy very similar to that which is used for TDE where we protect the symmetric key with a certificate; that certificate is in turn protected by the Database Master Key (DMK) which is in turn protected by the Service Master Key (SMK). However your hierarchy works, it always has a potential weakness at the top of the chain – anyone who can access the root-level object will likely be able to read your data. Equally if you use passwords, anyone who has the password will be able to do so.

Where we use an asymmetric key, we can use Extensible Key Management (EKM) to store the key with an external provider. We looked at this in the last chapter. This is almost exactly the same as we did for TDE, and you can follow the steps there up to the point where you create the asymmetric key object in SQL Server. Just make sure to create the asymmetric key object in the database where the symmetric key will exist. You can also use EKM to simply store the symmetric key itself directly with your provider.

If you choose to have your objects protected by SQL Server all the way to the SMK, then that means a database administrator can access the encrypted data, but it is easier to work with. The reason you might choose to use a password therefore is to avoid this. However, the password then becomes the vulnerable point of attack so itself must be well protected. Either way, someone who gains access to memory on the SQL box via a debugger, or who can access network traffic, will be able to see unencrypted data. I'm repeating myself, but this is why we want to use Always Encrypted – so we can avoid these headaches.

For the sake of this, in brief, look at other methods of column encryption; we're just going to look at a few of the most likely scenarios you might follow. These are:

- Relying fully on SQL Server to manage your keys. So, your symmetric key is protected by a certificate, which is in turn protected by the DMK, in turn protected by the SMK. This is known as Automated Key Management.

- Using much of the same hierarchy, but we remove any relation between the DMK and the SMK. Instead, the DMK is protected by a password.

- Using a symmetric key that is protected directly by a password.

To examine these options it's easiest if we dive in and look at how we set things up and the code to encrypt and decrypt data. We'll start with the Automated Key Management example and go over everything you need to do to work with encrypted data, and then we'll discuss the differences when you use one of the other two options.

Working with Automated Key Management
Creating the Keys

The first thing we create here is our DMK. This must exist in the database that we will be working in to encrypt data. We'll call our database TestColumnEncryption. You can create it and the DMK with the following SQL:

```
CREATE DATABASE TestColumnEncryption;
GO

USE TestColumnEncryption;
CREATE MASTER KEY
ENCRYPTION BY PASSWORD = 'SomeLongAndComplicatedPassword!';
```

Even though we've discussed that our DMK is going to be protected by the SMK, we still need to specify a password. This is in case we need to recover the database to another server where the original SMK will not be available. If we didn't have a password to access the DMK, then we wouldn't be able to access any objects that are in turn protected by it. That would mean we have lost access to our encrypted data. Even though we specify a password, the DMK is also protected by the SMK by default.

Next, we're going to create our certificate with this SQL:

```
CREATE CERTIFICATE MyColumnEncryptionCert
WITH SUBJECT = 'Certificate used for column encryption in the
TestColumnEncryption database';
```

Then finally we create our symmetric key. We specify the encryption algorithm to use, in this case AES_256 which we've used before in this book, and the certificate to use to protect the key. You can create the key with this code:

```
CREATE SYMMETRIC KEY MySymmetricKey
WITH ALGORITHM = AES_256
ENCRYPTION BY CERTIFICATE MyColumnEncryptionCert;
```

You can't export symmetric keys directly, so if you wish to be able to create the same key on a different SQL Server instance, you need a couple of additional parameters, KEY_SOURCE and IDENTITY_VALUE. You can see their usage in this code example:

```
CREATE SYMMETRIC KEY MySymmetricKey2
WITH ALGORITHM = AES_256,
    KEY_SOURCE = 'Pass phrase to generate the key',
    IDENTITY_VALUE = 'Pass phrase to generate the key GUID'
ENCRYPTION BY CERTIFICATE MyColumnEncryptionCert;
```

KEY_SOURCE is used to generate the actual key value – so the same phrase will generate the same key. IDENTITY_SOURCE is used to generate the key's GUID identifier. This gets stored as part of the metadata included with an encrypted value, so it must match if a newly generated key is to be able to decrypt data encrypted by another key even where the key value is the same.

Encrypting and Decrypting Data

Now we're ready to look at encrypting and decrypting data. Before you can use a symmetric key, it must be opened. You can do so with the following SQL:

```
OPEN SYMMETRIC KEY MySymmetricKey
DECRYPTION BY CERTIFICATE MyColumnEncryptionCert;
```

The key remains open for the duration of the session. It's considered good practice to close the key explicitly once you're done with it, though they do get automatically closed when the session is disconnected. You can close a key with this SQL:

```
CLOSE SYMMETRIC KEY MySymmetricKey;
```

With the key in an open state, we can look at encrypting data. Here is an example using our key with the ENCRYPTBYKEY function to encrypt a value:

```
SELECT ENCRYPTBYKEY(KEY_GUID(N'MySymmetricKey'),'SomeText');
```

The first parameter specifies the key to use, but we must supply the GUID for it – which we obtain via the KEY_GUID function. The second parameter is the plaintext value you wish to encrypt; this can be supplied as any of the text or binary data types but cannot be numeric, so you must explicitly cast a numeric value to text or binary if you wish to encrypt it. Your output should look something like this:

```
0x00362256B65B9B4DBDF3705E081C5B4702000000939B518C0568472D777180A1C5583605
AAFF01223E03945E347466BF5D6757818DDC01F78B890523D9245C06029339E9
```

Now let's run the select statement again and look at the results; here is an example output:

```
0x00362256B65B9B4DBDF3705E081C5B470200000007E18B494111AF9A4F0D691AD5E4E130
4AA6561F71292677360EA7F9EB6700D812674E1D61372BB5549446F91F757E2E
```

We can see that the two encrypted values are the same for the first 42 characters, but after that they are different despite it being the same underlying plaintext value. From this we can see that ENCRYPTBYKEY implements a form of randomized encryption; that means that the same input being encrypted again will always produce a different output, so there is no way to compare two encrypted values to see if they are the same.

The encrypted output is a varbinary and as you can see is a lot longer than the plaintext value we encrypted. Part of that is because encrypted values can themselves be bigger depending on the bit size of the algorithm used; in addition to that, there is an encryption header that includes a GUID identifying the key used as well as other information. In general, you're going to see the varbinary is up to about 85 bytes longer than your plaintext value. Where you wish to store these values in a table, I would make the columns 128 bytes bigger than the maximum data size just to be on the safe side. It's worth noting also that the maximum size of the output is 8000 bytes; that means you can only encrypt values up to a size slightly smaller than that.

We can decrypt the data as per the following example. Note this exact code will return Null if you run it on your machine as the encryption header specifies the Key GUID for my key and yours will be different. If you want to try this, you should substitute a binary value you have obtained by running the ENCRYPTBYKEY function yourself:

```
SELECT CAST(DECRYPTBYKEY(0x00362256B65B9B4DBDF3705E081C5B4702000000F777777
9B3530A9720241C13E2025BB75AF6A6E6EFFA43BFB712E03278BEB14B33E1D3602666A1E03
D679B30BBE3419E) AS varchar(50));
```

In addition to using the DECRYPTBYKEY function, we also have to cast the result (which is received as a binary value) back to the original data type in order to view it. We don't need to specify the key to use for decryption as the key's GUID identifier is included with the encrypted value, so the DECRYPTBYKEY function can identify which key to use.

It's worth noting what happens if you neglect to open the key before executing ENCRYPTBYKEY or DECRYPTBYKEY. In both cases you do not receive an error but instead a Null value is returned. That's something to watch out for; if you had buggy code that neglected to open the key – or relied on it being opened elsewhere – then you could think you are storing important values in a table but instead you are just storing Nulls.

Using an Authenticator

A final point to note about these functions is the use of an authenticator to prevent substitution attacks. A scenario that is commonly given for where an authenticator is useful is where we are storing salary information (or account balances). Let's suppose I have write access to a database, but I can't access the keys. If there is salary table that includes myself and the CEO, I can't tell what those values are exactly, but I can be fairly sure the CEO is paid more than me, so I might copy the encrypted value from the CEO's record and replace my own value with that one.

Let's create a table with some data using the following code so we can demonstrate how an authenticator works:

```
CREATE TABLE dbo.Salary(
    ID int IDENTITY(1,1) PRIMARY KEY,
    EmployeeName nvarchar(100),
    Salary decimal(12,2),
    EncryptedSalary varbinary(200) NULL
);
GO
INSERT INTO dbo.Salary(EmployeeName, Salary)
VALUES
('Me', 10000),
('CEO', 1000000),
('Geoff', 10000);
```

Now I'll encrypt the salary values and store them in the EncryptedSalary column. Note I have to cast the decimal values to a text type first as you can see in the example:

```
OPEN SYMMETRIC KEY MySymmetricKey
DECRYPTION BY CERTIFICATE MyColumnEncryptionCert;

UPDATE dbo.Salary
SET EncryptedSalary = ENCRYPTBYKEY(KEY_GUID(N'MySymmetricKey'),
CAST(Salary AS varchar(20)));

SELECT * FROM dbo.Salary;
```

We can see the encrypted values now stored in the table (Figure 21-1):

	ID	EmployeeName	Salary	EncryptedSalary
1	1	Me	10000.00	0x00362256B65B9B4DBDF3705E081C5B47020000007A55E8...
2	2	CEO	1000000.00	0x00362256B65B9B4DBDF3705E081C5B4702000000AA6A20...
3	3	Geoff	10000.00	0x00362256B65B9B4DBDF3705E081C5B4702000000C86491...

Figure 21-1. *Viewing encrypted values in our table*

I'm now going to update the value stored against my record and replace it with the encrypted value from the CEO. I'll then show the values stored using the DECRYPYBYKEY function. I'll have to CAST the output of DECRYPTBYKEY twice, once back to the varchar that was what I actually encrypted and then back to the original decimal. Here is the code for that – if you want to execute it yourself, you will need to substitute the EncryptedSalary value with the one from your own table:

```
UPDATE dbo.Salary
SET EncryptedSalary = 0x00362256B65B9B4DBDF3705E081C5B4702000000AA8...
WHERE EmployeeName = 'Me';

SELECT
    ID,
    EmployeeName,
    Salary,
    CAST(CAST(DECRYPTBYKEY(EncryptedSalary) AS varchar(20)) AS
    decimal(12,2)) AS DecryptedSalary
FROM dbo.Salary;
```

We can see the results in Figure 21-2:

	ID	EmployeeName	Salary	DecryptedSalary
1	1	Me	10000.00	1000000.00
2	2	CEO	1000000.00	1000000.00
3	3	Geoff	10000.00	10000.00

Figure 21-2. *Viewing the hacked salary value in the table*

We can see I've successfully given myself a 10,000% pay rise. This type of exploit can be avoided by using an authenticator. The authenticator is a value that is supplied to the ENCRYPTBYKEY function and gets stored within the encrypted output. To decrypt a value in the column, the same authenticator value must be supplied. We'll simply use the ID value as our authenticator and encrypt the Salary column again. We have to supply a couple of extra optional parameters to ENCRYPTBYKEY now; the third parameter is *add_authenticator* which we set to 1 to denote an authenticator will be used, and then we supply the authenticator value itself, in this case my ID value cast to a varchar. Here is the code:

```
UPDATE dbo.Salary
SET EncryptedSalary =
    ENCRYPTBYKEY(
            KEY_GUID(N'MySymmetricKey'),
            CAST(Salary AS varchar(20)),
            1,
            CAST(ID AS varchar(20))
            );
```

Now I repeat the same exercise as before; I replace the encrypted value for my record with the one from the CEO's record. I then decrypt the results to view them. Again, I have to supply two extra parameters to DECRYPYBYKEY, a 1 to denote an authenticator should be used and then the authenticator value:

```
SELECT
    ID,
    EmployeeName,
    Salary,
    CAST(CAST(DECRYPTBYKEY(EncryptedSalary,1,CAST(ID AS varchar(20))) AS
    varchar(20)) AS decimal(12,2)) AS DecryptedSalary
FROM dbo.Salary;
```

The results are shown in Figure 21-3:

	ID	EmployeeName	Salary	DecryptedSalary
1	1	Me	10000.00	NULL
2	2	CEO	1000000.00	1000000.00
3	3	Geoff	10000.00	10000.00

Figure 21-3. *Using an authenticator to prevent substitution attacks*

We can see my salary is returned as Null, so my attempted hack has failed. It's worth also mentioning that if an authenticator has been used to encrypt data – and you attempt to decrypt without supplying the authenticator – then all the values will be returned as Null.

That's pretty much all we need to cover on encrypting and decrypting data with a symmetric key, so let's go over the other key hierarchy scenarios we mentioned earlier.

Where the DMK Is Not Protected by the SMK

As mentioned, you can consider having the DMK that is not protected by the SMK to prevent database administrators from accessing your data without the password.

When we created the DMK earlier, this was the command:

```
USE TestColumnEncryption;
CREATE MASTER KEY
ENCRYPTION BY PASSWORD = 'SomeLongAndComplicatedPassword!';
```

When we create a DMK like this, it is automatically protected by the SMK. Effectively there are two copies of the DMK created, one encrypted using the SMK and one with the password. We can remove the copy that is protected with the SMK with the following command:

```
ALTER MASTER KEY
DROP ENCRYPTION BY SERVICE MASTER KEY;
```

The effect this has is that the DMK cannot now automatically be accessed by SQL Server. If we try now to open our symmetric key with the following SQL, we will see it fails:

```
OPEN SYMMETRIC KEY MySymmetricKey
DECRYPTION BY CERTIFICATE MyColumnEncryptionCert;
```

This is the error you get:

```
Msg 15581, Level 16, State 7, Line 113
```

Please create a master key in the database or open the master key in the session before performing this operation.

The error message is pretty clear. Now that we have dropped protection by the SMK, we must explicitly open the DMK (on which our certificate depends) in order to then open the symmetric key. We do that as follows:

```
OPEN MASTER KEY
DECRYPTION BY PASSWORD = 'SomeLongAndComplicatedPassword!';

OPEN SYMMETRIC KEY MySymmetricKey
DECRYPTION BY CERTIFICATE MyColumnEncryptionCert;
```

Then the open operation succeeds, and we can work with our symmetric key as before.

Where the Symmetric Key Is Just Protected by a Password

We can also create a symmetric key that is just protected by a password with the following SQL:

```
CREATE SYMMETRIC KEY MySymmetricKey_PasswordOnly
WITH ALGORITHM = AES_256,
IDENTITY_VALUE = 'Some Text',
KEY_SOURCE = 'Some More Text'
ENCRYPTION BY PASSWORD = 'OneMoreLongAndComplicatedPassword!'
```

In this case, to open the key in order to use it to encrypt or decrypt data, we just need to supply the password as follows:

```
OPEN SYMMETRIC KEY MySymmetricKey_PasswordOnly
DECRYPTION BY PASSWORD = 'OneMoreLongAndComplicatedPassword!';
```

It's an obvious question to ask why, if we are using a password, do we not just do it this way at the symmetric key level and dispense with having the asymmetric key and DMK we used in the previous example. The answer is really around how you want to manage your keys and passwords. You may want to have separate keys for each column of data you encrypt, but you may not want to manage having lots of different passwords. By having an intermediate certificate and key pair, you can also rotate that periodically without having to decrypt and re-encrypt your underlying data.

As discussed earlier you have a number of options of how you structure and protect your key hierarchy. The choices you make are likely to be governed by factors such as:

- Policies and regulation you must adhere to.

- Ease of management/need to maintain copies of keys and passwords outside the database.

- How you want to manage lifecycle tasks such as key rotation. We discuss key rotation extensively in the sections and TDE and Always Encrypted, so refer back if you want more detail.

Working with and Indexing Encrypted Columns

You're quite limited in the ways you can interact with encrypted columns. In general, if you want to perform calculations or similar activities against them, then you will need to retrieve the encrypted value, decrypt it in your application or stored procedure code, and then perform the actions you require. If you need to store an updated value, you encrypt the new value and store that against the record.

If you want to search for particular values in an encrypted column, then you are very restricted in how you can do so. In general, we will want to avoid encrypting columns that we need to search on. We saw earlier that ENCRYPTBYKEY implements randomized encryption, so there is no way to compare two encrypted values to understand if the underlying plaintext matches. Thus, this sort of pattern for searching columns will not work:

```
DECLARE @EncryptedSalary varbinary(200)

OPEN SYMMETRIC KEY MySymmetricKey
DECRYPTION BY CERTIFICATE MyColumnEncryptionCert;

SET @EncryptedSalary = ENCRYPTBYKEY(KEY_GUID(N'MySymmetricKey'),
CAST(10000 AS varchar(20)));

SELECT *
FROM dbo.Salary
WHERE EncryptedSalary = @EncryptedSalary;

CLOSE SYMMETRIC KEY MySymmetricKey;
```

This will return no results. The only way to search an encrypted column is to decrypt the contents and match against the search value as we see in this code example:

```
DECLARE @EncryptedSalary decimal(12,2) = 10000

OPEN SYMMETRIC KEY MySymmetricKey
DECRYPTION BY CERTIFICATE MyColumnEncryptionCert;

SELECT *
FROM dbo.Salary
WHERE CAST(CAST(DECRYPTBYKEY(EncryptedSalary) AS varchar(20)) AS
decimal(12,2)) = @EncryptedSalary;

CLOSE SYMMETRIC KEY MySymmetricKey;
```

This is not a good querying pattern from the point of view of performance. We are forcing SQL to decrypt every row in the table which, in the case of a large table, is going to be an intensive operation.

Indexing is also not going to help. We can create an index on an encrypted column, but as our column is effectively a series of randomized values, the index is going to be meaningless. It still can't be used for matching values, and it has no sense in terms of the order or distribution of our data.

From this we can see that we really need to avoid encrypting columns in this manner that we need to search against in our application. If you really need to do it, and you can't use Always Encrypted for some reason, then there only a few options:

- Store a partial version of your plaintext data unencrypted that you can search against. Even if this only narrows down the result set, at least then you can perform the more intensive decryption against a smaller number of rows. An example of this might be that you store the last four digits of a credit card number.

- Store a hashed version of the plaintext alongside the encrypted version. You can refer to Chapter 19 to understand how hashing functions can be used. Search terms can then be hashed and matched against the hashed value of the data stored in the database. You still may want to check the plaintext values actually match due to the very small possibility of a collision where the hash function has created the same hashed output for two different input values.

- Combine the aforementioned two methods so that you are only hashing a partial version of your data. This prevents the hashed version of the data being vulnerable to dictionary-type attacks; again we discussed such attacks in Chapter 19.

In each of these cases you can then also use an index on the actual column being searched.

Migrating or Restoring a Database with Column Encryption

When you need to restore a database that uses column encryption to another SQL Server instance, your biggest concern is going to be whether the keys used to encrypt data remain available and usable. In particular where you have an encryption hierarchy of keys, that all objects in the hierarchy are present on the new instance.

This is most likely not to be the case where you rely on automated key management and your Database Master Key (DMK) is protected by the Service Master Key (SMK).

This is the main example we've focused on in this chapter. The SMK is unique to your SQL instance, and while it is technically feasible to migrate it to another instance, you really don't want to do that. It is however straightforward to alter your DMK to use the SMK belonging to the new instance.

First let's quickly demonstrate the issue. I back up my TestColumnEncryption database and restore it to another server. Now on that server I'm going to issue the command to open my symmetric key:

```
USE TestColumnEncryption;

OPEN SYMMETRIC KEY MySymmetricKey
DECRYPTION BY CERTIFICATE MyColumnEncryptionCert;
```

I get the following error:

```
Please create a master key in the database or open the master key in the
session before performing this operation.
```

SQL Server is unable to automatically open my DMK as it isn't protected by the current SMK. This is part of the reason we protect the DMK with a password as well as the SMK. We can use the password to open the DMK and then drop its protection from the old SMK before adding protection from the current one:

```
OPEN MASTER KEY
DECRYPTION BY PASSWORD = 'SomeLongAndComplicatedPassword!';

ALTER MASTER KEY
DROP ENCRYPTION BY SERVICE MASTER KEY;

ALTER MASTER KEY
ADD ENCRYPTION BY SERVICE MASTER KEY;

CLOSE MASTER KEY;
```

Now let's try and open the symmetric key again:

```
OPEN SYMMETRIC KEY MySymmetricKey
DECRYPTION BY CERTIFICATE MyColumnEncryptionCert;
```

This time the command succeeds, and we are able to use the key for cryptographic activities. If you use other encryption hierarchies, make sure you have thought through if there are any issues in such a recovery scenario and make sure you test a backup and restore to make sure your assumptions are correct.

Temporary Keys

Besides creating symmetric keys that reside in the database for encrypting data, you can also make use of temporary keys. A temporary key is one that only exists in, and for the duration of, the session in which it was created.

You might use a temporary key where you wish to encrypt data that's just being stored for the duration of your session. Alternately, you may wish to encrypt data to store in the database, but you don't want to store the keys in the database also. In that case you can create a temporary key, specifying a KEY_SOURCE and IDENTITY value so that it can be recreated when you next need it

Creating a temporary key is similar to creating a temporary table (or stored procedure); you simply prefix the name with a hash sign when issuing a create statement:

```
CREATE SYMMETRIC KEY #MySymmetricKey
WITH ALGORITHM = AES_256,
IDENTITY_VALUE = 'Some Text',
KEY_SOURCE = 'Some More Text'
ENCRYPTION BY CERTIFICATE MyColumnEncryptionCert;
```

In this case I've created a temporary symmetric key protected by our certificate that exists in the database. You can then work with the key in much the same way as with a persisted key:

```
OPEN SYMMETRIC KEY #MySymmetricKey
DECRYPTION BY CERTIFICATE MyColumnEncryptionCert;

SELECT ENCRYPTBYKEY(KEY_GUID(N'#MySymmetricKey'),'SomeText');

CLOSE SYMMETRIC KEY #MySymmetricKey;
```

When you are done with your key, you can remove it with the following code, or if you don't, then it will be automatically cleared up when your connection closes:

```
DROP SYMMETRIC KEY #MySymmetricKey;
```

If you need to create it again, you can use the same IDENTITY_VALUE and KEY_SOURCE, and you will then be able to use the new temporary key to decrypt data encrypted by the previous version.

Encryption by Passphrase

We mentioned earlier than in addition to encrypting your data using symmetric keys, you can also choose to do so simply with a passphrase. We say passphrase rather than password as you are not limited to a single word. In this case encryption is carried out using the ENCRYPTBYPASSPHRASE function and decryption by the DECRYPTBYPASSPHRASE function. Let's look at a quick example:

```
DECLARE @EncryptedText varbinary(max);

SET @EncryptedText = ENCRYPTBYPASSPHRASE('My Pass Phrase','Some text to
encrypt');
SELECT @EncryptedText AS EncryptedText;

SELECT CAST(DECRYPTBYPASSPHRASE('My Pass Phrase',@EncryptedText) AS
varchar(max)) AS DecryptedText;
```

We can see the results showing our encrypted value and the same value decrypted in Figure 21-4:

	EncryptedText
1	0x02000000A3CD899F1B6FAB421A9097E598522452CBDFCB...

	DecryptedText
1	Some text to encrypt

Figure 21-4. *Encryption and decryption using a passphrase*

In the background ENCRYPTBYPASSPHRASE works by generating a 128-bit key based on the pass phrase value and then encrypting the data using the triple DES (3DES)

313

algorithm. You may notice that almost everywhere else in this book we've used the AES algorithm. DES is considered less secure, so that may be something that you want to consider before using this. It's not much different in terms of usability if you decide to use a temporary or persisted key which is itself protected by a password.

When using a pass phrase, you are also forced to decrypt and re-encrypt all the data if you ever want to change (rotate) the pass phrase.

Protection of Key Passwords Being Sent to SQL Server

We've discussed that you might choose to have keys protected by a password, rather than using automated key management where protection ultimately stops with the built-in Service Master Key (SMK). You do this if you do not want encrypted data accessible by administrators to the SQL Server instance. In that case then, how do we stop someone with administrative privileges from accessing the passwords as they are issued to SQL Server as part of executable queries?

The answer is that such protection is in-place by default. We can see this if we run an XEvent Profiler session and attempt to capture such information (we looked at how to create such a session in Chapter 8).

I'm going to set XEvent Profiler running and then execute the following query:

```
OPEN SYMMETRIC KEY MySymmetricKey_PasswordOnly
DECRYPTION BY PASSWORD = 'OneMoreLongAndComplicatedPassword!';
```

If I go to view the live data for my trace, I can see the query that I have just executed. I'm going to go to the event and extract the batch_text field. This is what I see:

```
--*OPEN SYMMETRIC KEY-----------------------------------------------------
```

You can see that most of the command has been masked so I can't view the password, and I can't even see what key is being opened. Let's look at another example from the previous section where we looked at encrypting data using a passphrase:

```
DECLARE @EncryptedText varbinary(max);

SET @EncryptedText = ENCRYPTBYPASSPHRASE('My Pass Phrase','Some text to encrypt');
```

This time I get the following text captured:

```
DECLARE @EncryptedText AS VARBINARY (MAX);

--*ASSIGN-----------------------------------------------------------------

SELECT @EncryptedText AS EncryptedText;

--*SELECT WITHOUT QUERY---------------------------------------------------;
```

You can see again that any critical parts of the command have been masked, so an administrator cannot simply run traces to capture the passwords we use to protect our keys or pass phrases that might be used to encrypt data directly. SQL Server parses query text where commands are issued directly and commands that can contain sensitive information of this type are not shown in trace outputs. Note however that if you issue the command via dynamic SQL, this will not be the case.

That still doesn't mean they are 100% secure, however, even for direct commands. Someone with debug rights at OS level over the server SQL runs on could use a debugger to view memory and retrieve actual passwords.

Summary

This chapter looked at other methods of column encryption, but we've gone over things quite briefly as the recommendation of this book is that you should use Always Encrypted for column encryption.

Key points are:

- We usually encrypt data using a symmetric key.

- The symmetric key is itself encrypted using a password or another key object (often an asymmetric key).

- You have many options regarding how to structure your encryption hierarchy. Usually you either have a hierarchy which goes all the way up to the SQL Server Service Master Key (SMK) at the top, or you manage your own keys and at some point in the hierarchy a password is required. You can also use temporary keys that only exist within the connections they are being used.

- When using keys, we encrypt data with ENCRYPTBYKEY and decrypt it with DECRYPTBYKEY.

- We can use an "authenticator" value to ensure that data isn't tampered with by replacing an encrypted value with one from another row.

- When using these methods of column encryption, it is best not to encrypt columns you need to search on. If you do have that requirement, then you need to work around it using hashing or by storing partial versions of your plaintext.

- You can also encrypt using a passphrase rather than a key though this is less secure.

- Commands that contain sensitive information, such as passwords used to protect keys, are prevented by SQL Server from appearing in trace outputs – though they may still be accessible using a debugger to view memory.

APPENDIX A

Glossary of Terms

This appendix provides a quick reference of the terms related to encryption we've used in this book, along with common abbreviations for those terms.

A

Advanced Encryption Standard

Advanced Encryption Standard is an algorithm designed to encrypt and decrypt data via symmetric encryption. Advanced Encryption Standard is the latest and most secure method for encrypting your data.

AES

See Advanced Encryption Standard.

Always Encrypted

Always Encrypted is a method of column encryption added to SQL Server in the 2016 version. "Always" means that data is encrypted at-rest, in-memory, and in-transit across the network. Encryption and decryption occurs client side on the application server and is carried out automatically by the client driver.

© Matthew McGiffen 2022
M. McGiffen, *Pro Encryption in SQL Server 2022*, https://doi.org/10.1007/978-1-4842-8664-7

Always Encrypted Wizard

The Always Encrypted Wizard is a GUI within SSMS that automates setting up the desired Always Encrypted configuration for your database and can also be used for encrypting existing data.

Asymmetric Encryption

Asymmetric Encryption works with an asymmetric key where the public key can be used to encrypt data, but only the private key can be used to decrypt data. Asymmetric encryption is more resource intensive than symmetric encryption, so in the context of SQL Server we mostly only use asymmetric encryption to protect objects rather than data.

Asymmetric Key

An asymmetric key consists of a public and a private key that can be used for asymmetric encryption.

At-Rest Data

At-rest is another way of referring to data where it is stored on disk.

Attestation

When working with Always Encrypted with Enclaves, attestation is the process of verifying that the enclave on the SQL Server box is trusted.

Authenticator

An extra value passed to the ENCRYPTBYKEY function to prevent substitution attacks. The authenticator value is usually stored alongside the encrypted value in the table and must match that used to encrypt the data in order to be able to decrypt it.

Automated Key Management

Automated Key Management is where our symmetric keys are protected by a key hierarchy that is fully managed within SQL Server. Commonly this will involve protection by a certificate which is in turn protected by a Database Master Key (DMK), in turn protected by the Service Master Key (SMK).

Azure Key Vault

Azure Key Vault is an HSM (Hardware Security Module) backed cloud service provided by Microsoft that you can use to store and manage encryption keys.

B

Backup Encryption

Backup Encryption is functionality that exists within SQL Server (from SQL Server 2014) that allows you to encrypt full, differential, and log backups of databases.

C

CA

See Certification Authority.

CEK

See Column Encryption Key.

Certificate

A certificate is a digitally signed object that contains a public key and often a private key as well to make up an asymmetric key pair.

Certification Authority

A Certification Authority is a trusted organization that stores, signs, and issues digital certificates.

Certificate Store

The Certificate Store is a location on your machine that is used to store local copies of digital certificates.

CMK

See Column Master Key.

Code Integrity Policy

A Code Integrity Policy is used to ensure that software installed on a machine comes from a trusted publisher and has not been tampered with.

Column Encryption Key

A Column Encryption Key (CEK) is a symmetric key used by Always Encrypted to encrypt and decrypt data. It is stored in the database encrypted by the Column Master Key (CMK).

Column Master Key

A Column Master Key (CMK) is an asymmetric key (often belonging to a certificate) that is used to protect Column Encryption Keys used by Always Encrypted. The CMK exists outside of the database server, though we have a CMK object within the database which is a pointer for where the actual CMK can be found.

D

Data Encryption Standard

Data Encryption Standard is an algorithm used to encrypt and decrypt data using symmetric encryption. Data Encryption Standard is no longer seen as being sufficiently secure, so you should use Advanced Encryption Standard instead.

Database Encryption Key

The Database Encryption Key (DEK) is a symmetric key that exists within a database and is used by Transparent Data Encryption (TDE) to encrypt the data in the database. The Database Encryption Key is itself encrypted by an asymmetric key (possibly belonging to a certificate) that exists outside the database.

Database Master Key

Each database can have its own (but only one) Database Master Key (DMK). The Database Master Key is a symmetric key that can be used to protect other objects within the database.

DEK

See Database Encryption Key.

DES

See Data Encryption Standard.

Deterministic Encryption

Deterministic Encryption is where an encryption algorithm will always produce the same output where the same input value and key are used.

Diffie Hellman

Diffie Hellman key exchange is a method of securely exchanging encryption keys across a public channel.

DMA Protection

DMA (Direct Memory Attack) Protection protects against attacks from connected hardware that can access memory directly. In the context of VBS this is used to protect memory inside the enclave.

DMK

See Database Master Key.

DPAPI

See Windows Data Protection API.

E
EKM

See Extensible Key Management.

Enclave

An enclave is a secure partition within memory where protected operations can take place securely. With SQL Server 2019, enclaves can be used with Always Encrypted to allow cryptographic operations to occur on the database server itself.

Encryption Scan

The Encryption Scan is the background process used by TDE for encrypting existing data on the disk.

Extensible Key Management

Extensible Key Management is functionality that exists within SQL Server to allow us to connect to an external store for our encryption keys (such as Azure Key Vault). This can offer an extra level of security for our keys as well as improved ease of management.

H

Hardware Security Module

A Hardware Security Module is a specialized computer designed to create a trusted environment for cryptographic operations, most commonly key management, but one can also be used for encryption and decryption activities.

Hash

A Hash is a fixed length binary value created from an input value using a hashing function that can be used to verify the input value is unchanged but cannot be reverse-engineered to find the original value.

HGS

See Host Guardian Service.

Host Guardian Service

Host Guardian Service (HGS) is a Windows service that provides attestation – verifying that another server is trusted and has not been tampered with. We use HGS when working with Always Encrypted with Enclaves to ensure that the enclave is secure.

Host Health Certificate

A Host Health Certificate can be issued by HGS to verify the health of a registered server. In the case of Always Encrypted with Enclaves, the certificate is issued to the SQL Server which can then pass it back to the client to prove its trustworthiness.

Host Key

In the context of Always Encrypted with Enclaves, the Host Key is an asymmetric key pair belonging to the SQL Server that can be used to verify its identity.

HSM

See Hardware Security Module.

I

In-Transit Encryption

In-transit encryption is the encryption of data that is being passed across the network. In the context of SQL Server, we use Transport Layer Security (TLS) for this.

K

Key Rotation

Key rotation is the process of periodically replacing your encryption keys. This helps maintain security of our encrypted data and is required to meet industry standards and best practice.

P

Parameterization for Always Encrypted

Parameterization for Always Encrypted is functionality that exists within SSMS to convert variables to parameters and execute your queries as parameterized queries. This is required to be able to execute queries against tables using column encryption with Always Encrypted.

Private Key

A private key is usually one half of an asymmetric key pair which can be used to decrypt data encrypted using the public key.

Public Key

A public key is usually one-half of an asymmetric key pair which can be used to encrypt data. It cannot decrypt data; instead, the private key must be used.

R

Randomized Encryption

Randomized encryption is where an encryption algorithm will always produce a different output even where the same input value and key are used.

S

Salt

A Salt is a random value added to an input before hashing to improve the security of the hashed values. This process is known as salting and prevents attacks that may use a dictionary of known hashed values for given inputs.

Secure Boot

Secure Boot is a security standard designed to make sure that a device boots only using trusted software that has not been tampered with.

Secure Hashing Algorithm

Secure Hashing Algorithm (SHA) is designed to provide a unique hash digest for a given input. In the context of SQL Server, we generally use SHA2 which is more secure than predecessors.

Service Master Key

The Service Master Key (SMK) is a symmetric key that is created the first time a SQL Server instance is started. It sits at the top of the encryption hierarchy in SQL Server and is used to protect objects beneath it.

SHA

See Secure Hashing Algorithm.

SMK

See Service Master Key.

Symmetric Encryption

Symmetric encryption is a form of encryption where the same key is used to both encrypt and decrypt data. Symmetric encryption is faster than asymmetric encryption, so we generally choose to use it over the latter for encrypting our data.

Symmetric Key

A single encryption key which is used for symmetric encryption.

T

TDE

See Transparent Data Encryption.

TDS

TDS (Tabular Data Stream) is a protocol used to transfer data between a database server and client.

Temporary Key

A Temporary Key is an encryption key that just exists within, and for the duration of, the session in which it is created, and does not get persisted to a database.

Thumbprint

Each certificate has a unique thumbprint. This is a hash value created from the whole data of the certificate combined with the certificate's signature.

TLS

See Transport Layer Security.

TPM

See Trusted Platform Module.

TPM Baseline

During the boot process for a machine, the TPM captures a number of items known as platform control registers (PCRs) that measure the firmware and OS configuration. This is known as the TPM baseline or fingerprint and can be checked to ensure that nothing has changed or been tampered with.

TPM Endorsement Key

Every TPM chip has a certificate with a unique asymmetric key. This is known as the TPM Endorsement Key. The key can be used to uniquely identify the TPM and can't be impersonated.

Transport Layer Security

Transport Layer Security (TLS) is a security protocol designed to encrypt data being passed across a network. In the context of SQL Server, TLS encrypts both data and queries being passed between the client and server.

Transparent Data Encryption

Transparent Data Encryption (TDE) is a SQL Server feature that allows you to encrypt your data where it is stored on disk.

Trusted Platform Module

A Trusted Platform Module (TPM) is a chip installed on the motherboard of most modern computers. The TPM contains a unique Endorsement Key that can be used to verify the identity of the computer. TPMs also store information about the boot processes of the computer as hashed measurements. You can also have Virtual TPMs on virtual machines.

V

VBS

See Virtualization Based Security.

Virtualization Based Security

Virtualization Based Security is technology based on Windows Hypervisor that is used to host secure enclaves.

W

Windows Data Protection API

The Windows Data Protection API is an application programming interface for encrypting data that is built-in to Windows.

APPENDIX B

Encryption in the Cloud

If you are running SQL Server on a cloud platform, the key thing to remember is that it is still just SQL Server. Most features remain the same and you work with them in the same manner. There are differences in some cases though, and we'll go over them briefly in this appendix. We're just going to look at Azure and AWS (Amazon Web Services); if you're using a different cloud provider, then much of the same will apply but you'll need to check their documentation. A key point to make is that cloud services change rapidly so where I state a restriction it's entirely possible that the cloud provider has changed that by the time you read this.

As a general point, if you are running SQL Server on a VM in the cloud, then the features available are mostly unchanged; it's only when using a Platform as a Service (PaaS) option for SQL Server that you are likely to see much difference. PaaS offerings are Azure SQL Database, Azure SQL Managed Instance, and AWS Relational Database Service (RDS).

We'll go through each option for cloud hosting and detail whether the features we've discussed in this book are available – with additional notes that you might find helpful.

Azure VM

When running SQL Server on a VM in Azure, there is no change to the features available for encryption or how you work with them.

Azure SQL Database or Managed Instance

In terms of encryption features and how you work with them, there is no difference between SQL Database and Managed Instance, so we'll discuss them together. Almost all the features are still available and work in the same manner, but there are some points to be aware of.

© Matthew McGiffen 2022
M. McGiffen, *Pro Encryption in SQL Server 2022*, https://doi.org/10.1007/978-1-4842-8664-7

TDE

TDE is on by default and the keys are automatically managed for you, including rotation of them on a periodic basis. You can however bring your own keys if you wish and manage them yourself.

Backup Encryption

Backup encryption is not available but is also not a relevant feature. Backups are managed for you, and they are automatically encrypted.

Always Encrypted with Secure Enclaves

Working with the basic version of Always Encrypted is exactly the same as with an on-premises server. If you wish to use enclaves, then you use the Azure Attestation Service (AAS) as your attestation service. To use enclaves, you must make sure your hardware configuration is "DC series." After that, it is much easier and more reliable to configure Always Encrypted to work with enclaves, so you may as well enable enclaves unless you have a specific reason you don't want to.

TLS

Is on by default and you can't change this.

AWS VM (EC2)

AWS VMs are known as EC2s (Elastic Cloud Compute). An EC2 with SQL Server installed supports the full encryption feature set. There are a few points however that are worth mentioning.

EKM

You can use EKM with SQL Server installed on an EC2; however, you can't use AWS Key Management Service (KMS) as your key store as KMS does not supply a provider module you can install on the SQL Server EC2. This means that if you want to use EKM with your SQL Server, you must use a different provider. You could, for instance, use Azure Key Vault as mentioned in the examples in the EKM chapter. If you wish to keep everything within AWS, there are also third-party providers that you can use.

Always Encrypted with Secure Enclaves

If you wish to use enclaves with an EC2 instance, then it must be a "bare metal" instance. AWS provide instructions on how you can set this up, though it is pretty much the same as we looked at in the chapter on setting up TPM attestation.

AWS RDS

RDS supports most (but not all) of the encryption features available in SQL Server. In some cases however there are differences you need to be aware of.

TDE

You can use TDE with RDS, but you configure this through what's called an Option Group rather than through T-SQL. Option Groups are used for configuring database-level (rather than server-level) settings in RDS. AWS automatically creates the certificate for you and manages that through the AWS Key Management Service (KMS).

You can also migrate on-premises databases that have TDE enabled to RDS. This is relatively new functionality (June 2022). Previously you had to remove TDE before migrating your database to RDS and then turn it back on afterward.

RDS also provides its own encryption functionality which you can use instead of TDE. The built-in encryption works by encrypting the file system for the underlying EC2 VM that hosts your SQL Server instance.

Backup Encryption

This functionality isn't available through T-SQL, as backup and restore commands also aren't available. You perform native backup and restores through built-in RDS stored procedures to achieve the same functionality. These stored procedures give you the option to encrypt your backups.

Always Encrypted with Secure Enclaves

While you can use the basic version of Always Encrypted on RDS, you cannot (at the time of writing) use enclaves. This is because working with enclaves requires OS-level access that is not available to you.

EKM

You can't use EKM on RDS as you do not have access to install a provider module. As mentioned with regard to TDE though, AWS will effectively use EKM to manage your TDE keys for you in AWS Key Management Service (KMS).

APPENDIX C

Encryption Algorithms

This appendix will look briefly at some of the algorithms we've used in this book, their history, and how they work. The implementation of encryption algorithms is a complex and deep subject, and there are many books devoted specifically to that topic, so I'd recommend you look at one of those if you want to know more. In most cases though, you shouldn't be considering coding your own implementation except as an academic exercise.

The history of encryption is also an interesting topic and can be fun to play with. I can recommend *The Code Book* by Simon Singh as an interesting and accessible guide to encryption through the ages.

Advanced Encryption Standard (AES)

Before AES, there was DES (Data Encryption Standard), developed by IBM in the 1970s. DES was considered good at the time, but as computer power and cracking methods improved, it started to look vulnerable. A number of projects were able to demonstrate breaking the encryption of a DES message in the late 1990s, so it was clear that a successor was required. We've mentioned earlier in the book that while SQL Server does allow you to use DES, in most cases it is deprecated functionality. The US government's National Institute of Standards and Technology (NIST) embarked on a program to evaluate a number of different methods of encryption, and a new standard (AES) was approved in 2002.

AES is based on something called the Rijndael block cipher, developed by John Daemen and Vincent Rijmen, two cryptologists from Belgium. Rijndael was chosen due to a combination of good performance – it's important that encryption and decryption are fast activities – as well as its security and ease of implementation.

© Matthew McGiffen 2022
M. McGiffen, *Pro Encryption in SQL Server 2022*, https://doi.org/10.1007/978-1-4842-8664-7

How AES Works in Practice

We'll take a brief look at how AES works, but this is just a general description and avoids some of the more complicated aspects.

Breaking the Message into Blocks

Rijndael works with 128-bit blocks regardless of the length of your key. The data is broken up into blocks of this size – which is 16 bytes. Each block can then be logically arranged into a 4x4 matrix. For instance, "My basic message" can be arranged as:

```
M y   b
a s i c
  m e s
s a g e
```

Key Expansion

This takes the encryption key supplied and uses it to generate a series of new keys to be used for each round of the encryption process. These are called "round keys" and will be 128 bits in size, so they can be logically arranged in the same manner as the message blocks. For instance, if an initial key was "Some initial key", then that can be arranged like this:

```
S o m e
  i n i
t i a l
  k e y
```

Add Round Key

We then start a series of "rounds" where the data goes through an iterative encryption process. The number of rounds depends on the size of your key. For instance, with AES_128 there are 10 rounds and with AES_256 there are 14 rounds.

First, the round key (for the first round this will just be our initial key) is "added" to the message block using a XOR cipher, which is an additive encryption algorithm. The output is another 4x4 matrix of binary values which already is an encrypted version of our original message. It could look something like this if we express it in hexadecimal:

```
cc 6e 5d 9a
94 b2 6d a9
f4 64 88 6d
30 49 cc 3d
```

Substitute Bytes

Each of the preceding hexadecimal byte vales is then "substituted" with another predefined value to create a new 4x4 array. Effectively the algorithm implements an internal lookup table for this purpose. The idea behind this step is to reduce the correlation between the input and output values. So we end up with a whole new 4x4 array similar to this:

```
53 58 44 22
bd ef 84 b7
9a 75 a2 c4
73 21 53 42
```

Shift Rows

Then we start a couple of transformations on the data. "Shift rows" moves the second row one space to the left, the third row two spaces to the left, and the fourth row three spaces to the left. If we use the sample values I showed previously for the result of the substitute bytes step, then this transformation gives us the following:

```
53 58 44 22
ef 84 b7 bd
a2 c4 9a 75
42 73 21 53
```

Mix Columns

This is the final transformation. In mathematical terms, each column is multiplied by a predefined 4x4 matrix to produce a new set of values. We end up with a new 4x4 matrix of values:

```
3e 72 60 d4
b9 b0 15 27
```

```
33  4a  06  ac
73  04  85  d5
```

Repeat Rounds

This whole process is now repeated a number of times. A new round key is applied using the XOR cipher, and then we substitute bytes, shift rows, and mix columns until we get to the last round where just the final round key is applied – as the other steps wouldn't make the result particularly harder to crack. The result is seemingly random data as compared to the plaintext that we started with. The number of rounds taken is to prevent attacks that have shown to be more effective than brute force cracking for small numbers of rounds while balancing the need to perform well. We could always do more rounds, but each takes additional CPU processing.

Decrypting Data

Decryption simply follows the preceding steps in reverse until the plaintext value is reached.

Security of AES

There is continual research to probe AES for weaknesses, to find a shortcut to cracking data that doesn't require trying every possible key using a brute force method. So far nothing has been found that will beat the algorithm itself, but exploits have been found where there has been poor implementation of the algorithm. This is why you wouldn't want to try developing your own version unless you were a cryptographic expert. We can trust that the versions implemented for us in SQL Server are sound.

Secure Hash Algorithm 2 (SHA2)

We discussed hashing functions in Chapter 19, in particular using the SHA2_256 algorithm with the HASHBYTES function. Hashing algorithms are not encryption per se, but rather they are used to create a fingerprint that can be used to verify a piece of information, such as a password, or to identify that an item has not been changed or tampered with. We talked about some of the properties of hashing algorithms in Chapter 19, but here they are again:

- They are deterministic. This means that the same value passed in will always return in the same output.

- Small changes in the input value will cause large changes to the output. There is no way of comparing the two output values and understanding that the inputs were similar. This is known as the Avalanche effect.

- Functions are one-way. This means that there is no way to take the output value and reverse-engineer it to find the input.

- Hash functions are generally engineered to minimize the chance that two different inputs will produce the same output, though it is always theoretically possible that such an event – known as a collision – should occur.

We have seen that the HASHBYTES function supports a number of algorithms though all but SHA2 are deprecated. Before the SHA algorithms arrived on the scene, we had the MD (Message Digest) algorithms introduced in the late 1980s. These were shown to suffer from collisions, a discovery which could be used by hackers to breach the protection they offer, so they are now longer seen as secure. The SHA algorithms first arrived in 1993 with SHA0 (also just known as SHA) and then SHA1 a few years later which has been shown since to have vulnerabilities. SHA2 is the latest version implemented in SQL Server and is still considered secure (no one has cracked it yet). However, SHA3 has been defined; it is just not widely implemented yet. In SQL Server, we use SHA2_256 or SHA2_512. These are often referred to outside of SQL Server as SHA256 or SHA512 but are still based on SHA2.

How SHA2_256 Works

The number after the algorithm (256, 512, etc.) refers to the size of the hashed output. In terms of the algorithms themselves, the main differences the bit size makes is the number of rounds carried out, as well as the size of the shift amounts and the values of the additive constants. SHA2_256 has 64 rounds before an output is produced.

In very simplified terms, SHA2_256 works like this:

1. Data is converted to binary.

2. The binary is then broken up into blocks of 512 bits. The last block is padded out to make sure it is exactly 64 bits short of 512. This provides space for the "length bits" to be added.

3. The MD buffer is initialized. This consists of eight 32-bit values that are used during the rounds.

4. The keys are initialized. Sixty-four keys are used (similar to encryption keys), one for each round.

5. The message is further divided into 32-bit blocks.

6. Sixty-four rounds are carried out where the blocks go through a compression function, taking the output of the previous round and the key allocated for the current round. They are then rotated in a specific pattern and additional data gets added.

7. After the rounds are complete, a single 256-bit hash value is created and that is our output.

SHA2 is fairly complex, so we've just aimed here to give a flavor of the process that's followed.

Always Encrypted (AEAD_AES_256_CBC_HMAC_SHA_256)

With Always Encrypted, we have the choice (currently) of exactly one algorithm we can use. It has a long name due to the number of different algorithms being combined. Let's look at what each of these algorithms is:

- AEAD (Authenticated Encryption with Associated Data). This is generally used to check the integrity of stored encrypted values.

- AES (Advanced Encryption Standard). We've looked at this already.

- CBC (Cipher Block Chain). Cipher block chaining is where the encrypted result from one block is combined with the next block's plaintext before that block is encrypted.

- HMAC (Hash Message Authentication Code). HMAC is used to verify the integrity of hashed values.

- SHA (Secure Hashing Algorithm). We've looked at this already.

How the Algorithm Works in Practice

Microsoft provides full reference about how the algorithm used by Always Encrypted works. Let's look at the steps involved as it's fairly interesting to see how the various algorithms combine to make our data extra secure.

Step 1: Generating an Initialization Vector (IV)

The IV is a 128-bit value. For randomized encryption, it is just generated randomly. For deterministic encryption, first an iv_key is derived from the CEK:

```
iv_key = HMAC-SHA-256(CEK, "Microsoft SQL Server cell IV key" + algorithm + CEK_length)
```

Then the IV itself is generated using the same function and truncating the output to 128 bits:

```
IV = HMAC-SHA-256(iv_key, cell_data)
```

The IV is included in the encryption metadata that forms part of the encrypted value that is stored in the table. The IV will always be the same for the same CEK and plaintext value, and that is how we achieve deterministic encryption. This method of deterministic encryption, the way the IV is generated, makes it much more difficult to discern patterns than other methods that might use a static IV.

Step 2: Computing the Ciphertext

The ciphertext is generated using AES 256 combined with CBC:

```
aes_256_cbc_ciphertext = AES-CBC-256(enc_key, IV, cell_data)
```

What happens here is that the data is broken into blocks of 128 bits. The first block is then encrypted with AES using the IV and the CEK. For subsequent blocks the same is done, but the IV is replaced with the encrypted value of the previous block (which is cipher block chaining in action).

Step 3: Calculating the Message Authentication Code (MAC)

The MAC can be used to verify that the ciphertext has not been tampered with. Effectively it has been signed. Calculating the MAC requires a few additional parameters:

```
versionbyte = 0x01
versionbyte_length = 1
mac_key = HMAC-SHA-256(CEK, "Microsoft SQL Server cell MAC key" + algorithm
+ CEK_length)
```

Then the MAC itself can be calculated:

```
MAC = HMAC-SHA-256(mac_key, versionbyte + IV + Ciphertext +
versionbyte_length)
Step 4: Creating the Actual Value We Store in the Table
```

Finally, we produce the value we actually store in the table with the following concatenation:

```
aead_aes_256_cbc_hmac_sha_256 = versionbyte + MAC + IV + aes_256_cbc_
ciphertext
```

Index

A

Accelerated Database Recovery,
  227, 233–235
Advanced Encryption Standard
  (AES), 28, 317
  blocks, 336
  data encryption, 335
  decryption, 338
  key expansion, 336
  mix column, 337
  repeat rounds, 338
  round key, 336
  security, 338
  shift rows, 337
  substitute bytes, 337
  working process, 336
Always Encrypted, 3, 8, 9, 12, 97, 278,
  317, 334
  algorithms, 340
    actual value creation, 342
    ciphertext, 341
    initialization vector (IV), 341
    MAC requirements, 342
  cloud platform, 332
  CMK creation, 85–89
  column creation, 92–94
  Column Encryption Keys, 89–92
  considerations, 169
    approaches, 170
    case-insensitive searching, 170
    client drivers, 177, 178
    ETL, 175, 176

  key points, 178
  limitations, 169
  performance
    impact, 176, 177
  source control/release
    management, 170–175
decrypt data, 82
deterministic encryption, 93, 94
EKM, 290–295
enclaves (*see* Enclaves)
encryption hierarchy, 79
existing applications (*see* Existing data
  applications)
features, 77
issue query, 80
key difference, 77
key rotation, 164–167
key scenarios, 82
keys/certificates, 85
limitations
  client-side encryption, 146
  data types, 148, 149
  deterministic *vs.* randomized,
    147, 148
  requirements, 145
  SQL Server, 146
  strong encryption, 147
parameterization, 325
parameters, 81
queries (*see* Query execution)
randomized encryption, 93
request metadata, 80

Always Encrypted (*cont.*)
  results, 82
  return metadata, 81
  rich querying (*see* Rich querying)
  role separation, 77
  secure enclaves, 219
  set up information, 85
  source control/release management
    approaches, 171
    database project, 172, 173
    database/server
      configuration, 171
    DevOps, 170
    implementation, 171
    limitations, 170
    publish settings, 173, 174
    sensitive data, 171
    SSDT database project, 171, 173
  SQL Server 2016 *vs.* SQL Server
    2019, 78
  Wizard configuration, 318
  working process, 78–80
Amazon Web Services (AWS), 13,
    278, 331–334
Asymmetric encryption, 24, 33, 67, 298,
    318, 326
Asymmetric key, 24, 31, 65, 77, 85, 184,
    247, 260, 287–289, 318
At-rest data, 8, 17, 65, 318
Attestation server, 187, 188, 191, 198, 201,
    202, 204, 212, 246
Automated Key Management, 299, 319
  authenticator, 303–306
    DECRYPYBYKEY
      function, 304, 305
    ENCRYPTBYKEY function, 305
    encrypted values, 304

hacked salary value, 305
  source code, 305
  substitution attacks, 306
  working process, 303
DECRYPTBYKEY function, 303
ENCRYPTBYKEY function, 302
encrypting/decrypting data, 301–303
key creation, 300
KEY_SOURCE/IDENTITY_VALUE, 301
symmetric key, 300
AWS Key Management
    Service (KMS), 278
AWS virtual
    machine (EC2), 278, 333, 334
Azure Attestation Service (AAS), 332
Azure Key Vault, 10, 85, 277,
    286–287, 290–293
Azure object creation, 278
  access policy, 285
  Active Directory, 280–283
  application registration details, 282
  authentication purposes, 281
  client secret, 283
  key vault, 283–286
  resource groups, 278, 279

B

Backup Encryption, 8, 9, 319, 334
  asymmetric key, 65
  certificate creation, 67
  cloud platform, 332
  compression, 72
  DMK, 66
  FULL backups, 68
  performances, 70, 71
  permissions, 67

RESTORE HEADERONLY
command, 68
restoring data, 69
test database, 66
unencrypted backup, 71

C

Certification authority (CA), 260–262,
319, 320
Cipher Block Chain (CBC), 340
Code Integrity Policy, 247, 251–254, 320
Column encryption
Automated Key Management, 300–306
DECRYPTBYPASSPHRASE
function, 313
DMK/SMK, 306, 307
indexing encryption, 308–310
key points, 315
key protection, 314, 315
in memory/in transit network, 297
migrating/restoring
database, 310–312
symmetric keys, 298–300, 307, 308
temporary key, 312, 313
Column Encryption Keys (CEKs), 79, 151,
171, 184, 208–210, 232, 234, 235,
319, 320
encryption/decryption, 164
existing data, 126
in-place encryption, 215–217
key creation, 89–92
object browser, 90
remove option, 166
rich querying, 225
Set-SqlColumnEncryption
command, 164
source code, 91

SqlColumnEncryptionSetting
object, 165
SqlServer module, 165
table view, 167
unencrypted value, 92
Column Master Keys (CMKs), 79, 81, 151,
171, 208–210, 290, 320
ALTER ENCRYPION KEY
command, 159
certificate, 85
current user store, 87
folder creation, 88
GUI, 86, 87
KEY_PATH, 88
key store, 87
PowerShell, 89, 160–164
SSMS GUI, 153–158
SSMS object explorer, 86
T-SQL, 88, 158, 159

D

Database administrator (DBA), 162–164,
299, 306
Database Encryption Key (DEK), 24, 31,
32, 34–35, 50, 290, 321
Database Master Key (DMK), 24, 50, 62,
299, 300, 306, 307, 310, 321, 322
backup encryption, 66
TDE database, 48
Data Encryption Standard (DES), 29, 313,
314, 321, 335
Data Protection API (DPAPI), 25, 322
Data protection regulation, 3, 5–7
Deterministic encryption, 93, 94, 148, 183,
219, 228, 230, 232, 321
Direct Memory Attack (DMA), 249,
250, 322

E, F

Elastic Cloud Compute (EC2), 322
Enclaves, 78, 98, 123, 164, 169, 207, 322,
    See also In-place encryption
  ALTER TABLE command, 184
  attestation, 184, 185
  categories, 183
  comparison operators, 183
  HGS installation/configuration, 203
  host key attestation, 191
  Hyper-V virtual machines, 192
  limitations, 183
  networking, 200–202
  queries, 185–189
  rich querying, 219
  SQL Server/configuration, 203–205
  VMs, 193–201
ENCRYPTBYKEY function, 301, 302,
    305, 318
Encryption
  algorithms, 335–340
  Always Encrypted (*see* In-place
      encryption)
  approaches, 11, 12
  backup encryption (*see* Backup
      encryption)
  cloud environments, 12, 13
  cloud platform, 331
    Always Encrypted, 332
    Azure VM, 331
    backup encryption, 332
    EC2, 332
    secure enclaves, 333
    SQL Database/Managed
        Instance, 331
    TDE rotation, 332
  column encryption, 297–315

data protection
    regulation, 5–7
  definition, 4
  ENCRYPTBYPASSPHRASE
      function, 313
  functions, 8, 10
  implementation, 5
  overview, 4
  passphrase, 313, 314
  scan, 323
  TDE (*see* Transparent Data
      Encryption (TDE))
  types of, 4
Endorsement Key, 184, 248, 249, 328
Existing data applications
  Always Encrypted wizard
    CEK configuration, 126
    column encryption, 126
    results, 129
    run settings page, 126, 127
    scripting data, 124
    setup option, 124
    SSMS Object Explorer, 125
    table's definition, 128
  fundamentals, 123
  Import and Export Wizard
    advantages, 134
    approaches, 133, 134
    column encryption, 138, 141
    data source configuration, 137
    data transfer, 138, 139
    methods, 142
    progress and completion
        view, 141
    records, 142
    source and destination tables,
        139, 140

SQL table, 135

SSMS Object Explorer, 135, 136

unencrypted version, 134

PowerShell code

column encryption, 129

connection/database, 131, 132

definition, 132

results, 133

run settings, 130

Extensible Key Management (EKM), 8, 24, 31, 65, 299, 322, 323, 334

advantages, 277

application code, 295

Azure object creation, 278–286

CMK, 290

CMK application, 277, 291–293

column encryption, 293, 294

definition, 10

error logging, 291

Key Vault, 295

policies page, 293

TDE key vault, 286–290

Extract, transform, and load (ETL), 175–176

G

General Data Protection Regulation (GDPR), 6–7

H

Hardware Security Module (HSM), 10, 277, 319, 323, 324

Hashing (hash function), 323

key properties, 269

passwords, 11

salting (see Salting)

Secure Hash Algorithm 2, 338

storing passwords, 269

Hash Message Authentication Code (HMAC), 341

High availability (HA), 62, 63

Host Guardian Service (HGS), 184, 187, 188, 191, 203, 205, 245, 247, 248, 323

I, J

In-place encryption

CEK rotation, 215–217

data decryption

ALTER TABLE command, 212

output window, 213

select query, 213

SQL table/data, 211

table definition, 213

URL connection, 212

key points, 217

network issues, 207

performances, 214, 215

test database/keys, 208–210

Input-output memory management unit (IOMMU) policy, 253, 255

In-transit encryption, 324

K, L, M

Key Management Service (KMS), 278, 333

Key rotation, 53, 54, 151–168, 324

N, O

Network Address Translation (NAT), 200–202

P

Parameterization, 98–100, 122, 294, 325
Personally identifiable information
 (PII), 5, 169
Platform as a Service (PaaS), 331
Platform control registers (PCRs), 247, 328
PowerShell script, 97, 116, 124, 127, 129,
 140, 142, 164, 166
 CMK, 89, 160–162
 direct queries, 117
 existing data application, 129–133
 query execution, 118–120
 role separation
  database administrator, 162, 163
  definition, 162
  security administrator, 163
 trusted platform module, 250, 252, 254
Private/public key, 325

Q

Query execution
 attestation process
  action window, 186
  enclave report creation, 187
  health and trustworthiness, 187
  host health certificate, 187
  issue query, 186
  public key, 188
  request encryption metadata, 186
  return metadata, 186
  verification, 187
 background, 103
  insert query, 103–107
  select option, 108
  TSQL option, 103
  XEvent Profiler trace, 103
 database connection, 97–99

deterministic encryption, 112
direct queries, 117–119
enclaves, 185
encrypted column, 108–111
error messages, 111
indexes/statistics, 112, 113
inserting data, 99–102
insert query
 encryption metadata, 104
 key columns, 105
 metadata, 105
 parameters, 106
 plaintext parameters, 107
 results, 104
 SQL query, 103
 XEvent Profiler
  trace, 104, 106, 107
modification, 102
parameterization, 99
PowerShell code, 117–120
reading data, 102
request/return channel info, 189
results, 189
secure channel, 189
stored procedures, 113–116, 119–121
working process, 188

R

Randomized encryption, 92, 93, 102,
 110–112, 176, 221, 222,
 229–230, 325
Relational Database Service (RDS),
 331, 333
 Always Encrypted, 334
 backup and restore commands, 334
 EKM, 334
 TDE, 333

Rich querying
   client driver, 225
   database/data, 220–222
   enclave computation, 220
   encryption metadata, 224
   equality comparison, 222
   GROUP BY/DISTINCT, 219
   indexes, 242
   joins, 235–243
   LIKE query, 225, 226
   randomized encryption, 222, 242
      database recovery process, 233–235
      DBCC command, 229
      deterministic encryption, 228
      error message, 227, 231, 232
      execution plan, 229
      features, 227
      indexes, 228
      index rebuilds/reorganizations,
        232, 233
      operations, 228
      plaintext values, 228
      principles, 227
      reading operation, 228–231
      requirements, 233
      statistics, 230
      updating/inserting data, 231
      warning message, 227
   range query, 226
   SQL Server 2022, 220
   XEvent Profiler, 223

S

Salting, 325
   capabilities, 271
   concept, 271
   CRYPT_GEN_RANDOM function, 273
   HASHBYTES function, 274
   HASHBYTLES function, 271, 272
   hashed password view, 273
   hash function, 270
   password values, 270
   SQL Authentication, 271
   stored procedure, 273
   storing passwords, 272–274
Secure Boot, 245, 249, 250, 255, 326
Secure Hash Algorithm 2 (SHA2)
   HASHBYTES function, 339
   hashing algorithms, 338
   SHA2_256 working process, 339
Secure Hashing Algorithm (SHA), 326, 341
Secure Sockets Layer (SSL), 259
Service Master Key (SMK), 25, 31, 50,
      298–300, 306, 307, 310, 314, 326
SQL Server 2016 SQL *vs.* Server 2019, 78
SQL Server Data Tools (SSDT), 171
SQL Server Management
      Objects (SMO), 124, 131, 132,
      160, 164
SQL Server Management
      Studio (SSMS), 85, 177, 205, 267
   CEK/CMK view, 210
   CMK rotation
      certificate button, 154
      cleanup selection, 156, 157
      database view, 155
      key rotation, 153–155
      SQL query, 156–158
   query execution, 97
Stored procedures, 113–116, 119–121
Symmetric encryption, 311, 326
   key hierarchy, 298–300
   object protection, 299
   scenarios, 299
   types, 298

Symmetric key, 24, 28, 34, 298–301,
    306–308, 311, 312

T, U

Tabular Data Stream (TDS), 327
Temporary key, 312, 313, 327
Thumbprint, 49, 88, 158, 327
Transparent Data Encryption (TDE), 3, 8,
    12, 17, 31, 321, 327, 328, 333
  account information, 288
  asymmetric key, 289
  Always Encrypted, 18
  BACKUP CERTIFICATE
      command, 26
  BACKUP command, 26
  backup files, 33
  backup progress, 45
  benchmarking database, 39–41
  certificate/associated asymmetric key
      pair, 24
  certificate creation, 33, 34
  components, 22
  database, 35–37
  database backups, 60
    compression, 61, 62
    performance, 60
  Database Encryption Key, 290
  DEK database, 34, 35
  DEK encrypt and decrypt data, 24
  DMK database, 24, 32
  empty space, 21
  encryption scan, 44
  exceptions, 18
  existing system, 39
  hex editor, 20, 21
  hierarchy, 23, 25–27
  high availability (HA), 62, 63

key rotation
    certificate creation, 54, 55
    replace process, 53, 54
    rotation, 55
keys/certificates, 22, 23, 31
key vault, 286, 287, 289
management
    certificate/private key, 48, 50, 52
    DMK creation, 48
    instances, 51
    migration/recovering
        database, 47, 48
    restore database, 49
    service account, 50, 51
    SQL Server service, 52
meaning, 17
monitoring background process, 42
multiple databases, 33
performance impact, 55
    comparison, 59
    CPU cores, 59, 60
    database, 58
    differences, 59
    disk activity, 57
    production server, 59
    queries, 57
    query performance, 56
    scenarios, 57
    SET STATISTICS command, 58
remove option, 289
root keys, 37–39
scan performance problems, 43, 44
SMK database, 25
source code, 19, 287, 288
SQL databases, 17
TempDB database, 18
TLS scenarios, 18
viewing details, 36

Transport Layer Security (TLS), 8, 9, 12, 18, 259–268, 327, 328
    asymmetric key pair, 260
    certification authority (CA), 260–262
    implementation, 259
    performance, 268
    production database servers, 268
    SQL Server
        certificate tab, 265, 266
        configuration manager, 264, 266
        dynamic management view, 267
        encryption status, 267
        force encryption option, 265
        Server Process ID (SPID), 267
        service account permissions, 263
    symmetric encryption key, 260
Trusted Platform Module (TPM), 184, 328
    attestation (*see* Attestation server)
    baseline, 247, 327
    code integrity policy, 247, 251, 252
    collect/register attestation
        artifacts, 252
    cryptographic operations, 245
    enclave configuration, 255
    endorsement key, 247, 253, 328
    hardware and software, 245

host key attestation, 254–256
installation/configuration, 248, 249
requirements, 246
system information tool, 250
URL configuration, 250
VBS configuration, 249, 250
T-SQL, 88, 92, 158–159, 164

V

Virtual hard disk (VHD), 195
Virtualization Based Security (VBS), 245, 249, 250, 329
Virtual Machines (VMs)
    action menu, 199
    Hyper-V, 192, 193, 197, 198
    installation options, 196, 197
    memory assignment, 195
    specify generation, 193, 194
    vCPUs configuration, 198, 199
    virtual hard disk, 196

W, X, Y, Z

Windows Data Protection API, 329
Windows Defender Application Control (WDAC), 251, 252, 254

Printed in the United States
by Baker & Taylor Publisher Services